A
Woman
Making
History

MARY RITTER BEARD

THROUGH HER LETTERS

Edited and with an introduction by

NANCY F. COTT

YALE UNIVERSITY PRESS   NEW HAVEN & LONDON

A
Woman
Making
History

Title page illustration: Undated portrait of Mary Ritter Beard, probably in her twenties.

Set in Sabon type by G & S Typesetters, Austin, Texas.
Printed in the United States of America.

The paper in this book meets the guidelines for permanence and durability of the Committee on Production Guidelines for Book Longevity of the Council on Library Resources.

10 9 8 7 6 5 4 3 2 1

All photographs courtesy of Detlev Vagts unless otherwise noted.

Library of Congress
Cataloging-in-Publication Data

Beard, Mary Ritter, 1876–1958.
  A woman making history : Mary Ritter Beard through her letters / edited and with an introduction by Nancy F. Cott.
      p.   cm.
  Includes bibliographical references and index.
  ISBN 0–300–04825–4
  1. Beard, Mary Ritter, 1876–1958—Correspondence. 2. Feminists—United States—Correspondence. 3. Women historians—United States—Correspondence. I. Cott, Nancy F. II. Title.
HQ1413.B39A4   1991
305.42′092—dc20   90–12699
                                                          CIP

To L. C., my lifetime collaborator

Contents

Preface

This book is an attempt to restore Mary Ritter Beard's place in history by bringing to light her private letters, against her own wishes. Historian that she was, leader of a plan to establish a World Center for Women's Archives, she nonetheless intended to leave practically no archives of her own. She used the epigram "No documents, no history"—did she want, then, no history of herself? According to her own report in the mid-1930s, she did not systematically save correspondence sent to her. If she kept copies of letters she wrote (and that is doubtful), she destroyed them toward the end of her life. She wished none of her letters ever to be published.[1]

The closest Mary Beard came to explaining why she wanted to keep her letters private was in justifying her refusal to publish letters of her husband's. Two years after Charles Beard's death, she wrote to historian Merle Curti: "Charles destroyed some letters, indeed all his letters, a short time before he died. I did the same with all but current correspondence in my files about the same time. He had only kept confidential letters and he felt obligated not to release them. I shared that feeling." She felt that correspondents who had received private letters from her or her husband should respect their wish for confidentiality. "If one cannot write freely to personal friends . . . without fear of confidences being betrayed in print . . . then liberty as friendship can be sadly lost." "It should be a precious liberty to bypass the press and public life by communing in personal letters on matters of the heart or mind."[2] Beard felt that she was acting in accord with her late husband's intentions in limiting revelations about his private opinions and her own. Before and after his death in 1948 Charles Beard suffered virulent attacks on his character and judgment, because he outspokenly criticized President Franklin Delano Roosevelt's conduct of foreign policy leading to World War II and failed to endorse the United States' entry into the war. At the time that Mary Beard made these decisions about their letters (in the late 1940s and early 1950s) she was undoubtedly feeling defensive, even embittered about the "vultures'" attack.

In her organizational and scholarly work, however, Beard was devoted to locating and preserving women's documents of all sorts in order to make possible the recording of women's history. Without that record, she fervently argued, contemporary women could not fully understand their social role. During the years that she led the World Center for Women's Archives project she displayed marvelous creative talents in excavating women's documents from basements and attics, creating historical documents through oral interviews, and identifying, cataloging, and maintaining known records of women's history. Many answers—none fully satisfying—might be given to explain why she exempted her own documents from that search. The failure of the World Center for Women's Archives (in 1940) defeated her largest hopes for women's knowledge of their own kind. By the late 1940s, the lack of recording of women's history appeared less grievous to her than women's refusal to pay attention to the historical information that lay before them. She felt protective of her private communion and collaboration with her husband, who had ended his life surrounded by hostile commentators. Both Beards had always shunned and disapproved of journalists' wishes to delve into the personalities rather than the ideas of intellectuals. Moreover, Mary Beard's version of women's history always focused on women's activities in the public realm, and it is likely that she wanted the record of her own life to do the same: her published writings would stand for her accomplishment.

Yet anyone who comes across Beard's letters in the manuscript collections of her correspondents cannot fail to be impressed that they convey the aims and variations of her political and intellectual convictions, perhaps even more lucidly than her published work does. My own interest was piqued when, in the course of other research, I began to discover her letters among the manuscripts of other women. By looking systematically in relevant collections, I was able to locate several hundred letters that she had written between the 1910s and the 1950s. The letters do not range evenly over these decades, however; only a handful date from the 1920s, and virtually all from the 1910s have to do with her work for woman suffrage. Although she wished to protect them from view, Beard's extant letters show little of a markedly private or intimate character. They are witty, sarcastic, frank in expression of criticism. The voice, however, is always that of the thinker and historian—the woman devoted to her intellectual work. One gleans only an occasional hint of her sensual or aesthetic pleasures or of her qualities as a leader, friend, wife, mother. Historian Alma Lutz, after interviewing Beard in her rented rooms in Washington, D.C., in 1939, recorded: "The apt. was light and pleasant, freshly painted but the furniture was shabby. . . . I felt that none of this mattered to her at all. . . . She was decidedly the pure historian."[3] A similar impression is gained from Beard's letters.

In this volume her literary heirs—her grandchildren, Arlene Beard and Detlev Vagts—have allowed me to go against the wish that Mary Beard expressed late in life to keep her letters private, in order to follow her larger and more lifelong convictions about the importance of documenting women's history. I believe that her letters provide the most complete and usefully detailed overview of her life's work. I have provided commentary in between to knit the letters together. My introductory essay, "Putting Women on the Record: Mary Ritter Beard's Accomplishment," is intended to complement rather than to preview or distill what follows. Dwelling mainly on Beard's published works, my essay does not explore all of the themes and issues raised in the letters, and it is especially brief on the development of the World Center for Women's Archives, which the letters themselves more thoroughly cover.

In selecting letters to publish, besides looking for inherent interest and readability I have tried to illustrate Beard's character, activities, and intellectual interests as completely as possible. I have not included letters of the late 1940s and 1950s in which she vented her spleen at her husband's critics (although she wrote many of these). In all but a few cases the letters published are whole, not excerpts. My occasional deletions of mundane or inexplicable details are indicated with three ellipsis dots. (When Mary Beard used ellipsis dots herself in letter writing, she made them more numerous, and those I have left as is.) My insertions of a word or two to identify someone named in the letters appear in square brackets, as do dates that I have supplied. I have silently corrected Beard's typographical errors. Her handwritten additions to a typewritten letter (most of which were to correct a misspelling or make a clarification) are not generally noted as such. The locations of the original letters are listed at the end of the book.

This project was made much easier and more enjoyable by Jane Kamensky's cheerful and utterly conscientious work in transcribing the letters, and by the excellent research assistance that she, Ruth Oldenziel, and Jacqueline Dirks supplied. I am indebted to all three. I also wish to thank Gerda Lerner for suggesting that I explore the Miriam Holden collection, Merle Curti for responding with interest to my queries, and Dorothy Porter for sharing her recollections with me. The enthusiasm of both Gerda Lerner and Ellen Dubois for the project has been very important to me. I am grateful to the American Council of Learned Societies and the A. Whitney Griswold Fund of Yale University for financial support for transcribing and annotating the letters and for the goodwill, skill, and cooperation of my friends at Yale University Press, especially Karen Gangel, Caroline Murphy, and Charles Grench.

I have relied heavily on the willingness of archivists and librarians at the libraries where Beard letters are held to send me photocopies, and I appreciate their help very much. For permission to publish the letters, I thank the libraries listed at the back of the book. Most of all, I wish to thank Arlene Beard and Detlev Vagts for their agreement to publish their grandmother's letters. To Professor Vagts, who has been extremely generous with his time and effort on behalf of the project and has given me full use of the letters and photographs in his possession, I am deeply indebted.

Putting Women on the Record
Mary Ritter Beard's Accomplishment

Mary Ritter Beard spent the better part of her life trying to prove the utility of history, especially by recovering women's past. She insisted that history was not whole without women's story. She persevered in seeing women both as cooperators with men and as makers, themselves, of *civilization* (a word she imbued with particular meaning). A woman intellectual of major stature and a unique historian on her own, she was also the lifelong companion and collaborator of Charles A. Beard, the most influential historian in the United States in the first half of the twentieth century. Never an academic, always an organizer through ideas, Mary Beard spoke to and wrote for the community at large. She deserves to be better known to history.

Certain themes remained remarkably consistent throughout her life work (she objected to the term *career* for herself).[1] Her approach to history and society was holistic or integrative. She refused, for example, to isolate the woman question from challenges facing society as a whole. She looked for the social principle and the process of social interaction as driving forces of culture and history. Her history writing began from the premise that "everything is related to everything else," that it was essential to see the "interplay of government, politics, economics, modes of living and working, schools of thought, religion, power, class, society and family, the arts and ambition, and the biological and cultural aspects of sex."[2]

Beside her holistic concentration on the social she had a lifelong passion to count women in. In her books, that showed as early as the high school text *American Citizenship* (1914), the first work of the Beards' coauthorship. In the preface, they objected that previous civics texts had been written "almost wholly from a masculine point of view." They called "less than half a book" any that neglected "the changed and special position of modern women." In her own first book, *Women's Work in Municipalities* (1915), Mary Beard embraced the subject of women "not in an incidental way." So did she in her subsequent works, *On Understanding Women* (1931) and *Woman as Force in History* (1946). In her words, the "whole social fabric" was not woven without women's strands. Responding to a friend's criticism of her "obsession with women," she defended herself: "The work I have done in studying women makes me aware of the large social corollaries as I should not otherwise be."[3]

Mary Beard rowed against the stream. Perhaps that has relegated her to the backwaters. She rowed against the stream of professionalization and specialization that engulfed her generation. More like a nineteenth-century than a twentieth-century historian, she was a moralist and didact who addressed the educated public. She earned no degrees beyond the bachelor's and accepted no honorary ones; she had no employment but as a writer and invited lecturer; she had no particular audience but those who would listen.[4] In a principled way, she was scornful of belonging to any academic "gild," as she called it. All these conditions had their advantages but also their disadvantages as far as the continuity of her reputation was concerned, especially because she was an innovator in both substance and style. Her published works were loose-jointed, oddly organized, her prose florid, her references sometimes obscure. Not willing to simplify the wholeness of her vision for the sake of lesser minds, she sometimes sacrificed her reader, who was her lifeline to influence.

She also rowed against the ideological stream, provoking and needling the organized feminists who would have formed her likeliest constituency. Passionately convinced that sexual equality was a deficient goal for women if it meant measuring up to a male norm, she doubted that the framework of equal rights was the most promising structure for women's advancement. In her pioneering efforts on behalf of women's history she came to believe that women's rights advocates since the nineteenth century had terribly misrepresented the past, by emphasizing women's domination by men. Nonetheless she insisted zealously that it was "important to keep the insurgent spirit alive" among women.[5] She spoke before many women's organizations, associations, and colleges and collaborated with those that shared her political and intellectual goals, but, after the suffrage movement, she joined none.

She pushed on optimistically, for most of her life, feeling in good company because she was in the same boat with her husband. Her teamwork with Charles Beard from 1900 to 1948 was a central feature in her life, their jointly written works a representation of it. After *American Citizenship*, they moved on to textbooks of U.S. history. In 1927 they published the acclaimed *The Rise of American Civilization*—which "did more than any other such book of the twentieth century to define American history for the reading public," in a later historian's accepted judgment. Its sequels followed: *America in Midpassage* (1939) and *The American Spirit* (1942). They summed up with *A Basic History of the*

United States (1944), an inexpensive mass market paperback, which sold more copies than any of their previous works.[6]

Like many the accomplished wife of a more famous man, Mary Beard achieved much greater public prominence as her husband's collaborator than she gained on her own as a suffragist, reformer, or author. Charles Beard established his presence as a major social critic and intellectual early in the twentieth century and sustained that reputation until World War II. "Not only as an historian but also as a political scientist and educator, Charles A. Beard was one of the most influential social thinkers in the United States from about 1912 to 1941," reads the assessment of him in the International Encyclopedia of the Social Sciences. His wife rode his coattails into the limelight—yet she remained on the periphery even when the limelight was brightest. During her husband's life, she received inadequate recognition for her contribution to their jointly written work.[7] (The entry in *Current Biography* of 1941 under both their names, for example, sketched his life only!) In the 1940s, when Charles Beard's foreign policy views diverged from the mainstream and he advocated American "continentalism" rather than international war, her former advantage became her burden. She felt that she shared the ignominy heaped upon her husband, because she shared his views. His fading glory entirely eclipsed her. After Charles' death in 1948, his evaluators read her out of the record, calling *The Rise of American Civilization,* for example, "his" masterpiece, "his" greatest work. The postwar generation of historians who kept Charles Beard's reputation alive by concentrated efforts to demolish his works paid no attention to his wife's contributions. The normative thinking of male historians of that generation appeared in Howard K. Beale's striking non sequitur on the Beards' coauthorship: "No one knows the nature of their collaboration. . . . Hence, I have always spoken of the joint works as Charles Beard's."[8]

Little is known about the method of their work together, about which both were always reticent. It was "too complicated," Mary Beard said late in her life, after her husband's death. Both shunned personal publicity (as distinct from publicity for their ideas and programs) and hated to satisfy voyeuristic journalists' desires for descriptions of their working relationship. In response to the inquiries of male historians, Beard was never forthcoming and usually slighted her own contribution. To Merle Curti she wrote self-deprecatingly in 1938, shortly before *America in Midpassage* appeared, "I try to help CAB escape the burden of carrying me for he is so much a personality alone. I would not allow my name to be placed on our co-authorship if I could prevent it because the major

contribution is his." Although Charles Beard told Curti that the couple
worked in "equal" partnership, Mary Beard wrote to him, "you don't
have to include me. . . . It is commonly assumed that I injected women
into the thought of history and just that. Let it all ride." On second
thought she suggested—curiously—that Curti might treat her contribution to the *co*authored volumes by noting that she had published inde-
pendently, and not only on the subject of women. Her actual pride and
investment in the joint works surfaced more visibly in her sarcasm (conveyed only to another woman writer) about a reviewer's calling a work of
the Beards "inferior to a work on American history by Morison and
Commager, naturally, because in the Beard case only *one* scholar had
worked on the book."[9]

No letters between the Beards are known to exist. They were rarely
apart. Besides, late in life they both protected the confidentiality of their
private letters by destroying as many as possible. Mary Beard's letters
found in her correspondents' papers suggest, however, a thorough and
mutually supportive partnership in writing, politics and life. In her first
published essay, in 1900, she had envisioned, among other things, that
twentieth-century women's engagement in work and politics would
change marriage from "a one-sided arrangement, a boredom, a farce,"
into "a life-long comradeship with community of interest in humanity."
In their own lives the Beards attempted to realize that transformation.
After her husband's death, Mary Beard reflected on their working life together in a letter to her son, William: "*As for my being free now,* I have
had as much freedom all along as I really cared for. . . . I loved sitting at
home with my darling every night and being at his side all the days. . . .
Outsiders and even you and Miriam [the Beards' daughter] because of
your comparative youth could not fully comprehend our mutual happiness in working, jabbering, and getting such exercise as we took in our
simple ways. THIS IS AN ABSOLUTE TRUTH."[10]

THE BEARDS' PARTNERSHIP

Both Mary and Charles Beard came from Republican Indiana backgrounds, although her youth was spent in urban Indianapolis, his closer
to small-town and farm life. Their marriage in 1900, when she was
twenty-four and he twenty-six, followed a college courtship at DePauw
University. They then lived in England for two years. Charles Beard had
begun studying at Oxford in 1898; there he was instrumental in the

Mary Ritter as valedictorian of her high school graduating class in Indianapolis, Indiana.

Mary Ritter at DePauw University. (Photograph courtesy of DePauw University archives.)

founding of Ruskin Hall, a precocious "free university" offering evening and correspondence courses especially aimed at a working-class audience. The Beards lived first in Oxford and then in Manchester, where Charles directed an extension division of Ruskin Hall, while he was also pursuing research for an institutional history of the office of justice of the peace in England (which eventually became his doctoral thesis). There Mary Beard, reared in bourgeois comfort, was first exposed to the "ghastly deprivations" of working-class life in an industrial center, an experience that "deeply influenced" her "whole life after[ward]" and imbued her with her "first and immortal feeling for labor and its history," as she later described it. The analyses and approaches of English cooperative socialists made a great impact on both Beards during this sojourn. In Ox-

Mary Ritter (at far left) and her roommate, Mary Goodwin (at far right), in a group of DePauw students. (Photograph courtesy of DePauw University archives.)

ford Mary Beard also read *Women and Economics,* the persuasive indictment of Victorian gender roles published in 1898 by the American feminist Charlotte Perkins Gilman. She began to read history, and she began to write, publishing her first essay in the journal of Ruskin Hall, *Young Oxford.* Moreover, in Manchester the Beards lived across the street from the fiery widow Emmeline Pankhurst and her three daughters. They became "devoted friends" of Mrs. Pankhurst, the genteel socialist and labor sympathizer, who was shortly to become world-renowned for her outrages against order on behalf of votes for women. "It was she who spurred me to work for woman suffrage," Beard recalled many decades later. The friendship powerfully directed the visitor from the U.S. to focus on problems of the female working class and on the vote as a form of remedy.[11]

The Ruskin Hall experience seems to have crystallized convictions that both Beards shared for the rest of their lives about the sterility of learning not aimed at progressive social application. "Mere learning in the form of collection of facts will never free the world," said Charles Beard in a

Charles Beard calling on Mary Ritter at DePauw. The bicycle in the foreground may have belonged to one of them; both were avid cyclists at college. (Photograph courtesy of DePauw University archives.)

speech there in 1900; and in her last major book, Mary Beard wrote, "The value of learning lies not in sheer erudition, if there at all." To both Beards, freeing the world was the priority. They continued to share an optimistic belief that the study and writing of history could *change* the path of history. Their most admired work, *The Rise of American Civilization*, opened with the claim, "The history of civilization, if intelligently conceived, may be an instrument of civilization." Their conviction about the dynamic relation between past and present was typical of rebellious scholars of the Progressive Era, and Mary Beard carried it through her life, in her work in women's history.

Returning to New York City in 1902, the Beards joined the "revolt against formalism" of their intellectual generation. They shared an ani-

Mary Ritter, DePauw graduate, in 1897. (Photograph courtesy of DePauw University archives.)

Mary Ritter Beard stands third from the right, next to her husband, in the center of this portrait of the Ritter family taken about 1906. The couple is flanked by Mary's brothers, sisters-in-law, and sister. Her parents, Eli and Narcissa Lockwood Ritter, are seated in the center. Miriam Beard sits on her grandmother's lap, beneath her mother, with cousins on both sides.

mus against historical fact finding for facts' sake, which made them enemies as well as friends in the School of Political Science at Columbia University, where they both enrolled—she remaining only briefly—and he subsequently found academic employment.[12] During the fifteen years following their return, Charles Beard taught history and political science at Columbia. He also produced an astounding flow of arresting prose, both journalistic commentary and controversial books in political science and history, the most shattering of which was *An Economic Interpretation of the Constitution of the United States* (1913). His fervent scholarship quickly made a name for him. There is no ready information about Mary Beard's public activities during the first decade of the century, while she was raising their daughter, Miriam, born in 1901, and their son, William, born in 1907. The couple seem always to have employed household help, but the children, understandably, occupied their mother's time more in this decade than later. "I know how you feel about the restrictions of young motherhood as well as any mere man can know," Charles Beard wrote sympathetically to a woman friend in 1917, "for Mrs. Beard had

*Three generations photographed at the Beards' New Milford property, about
1909. Mary Ritter Beard stands at far left, her parents on either side. Charles
Beard sits on the grass, with his mother, Mrs. Henry Beard, in back of him, an
unnamed maid next to her. The wagon holds the Beard children, Miriam and
William.*

everything fall on her young shoulders simultaneously." He continued,
"But in spite of all its limitations I find her believing that one must somehow work from the family out to public activity." This suggested a preju-
dice that they shared, which he made more prescriptive by adding, "It does
seem that abnormality is more apt to exist without the great human experience of close association with child life, and some family responsibility." [13]

In the early 1910s, when Mary Beard emerged a visible suffragist, still
she made periodic amends to co-workers for delay because she "had
to make the boy some suits—no suffrage" or because she had to be in
their New Milford country house "for the family's sake," or because
she "couldn't leave the children" to whom she was "glued together for
a fortnight while Charles and the nurse were both away." Before her
second-born was three years old, Mary Beard became active in several
women's voluntary organizations, including the Equality League for Self-
Supporting Women (a suffrage group) and the New York Women's Trade
Union League. In 1909 and 1910, she worked with the former to defeat
an assemblyman hostile to woman suffrage and with the latter to support

Mary and Miriam Beard, probably 1905.

Mary, Charles and Miriam Beard, resting during a hike on the Palisades (New Jersey), probably 1906.

women garment-makers involved in massive strikes. For a short time in 1910–11 Beard served as editor of *The Woman Voter,* the newspaper of the New York state Woman Suffrage Party (led by Carrie Chapman Catt). She then focused her energies on the Wage-Earners' Suffrage League, an offshoot intended to organize working-class women. Her intense commitment to that cause, and her belief that class exploitation could be addressed by women's votes, undoubtedly had been shaped by her sojourn in England. After the disastrous Triangle Fire of 1911 incinerated nearly 150 trapped garment workers, Beard worked closely with the New York Women's Trade Union League, serving briefly as treasurer. She wrote to a close colleague, the working-class suffragist and unionist Leonora O'Reilly, "It has been my dream to develop working women to be a help in the awakening of their class." Her earnest and unconsciously condescending tone, if not her awareness of class, was characteristic of contemporary middle-class women facing their working-class "sisters." [14]

Beard broke completely with the Woman Suffrage Party in 1913, angered by Catt's failure to speak up for Emmeline Pankhurst, who was now roasted internationally for her destructive acts of civil disobedience. Beard's stomach for suffragist militance was tested by her joining the Congressional Union, a new national suffrage organization founded by Lucy Burns and Alice Paul in 1913. Paul and Burns, both of whom had served apprenticeships among the English militants, jolted the established state-by-state approach of the woman suffrage movement by working for a constitutional amendment through pressure on the "party in power" (the Democrats) at the national level. Beard was a prime mover in the new group. She worked with it through 1917, approving its political approach and flamboyant tactics, although never fully in sympathy with its leaders' single-issue approach. "I am so much more radical than either of the old political parties that, when I get off and think, I lose my whole absorption in the one fight for enfranchisement," she confessed to Alice Paul in mid-1916. Beard approved of the tactic of picketing in the nation's capital that the group, renamed the National Woman's Party, began early in 1917. She led a New York delegation to Washington, D.C., to protest the imprisonment of suffrage pickets early in November of that year. Later in the same month, however, for reasons not entirely clear, she resigned from the group's Advisory Council. [15]

Charles Beard not only marched in suffrage parades but also, at his wife's urging, committed himself to the unpopular position of the Congressional Union in the pages of the recently founded progressive political journal the *New Republic*. (Strenuous and noisy arguments preceded his conversion to "positive and valiant support" for woman suffrage, in the account Mary Beard gave her son many decades later. Childhood memories of his grandmother's management of a country estate made Charles Beard underestimate women's disadvantages and overestimate women's control of resources; he did not see their need for the ballot until his wife's constant disputation—carried on "impersonally," she assured their son—convinced him.) [16]

In the early 1910s both Beards tramped the sidewalks, climbed stairs, and rang doorbells for workers' causes and for local reform candidates. While Mary pushed for urban playgrounds, Charles labored intensively at the New York City Bureau of Municipal Research; he published a survey and comparison on *American City Government* in 1912, she a similarly structured overview of *Women's Work in Municipalities* in 1915. His scholarly work on constitutional history—most notably, his reinterpretation of the motives of the framers of the U.S. Constitution to highlight their economic interests—intersected with the aims of both of them to change constitutional provision and interpretations. Both saw scholarship in service of social change. The high school civics text that they wrote together in 1914 derived from both of their interests and was written at Mary Beard's instigation, in order "to bring women into the conception of citizenship," according to a much later account of hers. The book affirmatively intended to address not only boys but also girls— the majority of high school students, as the Beards knew. Assuming that women as mothers, workers, taxpayers, and citizens subject to the laws were deeply interested in government, the Beards urged, "Civics concerns the whole community, and women constitute half of that community." [17]

Both husband and wife sustained the alternative vision of education that had inspired them at Ruskin Hall. Both remained deeply skeptical that conventional establishments of higher learning furthered the goals of democratic progress and social enlightenment. In 1917 Charles Beard resigned from the faculty of Columbia University in a celebrated defense of academic freedom during wartime, and thereafter neither Beard relied on support from an established institution of higher education. Both fostered unconventional "counter"-institutions. Charles Beard was one of the founders of the New School for Social Research (from which he rather quickly departed, however), and in 1920–21 both were among the initiators of the Workers' Education Bureau of the United States, intended to promote educational efforts among trade unionists. Mary Beard's *A Short History of the American Labor Movement*, published in 1920, was a contribution to the "Workers' Bookshelf" series of the Bureau. [18]

Both of them continued to criticize the barrenness of academically generated scholarship and to express exasperation with deficiencies in the higher learning. As her interests in women's history deepened, Mary Beard excoriated educational institutions for their muteness on women's constructive presence in civilization. "What we now have is the instruction of young men and women in the history of men—of men's minds and manners," she pointed out in 1935; "in not one college of this country— man's woman's or co-educational—is there any comprehensive treatment of women's contributions to civilization and culture." In the 1930s and again in the 1950s she envisioned and tried to plan for a "real" woman's college or research institute, one that would instruct women neither in the home economics that she deplored as an academic course nor in the "masculine" knowledge that she felt was the staple fare in American higher education. As a result of her disaffection with conventional scholarship, she distanced herself not only from institutions but from the very name of professional. An advertisement for her last major book announced, "Mary Ritter Beard belongs to no professional guild and permits no designation of herself other than that of student and writer." [19]

From 1921, when their coauthored textbook *A History of the United States* was published, until the late 1940s, the two Beards were always involved in writing works of U.S. history together, whatever else they were doing. Their base of operations was their farmhouse in New Milford, Connecticut, which purposely lacked a telephone but boasted a library eventually stocked with seven thousand books. From it they began their travels and dispatched their missives via the printed word; to it their presence drew intellectuals, policy makers, international visitors, and would-be students. The style of life that both maintained as scholars and publicists had more in common with the gentlemen historians of the nineteenth century than with contemporary professional specialists. They were both intellectual loners of a peculiar sort, wanting to address and be heard by the wide audience of the public, frequently collaborating with others on an ad hoc basis, and yet avoiding constant collegial solidarity. [20]

In the decade following the spectacular success of *The Rise of American Civilization,* both of the Beards reached the height of their public influence. During the New Deal years the couple usually spent the winter months in hotel rooms in Washington, D.C., doing research at the Library of Congress and involving themselves in politics. Charles Beard more than once prepared and gave testimony before the House Naval Affairs Committee in the effort to keep U.S. foreign policy anchored on neutrality. In part because of her work to found a World Center for Women's Archives, which she took up in 1935, Mary Beard was among the dozen "leading feminists" of that year, in the wisdom of the *New York Sun.* She was also the only intellectual among the dozen organizational leaders and professionals named as possible female presidents of the United States that year, in a widely publicized interview with the editor of the *Pictorial Review.* At that point Charles Beard's economic interpretation of the U.S. Constitution had become accepted dictum in college textbooks. In 1938, a symposium among intellectuals by the *New Republic* on "Books that Changed Our Minds" placed him second on the list, ahead of John

Dewey and Sigmund Freud in influence (although trailing Thorstein Veblen).[21]

In their sequels to *The Rise,* the Beards expressed both their aggregated interpretation of American history and their shared political views. The work of the two in the 1930s showed their preoccupation with defining a workable "collectivism" in answer to economic crisis. In *America in Midpassage,* which covered the 1920s and 1930s and was published in 1939—"a kind of memoir of the time from 2 old birds," as Charles Beard described it to a friend—they stressed the need for national management of economic and technological resources and enterprise; they equally emphasized the crucial importance of democratic methods and values, using terms such as *humanistic democracy* and *economic democracy.* Their criticism of the New Deal was that it did not go far enough in these directions. These were their joint positions, Mary Beard explicitly told friends.[22]

The two volumes of *America in Midpassage* also echoed with their insistence on avoiding munitions build-up and on neutrality as an alternative to international intervention. Shortly after the Versailles Peace Conference, Charles Beard already referred to the Great War as the "First World War." As a result of his negative judgments of the conduct and results of the war and his perception of a parallelism between Japanese and American imperial intentions, he quickly became an acute critic of American military adventurism in the Caribbean and of dollar diplomacy. He was also perturbed by the foreign policies of America's European allies, which he saw as undemocratic and imperialistic. Such international ventures would threaten constitutional government and liberties in the United States, he believed. His wife shared his insistence on maintaining American neutrality and concentrating on national development rather than international order. "Our minds and hearts are devoted to the enterprise of trying to persuade Americans to care about the making of a decent order in the USA where they have everything to work with," she wrote to a friend in reference to *America in Midpassage.*[23]

The Beards' teamwork formed in mutual respect, shared intellectual and political convictions, and mutual dependence. Charles Beard's increasing deafness made him rely on his wife's help on many occasions. With reference to his testimony before a congressional committee in 1935, for example, Mary explained, "I just have to stick pretty close to CAB and his enterprises because he is so helpless without me, being so deaf and generally so dependent on my cooperation. Even so, we generally have the same urges and points of view, if not in every instance." In their last decade together, she wrote unembarrassedly to a friend that she would go with her husband to Baltimore, where he was to teach a year at Johns Hopkins University, because "we are still in love." Her own political projects and writing always intersected with her teamwork with him. "What I print has to be rushed along to get anything of my very own out between orgies of co-authorship with CAB," she seemed to apologize to Luella Gettys, who was also the wife of a more-renowned scholar (V. O. Key). Yet she went on, "The orgies have a pleasure all their own and so do the separate thrusts at self-expression." The balance between the two satisfied her.[24]

Mary Ritter Beard preserved her independence as a writer and public figure by never signing herself "Mrs. Charles Beard," yet constant companionship with her celebrated and enormously productive husband must have affected her self-assessment. Her private letters reveal a lifelong ambivalence. On the one hand, she was intensely sure that her reading of history was accurate and all-important; on the other, she leapt to call herself "insane," "the worst person" possible to launch a project on women and history, "a low-brow."[25] She understood her mission with utmost seriousness and yet had a hard time taking herself seriously. Probably the immediate comparison of her husband's position and influence magnified in her the insecurities and difficulties that any woman intellectual of her generation faced. Charles Beard won institutional rewards and prestige that eluded her, including the presidencies of the American Political Science Association in 1926 and the American Historical Association in 1933. Having earned advanced degrees and taught at a major research university, he kept his eager academic audience, while his wife never gained one. She knew that she was his crucial collaborator, yet she must have sensed simultaneously that she was not viewed as his equal. This made her inordinately self-critical; she found it stressful to be seen as an authority. On an occasion when she was addressing a group in Cincinnati, the concentrated attention of the mayor and university president (both men) made her laugh—"I felt positively ridiculous with respect to my role as speaker but then I came to grips with myself in that role and finished out my speech," she wrote to a friend. Yet she bristled at criticism and suffered from unfair barbs. Her magnum opus, *Woman as Force in History* (1946), was initially greeted by a newspaper editorial in Charlotte, North Carolina (where the Beards were spending their winter), which said that she had "wasted [her] time working on such a book." "All I needed to do," Mary Beard grimly recounted to a friend, "if

I wished to know about the force of woman, was to ask my husband and he would tell me!" The effect on her of this "slap in the face" was "stunningly bad."[26]

In the late 1930s and the 1940s, Beard shared the views of America's place in world politics for which her husband came to be condemned. They were both vigorous anti-Fascists but also (in her words) "'hard-boiled' noninterventionists" regarding the European war. Her stance distinctly separated her from mainstream American women's groups, as she was well aware. "The name 'Beard' is anathema in many quarters, I assure you," she warned a friend in 1944, "whether Charles or Mary is prefixed to it." Her lament was fiercer a few years later, after Roosevelt's death and the publication of two books by her husband raking over the late president's foreign policy: "Charles Beard is now viewed as a combined buzzard and snake . . . and [as] a Brutus slaying a Caesar venerated by a world which understands him and abhors Brutus." Not long after that caustic observation, Charles Beard was dead. Mary Beard carried on for another decade, acting on her conviction that "work on my part is courage," to be pursued "for the mastery of grief and the enrichment of the invisible continuing companionship." She was sustained by her "glorious memories and work," she wrote to her son: "I am so thankful I trained myself to work, in this way."[27]

THE EVOLUTION OF MARY RITTER BEARD'S VIEWS OF WOMEN'S HISTORY

Mary Beard's first article, published in two parts in the journal of Ruskin Hall, began: "The volumes which record the history of the human race are filled with the deeds and the words of great men . . . [but] The Twentieth Century Woman . . . questions the completeness of the story." From this until her very last, she focused on history and its meaning for contemporary women. Spanning the century break, "The Twentieth-Century Woman Looking Around and Backward" appeared in December 1900, "The Nineteenth-Century Woman Looking Forward" in January 1901— the two titles and their order foreshadowing her later creative play with narrative linearity in history.

At this point, Beard's reading of women's past was vastly different from the analysis she would later develop. In "universal history" she saw women contributing nothing but children; marriage was akin to slavery, and women were men's beasts of burden or their valued property. She put

did not erase the Gilman-like conviction that women had been a dependent sex in the long past. Neither had Beard during the years 1912 to
1915 yet formed a view of women's roles in long history. But as a booster
of women's constructive social activities she was angered by the scarce
esteem they received. Her developing belief in women as partners and
equals with men in the common life of civilization contested with her
awareness that men scorned or diminished women's efforts. The disparity
between what she saw as the reality and what was acknowledged in men's
eyes rankled her. More emphatically than at any other period of her life,
she alluded to differentiation between the sexes in terms of separation,
hierarchy, and injustice. In an unpublished essay, for example, she compared the overwhelming public welcome given to Hungarian revolu-
tionist Louis Kossuth in the United States in 1851 with the hostility
shown the English militant suffragist Emmeline Pankhurst in 1913. Both
rebels, she pointed out, had come across the Atlantic waving the banner
of political liberty—Kossuth to be lionized, Pankhurst to be denied ad-
mittance by the U.S. government until masses of suffragists demanded her
entry. "Can it be, merely, that this is a man's world still and that the deeds
women do are not of public worth?" Beard asked rhetorically, her own
implied answer clear. As in days of old, she concluded, "Men still count
most"; "what is feminine is hysterical, frenzied, or just idiotic—in a
man's world." [32]

Beard's involvement in the suffrage cause compounds the difficulty of
tracing the evolution of her views, for her rhetorical claims in suffrage
propaganda may have been keyed to her audience's expectations, oppor-
tunistic rather than deeply felt. In an essay intended to arouse working-
class men's sympathies for the ballot for women, for example, she focused
on women of their class and claimed that without the vote, "they have
no power to help themselves." She gave a different emphasis to an article
two years later, one that drew on her research for *Women's Work in Municipalities* and was published in the *Annals of the American Academy
of Political and Social Science,* destined for an audience of intellectuals
and reformers. There she argued strongly for recognition of "the legis-
lative influence of unenfranchised women," exercised through their lobbying, their organizational platforms, moral sanctions, and indirect "wire-
pulling," as well as through their joint efforts with men in voluntary
associations. Because she concluded that these activities marked "a long
journey from woman's old spheres, the three K's," she presumably had
not discarded the assumption that women had emerged to the political
scene only recently. But she made the argument for women's influence

thoroughgoing. "In the progress of modern social legislation of all kinds—the extension of educational functions, pure food laws, mothers' pensions, development of recreational facilities, labor laws, particularly for women and children, and measures directed against prostitution—not a single important statute has been enacted without the active support of women," she declared. She was speaking mainly about middle-class activists; she conceded that "women's weight has been almost negligible in many instances" with respect to "serious labor legislation affecting large employing interests." The difference between her earlier and later statement on unenfranchised women's influence may not reflect a change in emphasis over time but her perception that working-class women had less political clout than middle-class women and needed the vote more.[33]

If Mary Beard in the 1910s had not yet set herself the task of correcting the history books, she had seen the neglect of women in history as a major problem and had called history to her aid. Frequently drawing on her own and her husband's knowledge in American constitutional and political history in the suffrage cause, she argued analogies between the nineteenth-century attainment of white manhood suffrage in the United States and twentieth-century methods of woman suffragists; she went back to Jefferson and Madison to point out to Democratic congressmen that suffrage ought to be regarded as a federal question; she drew her suffragist colleagues' attention to the U.S. Supreme Court decision in *Minor v. Happersett* (1875). Just after the nation became a belligerent in the Great War she set before the Senate Committee on Woman Suffrage the history of American women's "vital services" and "equal and active participation" in the Revolutionary War, the War of 1812, and the Civil War as justification for giving women the ballot.[34] That leaning in the direction she would subsequently go did not continue into her next book, *A Short History of the American Labor Movement* (1920), which took a conventionally male-centered approach and treated women in trade unions very briefly.

Soon after, however, Beard's outlook on the long past showed that she had redrawn her portrait of 1900 in which women were either idle, engaged in trivial domestic pursuits, or purely exploited. When, in 1921, the suffrage goal attained, she wrote to her former suffragist associate Elsie Hill, she seemed convinced that women had typically attained more equality in access to work than feminists had been accustomed to admit, and she was, furthermore, newly critical of equality as a goal for women. During a trip to postwar Britain, France, and Italy, Beard had found that "there is so much industrial equality that women sweep the streets and till

The Beard family, met upon arrival at Yokohama, Japan, in 1923 by the son and son-in-law of the city's mayor. Miriam Beard stands at left, William Beard above his parents.

the land while men drink in the cafes." Her experience made her feel "how bourgeois our whole suffrage and equal opportunity movement is." She wrote to Hill: "Women have been having that equality in the fields of Europe since the days of the Roman Empire, for example. Of course real equality would have transferred the whip to her hands and let her hitch her husband and an ass together to the plow instead of having the sexes reversed; but is that the final answer?" Beard's European observations precipitated her new conviction that women had been occupied in "the world's work" all along, although there was nothing glamorous about it. Here she denied Charlotte Perkins Gilman's main accusation, that women had been excluded from meaningful and productive work in the world— work like men's. Beard also denied Gilman's assumption that what men had was worth women's striving for. She added by hand to her typed letter, as though she could not resist the impulse, "Half the goals they [men] set are ridiculous and [women's] pure imitation is both infantile and unin-

The Beard family seated for dinner in Japan (1923), with their host and hostess. Miriam and William are at the right.

telligent. A! Ha!" At the same time that she arrived at the opinion that women had shared "equality in the fields" of toil with men, she discarded equality with men as an adequate goal for women. Her revulsion from war and her bitter observation that women "rushed to recruit" reinforced the latter point.[35]

In her developing view, equality was not an adequate goal for women because the world at risk needed women to offer something different and better, more socially constructive, than war-making men had typically provided. A English-language newspaper report of a speech she made late in 1922 in Tokyo (where Charles Beard had been called to consult on municipal problems) put a unique spotlight on her thinking. If the report can be trusted, that speech marked the first time that Beard cited women's part in founding and sustaining civilization for the purpose of urging contemporary women to take leadership in social responsibility. "Time to Boast a Bit, Women Told," summarized the headline. Reiterating her earlier objection that history books had been partial—satisfying only men's vanity—Beard argued that such an account of the past was not only wrong but also "depressing for women to believe." Here, for the first time, she began to rewrite the long past. Women probably created settled agriculture, with the innovation of storing seed, she claimed; in archives and libraries lay materials that would show the vital part womankind had played in constructing and sustaining societies. Aware of herself as an American in a foreign land, she urged women of the world to join hands and make known their part in building civilization. She closed with a vague but telling admonition that women's newly gained tools of higher education, economic independence, equality before the law, and suffrage would mean nothing unless utilized socially, for the benefit of the whole community.[36]

Beard's Tokyo speech must have reflected her reading of anthropological works on women's contributions to the development of civilized society. The likely suspects were the books highlighted by the Beards in *The American Spirit* (1942), their intellectual history of the idea of civilization in the United States: Lewis Henry Morgan's *Ancient Society,* Lester Ward's *The Psychic Factors in Civilization,* Otis T. Mason's *Woman's Share in Primitive Culture,* and Anna Garlin Spencer's *Woman's Share in Social Culture.* All of these works revealed a primitive matriarchal social organization preceding the patriarchy of biblical times. Mason's, especially, reversed the theory that human society arose from paternal considerations and claimed that the kindly arts of civilization—agriculture, cooking, weaving, pottery, child nurture—sprang from women's work. All of these books except Spencer's were late Victorian productions, published before Mary Beard graduated from college. They could have been part of her intellectual repertoire long before 1922—but were they? The Beards wrote retrospectively in *The American Spirit* that works such as Ward's (1893) and Mason's (1894) had "brought more illumination and force" to woman's rights advocates at the time:

> Hitherto the sources upon which leaders in that movement had relied for information respecting the role of women in history had been largely limited to works on political, military, legal and ecclesiastic history written mainly by men for their own purposes. . . . Now anthropology penetrated the far past, ages beyond the oldest written myths and stories on which historians of politics, wars, laws and theologies had depended . . . . By its very scope it took into account all the arts and institutions for the maintenance and care of life. . . . And in its wide searchings anthropology found women at the very center of civilization in origin and development—as creators and preservers of the arts and of that perennial moral strength of civilization.[37]

This intellectual history sounded suspiciously like Mary Beard's own. True, late-Victorian anthropological theories of ancient matriarchy heartened some leaders in the woman movement (as the women's movement of that day was called). Elizabeth Cady Stanton, for example, cited the existence of a primitive matriarchate when she criticized the Bible in the 1890s, and Charlotte Perkins Gilman was inspired by the work of Lester Ward.[38] Most male scholars writing on the theme of matriarchy meant to document the superior virtues of the succeeding patriarchy, however. Their findings offered at best ambiguous encouragement for all but the most willful and purposive readers—such as Mary Beard.

The account in *American Spirit,* written decades later, does not clarify whether Beard read Mason's or Spencer's works when they were published, or not until shortly before 1922. It seems likely that she would have read *Woman's Share in Social Culture* upon its publication in 1913, since Spencer was part of the woman movement herself, one generation older than Beard. Spencer was a minister, writer, lecturer, and reformer active in child welfare efforts, a lifelong suffragist and leader in the National American Woman Suffrage Association. *Woman's Share in Social Culture* showed (even in the similar-sounding title) that Spencer was familiar with O. T. Mason's work; like Mason, she gave women the priority in initiating family organization and settled agricultural production. Much of her book, however, focused on family and social issues in the contemporary world, where she assumed that women's unique caregiving role might give rise to liberating ethical insights. Either Spencer's or Mason's book would have provided the framework that Beard needed to support her Tokyo talk, the title of which was, revealingly, "Women's Share in Civilization." Only Spencer supplied a link between the primitive past and the modern world, in an essay on the state that suggested a relative loss for women when men achieved the democratic "rights of man." Spencer argued that as the modern state broadened its social responsibilities beyond narrowly political to "ministrant" functions, it included "woman's sphere" of social services, thus making necessary the enfranchisement of women as members of the body politic.[39] Perhaps Beard read Spencer's book in 1913 or 1914—it would have supported her approach in her own book, *Women's Work in Municipalities*—and then, during the war years or after, sought more historical-anthropological confirmation of primitive women's importance in works such as Mason's and Morgan's.

Aside from traveling in the "old world" in the early 1920s, Beard was

necessarily delving into its history, because she assisted with Charles
Beard's textbook on European history (written with William Bagley),
Our Old World Background (1922).[40] Her objections to male-centered
histories of civilization also were gathering force. H. G. Wells' two-
volume *Outline of History* of 1920 aroused her particular animus. In her
Tokyo talk she accused Wells of partiality and vanity in treating only men
in history. She continued to take him to task in the 1930s, criticizing his
failure to discuss ancient female leaders and his use of the generic Man so
as to imply that males launched civilization, when, in her view, anthro-
pologists were "almost unanimous" that females had.[41] Although Beard
had incorporated the relevance of women's invention of civilization into
her thinking by the early 1920s, she did not speak of women's "force"
coursing freely through history. In Tokyo, she described primitive women's
skills as leading to their undoing: she reasoned that men, seeing value in
women's arts and industry, used physical and mental power to dominate
women and transform them into a species of property.

Such a bifurcated outlook was more or less her position when she and
her husband began planning *The Rise of American Civilization,* in November 1923, as they traveled home from a second trip to Japan, view-
ing their own country anew as a result of journeying to the Far East.[42]
Charles Beard characterized *The Rise* to its publisher for advance publicity in 1927: "Our book is essentially an organic book, not a collection
of friable molecules. It is an attempt to get at the inner motive forces, acting continuously in time, that have driven the American people forward
through three hundred years, displaying their unresting energies in the
conquest of a continent and on the battle fields of two hemispheres. It is
an effort to disclose the contacts of unity between economic, political,
and cultural life." Here Mary Beard's integrative vision of history began
to show itself. From the first reviewers' responses to *The Rise,* Charles
Beard insisted that the work was truly joint, and that if personal mention
were necessary in advertising, that feature would be the one to "play up."
Indeed, he directed Macmillan Publishers to avoid quoting reviewers' extracts that singled him out as the author, because these were "not true to
fact or just to my co-worker." "In reality the scope of the book outside of
the politics is due to Mrs. Beard's interest and her labors," Charles Beard
wrote. "The grand plan I should not have thought of or attempted to ex-
ecute alone."[43]

A few times in her correspondence with women friends Mary Beard
took credit for thus "widening the frames" of historical scrutiny in the
joint work. To an old friend who praised *The Rise* she wrote, "Reviewers

often imply that the whole product is C.A.'s in spite of the fact that he had never written on cultural themes before and so I appreciate your willingness to count me in, in view of the way I drudged on the work for three years and especially since the cultural side was my hunch—not just women." Decades later she confirmed that in their "cooperative enterprise" she had always insisted that "history is in fact the *whole* story of humankind including religion, literature, philosophy, and biology and everything else. . . . I have in my collaboration with CAB, from its beginning, widened politics, war and law and political economy to cover more aspects of human development. CAB has accepted my wide interest and done everything he could to work with me as I have done everything I could to work with him." [44]

Mary Beard likely supplied not simply the cultural side but the civilization concept itself, now deeply rooted in her thinking. Her husband's *Contemporary American History,* published in 1914, anticipated some of the interpretive themes and judgments of *The Rise* (for instance, on the significance of the Reconstruction period) but did not enunciate the concept of civilization. She, on the other hand, had long been sounding the theme that "woman as maker of civilization" was absent from written history. In line with her approach, the preface to *The Rise* alluded to women's agency in civilization, commenting sardonically that "there would be little more than caves and barracks or bare monastic walls in the wide world" without the very efforts condemned by "strong men" for "effeminacy." More specifically, *The Rise* proposed that twentieth-century women occupied a "strategic position in the unfolding of modern civilization," because their "power as the buyers of goods" put them in special "relation to the psychological centrum, the market, around which modern industry revolves." [45]

The preface to *The Rise* stated Mary Beard's now settled assumption that women were "involved in the whole process of human evolution from top to bottom, in war and in peace, as bearers of the heritage and workers in the arts and sciences." On women's participation in the European migration and establishment of a colonial economy the Beards were emphatic. "Absolutely imperative to the successful development of European civilization in America was the participation of women in every sphere of life and labor," they began, and after stressing the skills and strengths of seventeenth-century women in farming, handicrafts, and merchandising, concluded, "No doubt the migration of families was determined by domestic council, for the most part, and after the momentous step was taken, the women assumed their share of the hardships and their full burden of responsibilities."[46]

If the colonial era presented in *The Rise* thus accorded with Mary Beard's later readings of women's history, the treatments of eighteenth- and nineteenth-century women's work, politics, and education did not. Although the book cited statistics on women's proportion in the labor force at various points, its only discussion of women in developing indus- try took the point of view of the male labor movement, assuming that women, as also immigrants and blacks, were difficult to organize. Mary Beard had not yet entirely given up a mainstream feminist reading of gen- der hierarchy and sex discrimination. Remarking on the gathering force of the movement for woman suffrage, *The Rise* took the conventional view that "politics was a man's world." It asserted that "traditional discrimi- nations" closed girls out of schools beyond a very basic level, that men had an "age-old grip on higher learning" and that women school found- ers such as Emma Willard and Mary Lyon had to battle against the cus- tom of women's ignorance. It accepted the adage that war was "almost exclusively a man's business" until the late eighteenth century when the democratization of conscription meant that women as well as men were involved in national battles. It presented women's club activities and phil- anthropic ventures during the Gilded Age as evidence that "the gravity of women's interests steadily moved from the center of the family outward"; clubwomen discussed "questions long reserved for the masculine mind." In sum, by 1900, *The Rise* concluded, "American women had broken down the walls of the traditional sphere."

Credible as all of these interpretations were—and remain, for many readers—they are surprising only because in subsequent decades Mary Beard railed against them. She later refused to believe that politics and war had ever been "men's" domains, she insisted that women had found means of education equal to their brothers, she intentionally saw the home as central to rather than separate from the rest of public activities, and she never used the language or the concept of "spheres." While she and her husband made strides toward integrating women's vital presence into the history of American experience in *The Rise,* in other words, the narrative still half-clung to the framework of "woman as a subject sex" that Mary Beard later reprobated. As *The Rise* moved into the twentieth century and toward the present, the Beards emphasized the presence and power of women, especially their leverage as the nation's principal con- sumers, their share in producing goods and ideas, and their influence on public policy and political parties. "Having the means to buy and to com- mand, education to guide them, and freedom to superintend, women became powerful arbiters in all matters of taste, morals and thinking. In short, they called the tunes to which captains of industry, men of letters, educators, and artists now principally danced," the book summed up.[47]

Like the end of *The Rise,* Mary Beard's occasional writings in 1929 and 1930 took a very sanguine view of American women's attainments and prerogatives.[48] Possibly she saw the privileges of American women in a new light after direct observation of women in rural Japan and China during her travels of 1922–23. Although she left no such record, her husband later wrote that "after a trip to the Orient the Occidental is never the same" and that during their "first visit to Japan and China—both so different from the US and other Western countries—I became a changed person." Further eye-opening travels to Yugoslavia in 1927–28, where Mary Beard took special note of women eking out a living from the land, may have reinforced impressions gained in the Far East and influenced her to connect women's long past with their present through her own writing of history.[49] Many factors must have been involved in the shift in emphasis she undertook in her next book.

On Understanding Women, which was published in 1931, proclaimed Mary Beard's interest in women in *long* history. That interest diverged sharply from the coauthored work and from her husband's concern to encourage historians to write recent or contemporary history.[50] The book also clarified what was behind her insistence on the concept of civilization. Only that concept, in her view, made room for women in history. She argued that written history—"the chief source of knowledge about human affairs"—had been partial and fragmentary, "neglect[ing] one-half of the beings that have made up the human world." There was only one way to restore balance: "the narrative of history must be reopened, must be widened to take in the whole course of civilization as well as war, politics, gossip and economics."

> It is only by attempting to comprehend the wide course of civilization, therefore, that we can hope to understand women. In its evolution we see the interplay of government, politics, economics, modes of living and working, schools of thought, religion, power, class, society and family, the arts and ambition, and the biological and cultural aspects of sex. . . . Here are revealed the actions and reactions of social forces molding both the sexes.[51]

Such a concept of civilization justified placing women at the center with men, and thus was crucial to Mary Beard's inclusion of women in history. She developed that understanding long before the joint work, *The Ameri-*

can Spirit, explained both Beards' understanding of "civilization" not as
a neutral term or a synonym for culture but rather as an affirmative sign
for the purposeful movement from barbarism to humane living.[52]

Beard's venture into *On Understanding Women* may have been inspired by her reading of Robert Briffault's *The Mothers* as well as by her
travels outside the United States. The work of Briffault, a British maverick
anthropologist, published in the same year as *The Rise* (and by Macmillan, the Beards' publisher), confirmed Otis Mason's findings with
much greater sophistication of theory and method. More than once Beard
cited the significance of Briffault's three-volume work. In 1948, as Charles
Beard lay on his deathbed, she called it "her Bible." Not only Briffault's
words but also his references may have been highly instructive as she
wrote *On Understanding Women.* Of the more than two hundred works
she listed in her book's bibliography, she commented only on Briffault's,
"contains an extraordinary bibliography on the subject of women." A
few years later, when she composed a syllabus of readings and questions
for discussion called *A Changing Political Economy as it Affects Women,*
Beard remarked on Briffault's limitations. He was brilliant on the primitive era, she thought, but his accomplishments as a social historian were
less inspiring, because he believed that women's activities during cen-
turies of recorded time were basically domestic.[53] That was where Beard
went beyond Briffault.

In *On Understanding Women,* Beard not only explicitly theorized her
historical approach but also built, on top of anthropological findings on
women's roles in *pre*history, an initial rewriting of women's roles in recorded history. Beginning with a review of the female-instigated origins of
settled society, her book amounted to a revisionist, woman-centered outline of European civilization, with some excursions to consider oriental,
Indian, Mesopotamian, and Egyptian examples too. It focused on the
high points of the standard history—the Greeks, the Romans, the feudal
and medieval periods, enlightened and imperial Europe. It found in each
setting female personalities and activities central to social and political
life and to the civilizing process. Beard eventually regretted the title she
had chosen, because it suggested a psychological approach. What she intended to show was that only history could lead to understanding. As she
later made explicit, she saw the problematic of feminist history that
stressed male domination to be, "how a creature who had been nothing
or nearly nothing in all history could suddenly, if ever, become something—something like a man, his equal"?[54] *On Understanding Women*

attacked the problem head-on, by subverting its major premise—that is, by denying that women had been nothing in history.

The book anticipated most of Beard's subsequent themes. First she pointed out many historians' partiality in neglecting women (as she would again, more caustically, in *Woman as Force in History)*. Then she improved on their views, with her findings of women's appearance on all the stages on which men also paraded. More temperately than in her later work, she explained that women themselves had been partially responsible for the "one-sided view of their work in the world," because "unwittingly they have contributed to the tradition that history has been made by men alone":

> Women have been engaged in a continuous contest to defend their arts and crafts, to win the right to use their minds and to train them, to obtain openings for their talents and to earn a livelihood, to break through legal restraints on their unfolding powers. In their quest for rights they have naturally placed emphasis on their wrongs, rather than their achievements and possessions, and have retold history as a story of their long Martyrdom. . . . Feminists have been prone to prize and assume the traditions of those with whom they had waged such a long, and in places bitter conflict. In doing so, they have participated in a distortion of history and a disturbance of the balanced conceptual thought which gives harmony and power to life." [55]

This was the critique of feminist history that Beard would later accentuate, with less empathy. She did not yet heap particular blame on proponents of equal rights nor identify the theory of women's historic subjection to men as a great evil. *On Understanding Women* prefigured another core argument of *Woman as Force,* in its brief remark that a reliance on the jurist Blackstone's eighteenth-century *Commentaries* to explain women's legal status under the common law ignored the many "offsetting exceptions" in equity jurisdiction. Beard interpreted such reliance as a failing of "writers on historical jurisprudence" rather than (as she later would) a failing of equal-rights feminists.[56] Perhaps under the influence of Briffault, *On Understanding Women* laid more stress on women's differences from men, and especially on women's nurturant care-giving, than would Beard's subsequent works. The poetic cascades that opened the book—illustrating the "bewildering diversity" that the historian might hope to capture—were divided into two sections, one on the varieties of type in the "man's world" and one on the same in the "woman's world."

Mary Beard's later writings insisted that there was only one world in which both sexes acted; she used the term "man's world" only in sarcasm.

An ambiguity reigns through much of Beard's writing, oscillating between attributing special nurturant qualities to women, and assuming that woman manifested the full range of good and bad qualities also shown by men. *On Understanding Women* leaned in the first direction, her subsequent writings more toward the latter. The preface to Beard's next work of women's history, the anthology *America Through Women's Eyes* (1933), sounded with both voices. An innovative collection of excerpts from women's writings, the book followed a narrative of American history similar to that in *The Rise*, with a sharper edge of critique of bourgeois accumulation, befitting the era of the Great Depression. In Beard's preface, her doleful acknowledgement of women's instrumentality in the crumbling as well as in the construction of societies broke through her usual intent to place women "at the center of life—where operations are carried on efficiently for the care and protection of life"; she added "or where this fundamental cultural responsibility is discarded in the pursuit of self-interest." She tried to give the constructive side more weight, picking up paragraphs later with, "If there is in all history any primordial force, that force is woman—continuer, protector, preserver of life, instinctive, active, thoughtful, ever bringing thought back from sterile speculation to the center of life and work." Yet as if in counterpoint to *On Understanding Women*, *America Through Women's Eyes* was Beard's strongest statement of women's collaboration with men.

Beard intended the book to illustrate "the share of women in the development of American society—their activity, their thought about their labor, and their thought about the history they have helped to make or have observed in the making." Her headnotes to documents repeatedly stressed women's presence alongside men, in the Revolution, in peopling the wilderness, in social reform efforts, in the Civil War, in the era of robber-baron capitalism and imperialism. Typical statements were, "In this transformation of productive economy, women were actors"; "In all the activities of that conflict—economic, moral and intellectual—women participated on both sides"; "Having worked their way into every department of the political and social structure . . . women shared in the tempest of discussion."[57] In an important sense *America Through Women's Eyes* rewrote *The Rise*, for it avoided reference to male exclusionary practices in education, work, and politics. It also barely mentioned the women who rose to challenge such exclusions.

On the whole, this volume was as remarkable for its omissions as for its content. It virtually ignored the suffrage movement, including only one excerpt from a book by Carrie Chapman Catt and Nettie Shuler, which briefly summarized the campaign and its opponents and supporters among male politicians. The pioneers Elizabeth Cady Stanton and Susan B. Anthony were presented minimally, more as Civil War–era abolitionists and Union supporters than as complainants against male tyranny. Beard gave more space to Lucretia Mott than to Stanton or Anthony, highlighting, however, her social reform and antislavery rather than her women's rights views. Excerpts on women's emergence in the modern fields of law and medicine alluded to sex barriers there, but Beard titled this section "Breaking into Privilege" and, far from underlining male prerogative or female deprivation, observed that "inevitably, forceful and intelligent women demanded the full right to share in the golden profits of capitalism and attacked the legal and social restrictions that stood in their path." Beard's intent to document historical partnership rather than antagonism between the sexes was clear. Her approach was warranted by her developing interpretation of the nineteenth-century ferment over women's rights as a brief, almost anomalous phase in the longer history of women's agency, caused when "the domestic system of industry which revolved around the care of life—woman's prime concern—was demolished by the factory system." Beard reasoned that when the "sound" domestic and agricultural economy in which women "shared as workers, directors, and beneficiaries gave place to the feverish economy of capitalism," women "had to battle as individuals" and had "to think in terms of competition for place, income, and power."

Beard minimized the significance of women's rights advocacy as providing a framework for understanding women's history, but the premise of her book was that history looked different through women's eyes. Her headnotes occasionally suggested differences between women's perceptions and men's—for example, "Through the eyes of women journalists and diarists something besides elections, camp meetings and bar-room quarrels can be seen [in the West] by those who care to see." That theme was poorly developed in the documents, however, not only because Beard avoided revelations of gender conflict, but also and principally because she chose to focus on the public arenas of activity usually called men's, and found women speaking in ways parallel to men. For example, as she introduced antebellum Northern and Southern women's documents to show the development of two opposing cultures of "machine industry" and "plantation," Beard claimed, "Not a phase of the struggle . . . did they neglect and were all the speeches of Congressmen lost, the intellectual imagery of the verbal battle could be entirely recovered from the writings of women." Her intent to show parallelism and partnership between the sexes undercut her intent to distinguish women's ethical values and social contributions and thereby to revisualize history. The anthology amounted to what has recently been categorized by women's historians as "compensatory" or "contribution" history, which advances beyond a traditional narrative by including female subjects but places them within a conventionally male-defined framework of historical significance.[58]

The vagaries of the preface to *America Through Women's Eyes* (including a poorly developed proposition of the cyclical nature of the rise and decline of civilizations) reflected distinct shifts and complications in Beard's thinking about feminism and its relation to civilization, brought on largely by the depression. The economic crisis both vastly sharpened her critique of existing feminist ideology and raised her hope for a new kind of women's movement. Beard's own feminism had been forged in the early-twentieth-century civic, suffrage, and labor movements. She felt then that women would be much more effective in constructive reform work if they had the vote; the cause of justice for women alone did not ignite her unless it broadcast a social vision.[59] Beard's subsequent views were inevitably shaped by changing definitions and practices of feminism. Shortly after the Nineteenth Amendment was ratified, the National Woman's Party (NWP)—in which Beard had enlisted and worked for the vote—seized the name of feminism for its intent to "remove all remaining forms of women's subjection." Its program was a constitutional amendment assuring equality of rights regardless of sex. More than any other women's organization the NWP asserted that women as a group had to wage their own struggle for emancipation, although, paradoxically, their equal rights amendment proposed that the law treat women just like men.[60] Its leaders embraced a single-issue politics, which severed the party from the political left and from a multifaceted program of women's liberation. The NWP thus became in the 1920s quite different from what it had been in the 1910s, both its aims and its constituency narrowed.

In light of her holistic approach to gender questions and her postwar skepticism about equality as a goal for women, Beard did not support the equal rights amendment nor the National Woman's Party. (Many of the women in it remained her friends for decades, nonetheless.) Beard saw little meaningful difference between the position of the NWP and that of professional or business women who intended to strive for success on the basis of individual ambition and merit alone. In Beard's assessment, both outlooks amounted to advocacy of sexual equality with men in the context of laissez-faire individualism (something she reprobated before the crash of 1929). In brief remarks that she wrote for the journal of the National Federation of Business and Professional Women in mid-1929, for example, she reviewed feminist progress in terms of the commercial and professional gains that women had made, asking, "What is this equal opportunity in fact and in import? It is the mere chance to prove fitness and adaptability to a tooth-and-claw economic struggle reflecting the greed and destructive propensies of the traditional pacer. . . . If business and professional women had won their race in the days of rawest capitalism during the last quarter of the nineteenth century, would they have rested content and proud to be partners on a fifty-fifty basis in the practices and ethical justifications which marked the times?"[61]

Beard's evolving views rested on the premise that feminists had succeeded spectacularly in their immediate goals. Her rosy reading of American women's progress manifested a tendency recurrent thereafter in her historical writing, toward overly facile judgment that one woman's, or a few women's, attainment of a certain status or privilege signified that women in general had the same opportunity. In the late 1920s and early 1930s Beard seemed especially impressed with statistics citing women's control of economic resources. More than once she reiterated in print that women paid taxes on $3 billion of income and received 70 percent of the estates left by men and 64 percent of the estates left by women. The possibility that these facts represented only nominal economic control did not seem to have occurred to her. Beard asserted in 1930 that American women had gained a "genuine power of directorship"—a "status amounting almost to dictatorship in the nation's industrial and social order," she claimed by 1932. "In the old days," she wrote, "it was satisfying beyond present belief to prate of equality, for there was the wild freedom to philosophize about what women would contribute when they got the chance." Now, she believed, "the chance has come in large part." American women had raced through the doors of opportunity that feminists had flung open. They had attained "important political offices, novel business positions, unexampled wages and salaries, educational influence, laboratory advantages, scientific training, honorary degrees, prizes of many sorts, rare chances to explore the earth by land, sea or air, and international recognition." They had taken the "capitalist economy at face value—the face value assigned it by men," and had achieved, individualistically.[62]

Both Beards had long been critics of economic and philosophic individualism and of laissez-faire premises. The essence of the civilization concept, as adumbrated in *The Rise* and in all of Mary Beard's work, was communal or collective cooperation, as opposed to individualism. What was new in Mary Beard's work as the depression deepened was the plain identification of feminism with individualism. In *On Understanding Women* she saw feminism as a "sex antagonism" based on "legitimate grievances." It had seen "many honorable battles" but—being a phase "not fundamental" to civilization—it should pass, leaving open new possibilities for women to take part in social evolution. In *America Through Women's Eyes*, she pinpointed feminism as a reaction-formation phase occurring in the nineteenth century when men aggrandized political and economic control and women responded by mimicking the "rugged individualism" of the time.[63] Her assumption that equal-rights feminism was bred in laissez-faire individualism, and her objections to both, became major themes of hers during the economic crisis.

Beard's critique of feminist individualism was directed not only against laissez-faire but also against the sufficiency of the male model for female aspiration. The depression enormously enforced her view that equality— if it meant aping men's ways, as she felt it had—was a spurious and a world-threatening goal. "Equality with a spoliator of the nation's resources in commodities or life is a dead aim, whatever the exigencies may be of earning a livelihood; whatever the glories of a limelight fame," she wrote in 1930. "The opportunity to rise in professions, if they remain anti-social or plain stupid in their outlook, is of no importance from the standpoint of a progressive society or State. . . . Fixing the mind on man in a effort to pursue his course to the neglect of a consciousness of humanity in the large is a weakness—not a strength—in woman." Her most profound and seemingly most heartfelt commentary focused on women's adoption of men's view of knowledge and education. In contrast to her own efforts to change the male-centered reading of the history of civilization, she judged that women's presence in the academy, in general, had only meant more of the same. "That women frequently out-Herod Herod in academic sterility is an occasion for regret rather than exultation," was her withering assessment.[64] Worse, she thought, was that university-trained women absorbed and manifested typically male views of men's leadership and importance in human society and culture. Beard had looked skeptically on academic women before *On Understanding Women* was published, but the lack of enthusiasm for her book in women's colleges seemed to exacerbate her righteous indignation. More than once she recounted with rage and scorn the unsympathetic response of the women faculty at Vassar in 1931 when President Henry MacCracken invited her there to discuss the book. "The time has come to forget women," she remembered them saying. "We are human beings now." Beard retorted, "It is easy for you to forget women since you have nothing to forget, knowing none of woman's history." [65]

With the depression constricting university budgets and Ph.D.'s "actually selling ice-cream sodas at fountains," Beard pierced the veil of women's illusion, as she saw it, about university advantages. She seriously considered that women risked handicap rather than benefit from "university discipline," and not only for economic reasons. She perceived a danger that training mainly "by the male of the species in his own modes and manners . . . may unduly crush the initiative of the girl student and force her to believe that she must follow the masculine leadership or authority without deviation and at all costs." She went on: "There is considerable warrant for the thesis that university careers guided by men have deepened the intellectual cowardice of women instead of alleviating it. By accepting man's estimate of his own behavior, economic, political, industrial, and mental, at his own figures without considering the long and important drama of feminine behavior and feminine interests, women may lose ground both intellectually and economically." [66]

Not simply the matter of gender injustice in the universities but its social result concerned Beard. She had generally hoped and assumed that education and knowledge would equip women to exercise their particular genius at social construction and cohesion. Now, she realized, the result might be the opposite. Neither she nor her husband had ever seen the inculcation of knowledge in and of itself as a necessary good; both were constantly aware of the double edge of education. Back at Ruskin Hall, in a speech of 1900, Charles Beard had said, "Learning stands impeached in the court of history as the enemy of man as often as it stands glorified for its service to man." (He used as an example the teaching of antebellum Southern educators on the nature of blacks and slavery.) [67] In the 1930s, the rise of fascism in Italy and Germany piqued both Beards' sensitivities to the possibilities and consequences of mental indoctrination.

Mary Beard's constructive pessimism about women's indoctrination to men's views in the supposedly value-neutral universities and professions was virtually unique in the United States in this period. Critics of women's presence in the professions and the universities abounded, but they were critics who felt that women's place was behind men, at home. Beard was looking for women's leadership in social reconstruction, in values alternative to the ones that had brought economic crash and fascism. One other who sounded a similar alarm, warning that women who followed in the footsteps of educated men risked becoming like them, with all their destructive faults, was the British author Virginia Woolf. In *Three Guineas* (1938) Woolf brooded over questions similar to the ones that concerned Beard (although there is no evidence that either knew of the other's work). In an extended metaphor, Woolf imagined an imposing "procession of the sons of educated men," mounting to offices of power, and asked what it meant for the daughters to join them: "For we have to ask ourselves, here and now, do we wish to join that procession, or don't we? On what terms shall we join that procession? Above all, where is it leading us, the procession of educated men?"

Like Beard, Woolf looked to history to guide her, but she found little there to prevent an affirmative answer to her rhetorical question, "In another century or so if we practise the professions in the same way [as men], shall we not be just as possessive, just as jealous, just as pugnacious, just as positive as to the verdict of God, Nature, Law and Property as these gentlemen are now?" Woolf found a partial way out of this dilemma in the inspiration provided by biographies of distinguished women of the past, women who had made notable social contributions without having entered university discipline. These women, she wrote in a poignant combination of admiration and critique, had found their own teachers in "poverty, chastity, derision, and freedom from unreal loyalties." Only partially tongue in cheek, she recommended the same allegiances to modern professional women.[68]

Beard saw in history a much more continuous exertion of social leadership by women than Woolf did. By 1933 and 1934 Beard rejected and attacked outright the assumption that men had subjected women to their own will and domination in the long past. In her mind, certainly, the theory of subjection and the demand for equality were two sides of the same feminist coin. She did not attack the subjection theory directly until, at the turning point of the depression, the gleam on equality had thoroughly dulled for her. In speeches delivered in 1933 she referred to the notion of subjection as a "false theory which dominated the women of 1848"—her reference being to the "Declaration of Sentiments" composed that year, by Elizabeth Cady Stanton and others, denouncing male domination. In writings of 1934, Beard anticipated her main argument in *Woman as*

Force in History by pinning the prevalence of the subjection theory on credulous readers of Blackstone's commentaries on the common law. She attributed the "stranglehold on thought" achieved by that view to the writings of two nineteenth-century men, both advocates of greater liberty and equality for women: the German socialist August Bebel and the English liberal John Stuart Mill. Mill's book of 1869, *The Subjection of Woman*, indeed a bible to many feminists and a revelation to many liberals, gave the "dogma" its common name, in her view.

Beard had no doubt that both the subjection theory and the goal of equality with men had had historic reasons for being—"at a time when household industry was giving way to a machine economy"—and historic usefulness. "The dogma," she wrote in 1934, "knit them into a remarkably close sisterhood, simplified agitation, provided the emotional force for continuing the struggle for privilege on new lines, and left no room for disruptive questioning." [69] As a mover for social change (and as a veteran of Alice Paul's suffrage organization), Beard appreciated the utility and significance of these items but felt more strongly that this thinking, which once seemed to open the road, now led down a blind alley. As a historian, she recognized that an ideology might be progressive at one time and regressive at another. Charles Beard said as much, in a contemporary critique of "the myth of rugged American individualism." The individualist creed, he argued—in parallel to his wife's judgment of equal-rights feminism—had been "the great dynamic which drove enterprise forward" in the days of pioneering industry. But it was now archaic and destructive, superseded by the need for collective rationalization and planning. [70]

By the mid-1930s, Mary Beard moved from questioning and criticizing women's adoption of men's ways to expressing a renewed (if subdued) optimism that the world economic and political crisis would shock feminists into a more "cosmic" awareness. All of her historical findings were aimed toward rousing her contemporaries to reenact anew what she believed to be their historically documented role of creative social leadership. On her dark days in the mid-1930s, no doubt feeling that her message was falling on deaf ears, she blamed women—agents of their own lives as she saw them—for failing to see and grasp their historic potential. Criticizing Harry Elmer Barnes' *History of Civilization* (1935) for neglecting women, for example, she wrote to a friend "But I think his fault is women's fault in knowing nothing of themselves." "More and more I blame on women themselves their own supineness and oblivion," she wrote to another close associate. [71] Her own a priori belief in women's creativity usually won out, however, and in her most optimistic vision, she imagined that "rugged feminism" (as she called it in obvious parallel to nineteenth-century "rugged individualism") would retreat, and a new feminism emerge. The new feminism would be "less imitative than the old, more constructive and less acquisitive (therefore destructive), indicative of feminine concern with political economy as a whole as the old feminism was not, and in its collectivist vision betraying its realistic roots." It was such a vision, integrating women's struggle for gender justice with the encompassing "demand for decency of life and labor all around and security if possible," that Beard sought to foster in a course of readings and questions she composed at the invitation of the American Association of University Women in 1934, published as *A Changing Political Economy As It Affects Women.*[72]

Few other feminists understood what she was trying to do. "Mary Beard is a friend of mine but she has such a strange point of view. When have women had the power she gives to them?" one National Woman's Party activist wrote to another. To her friends in that group, Beard's announcement of her "disillusion" with the theory of subjection and the goal of equality was truly baffling. They did not sympathize with her intensified critique of a single-issue approach to gender justice during the depression. Loyal equal-rights seeker Doris Stevens identified Beard's interests in social renovation and collectivism with communism, not feminism—despite Beard's protestations that she was not a Communist. Stevens insisted "that a feminist can and must do one thing at a time," while Beard believed "that we have to do everything at once." Beard's desire to develop women's consciousness, values and leadership as such did not fit with the program of the Communist Party in the United States. She insisted—here in tune with Doris Stevens—on "admitting oneself to be a woman and making that reality and influence count as such." She deplored the "folly of pretending to represent something as neutral, as a 'human being' neither man nor women," an approach typical of women in professional and political posts (liberal or Communist) during the 1930s. Beard's claim that women had long been partners with men in the public domain also set her at odds with the educational approach of the League of Women Voters, which emphasized—to her annoyance—gradual training rather than immediate action for female newcomers to the political process.[73] Her support for U.S. neutrality (especially toward the end of the 1930s) was more thoroughgoing than that of middle-of-the-road organized women who also did not embrace her opposition to free-trade internationalism. At the mid-decade peak of neutrality senti-ment in the United States, however, she found political if not necessarily feminist allies in the National Council for Prevention of War and the Women's International League for Peace and Freedom.

In the most salient division among women activists of the 1920s and 1930s, over the equal rights amendment, Beard "held aloof from the fac-tional strife," in her own words. She criticized her former colleagues re-maining in the NWP, perhaps because she expected more of them. Al-though she easily conceded that a "woman's bill of rights," as she called the equal rights amendment, was "long overdue" and "should have run along with the rights of man in the eighteenth century," she believed that current advocates of equal rights ran the risk of "positively strengthening anachronistic competitive industrial processes; of supporting, if uninten-tionally, ruthless laissez faire; of forsaking humanism in the quest for feminism as the companion piece of manism." If the ERA were achieved, she contended, "it would be so inadequate today as a means to food, clothing and shelter for women at large that what they would still be en-joying would be equality in disaster rather than in realistic privilege."

Her reservations about the equal rights amendment were balanced by no fewer reservations about its opponents who stressed the need for sex-based legislation regulating wages and hours. These women, not so un-like Beard, considered the equal rights amendment a narrow-minded, na-ture-defying expectation of sameness between women and men. Their conception of women's difference from men echoed conventional views of women, centering on the home, however. They usually portrayed wage-earning women as vulnerable, passive, dependent victims of the man-made industrial system. Beard not only refused to see women as victims but, more positively, believed that constructive work in the world as well as in the home defined women's essence. The protectionists' determina-tion to prevent exploitation of women workers appealed to Beard, but she found their approach inadequate to the task of social leadership that feminists should provide, especially during the depression. "The mini-mum wage implies *a* wage and leaves out of account the millions of un-employed," she objected; it represented "too complacent, too sentimen-tal, an acceptance of capitalism" and was "too consistent with the economic rule of a plutocracy." The agenda of neither equal rightists nor protectionists, she thought, would really "make a dent" on the "anti-social American labor system."

"Sex protection . . . embodies the objectionable idea of dependence.

Equality leaves out of account the objectionable mores of 'free' men,"
Beard said concisely, expressing her lack of sympathy with both sides. In
her most stirring statement on the issue, in a letter of 1937, she charged
equal rights advocates and opponents both with "inadequacy against
women's and democracy's ruthless enemies—war, fascism, ignorance,
poverty, scarcity, unemployment, sadistic criminality, racial persecution,
man's lust for power and woman's miserable trailing in the shadow of his
frightful ways." Her agenda instead was "plenty-for-all, to be attained by
democratic co-operative planning on a broad scale, with state help where
needed." As that suggests, her own vision was only schematic. She spoke
of "community planning for the meeting of community needs," a "collectivist" approach "less solicitous of the interests of the few." She looked
for "decency of life and labor all round and security if possible to attain"
and gave this as high priority as equal opportunity for women. To advance her vision of security for all, she urged women to be "creative leaders in the vanguard," *more* than equal to men.[74]

The vision itself was one she entirely shared with her husband. As
collaborators whose views on both domestic and international politics
agreed, both Beards were moving in new intellectual directions during the
1930s. Dropping the hint in *America Through Women's Eyes* that the
Italian historian Benedetto Croce and other social theorists were encouraging her to see a revolution in thought and a more integrative understanding of human history on the horizon, Mary Beard confirmed that
she shared the intellectual background of her husband's celebrated presidential address to the American Historical Association (AHA) in 1933,
"Written History as an Act of Faith." Indeed, her own work in theorizing
and writing *On Understanding Women* may have contributed signifi-
cantly to her husband's interest in disputing the propositions that objective history could be known and that it was the professional historian's
task to capture it. Although Charles Beard's new accent has been seen by
some historians as an "intellectual conversion," a break from his former
reliance on economic determinism to an unprecedented historical relativism, a more persuasive case has been made for the essential continuity
and consistency of his purpose from the 1910s to the 1930s. As early as
the Ruskin Hall experience, the relation between the historian's found
facts and the usefulness or interpretation of those findings was an imma-
nent theme in his work. His address of 1933 assumed the impossibility of
conveying the past as it was in actuality and the inevitability that the historian would select events or facts (often on the basis of incomplete docu-

mentation) to make a purported whole picture. It was for these reasons that he called the writing of history an "act of faith," which relied on a subjective "conviction that something true can be known about the movement of history."[75]

Whether Mary Beard influenced her husband to address directly the issue of subjectivity in history is an interesting if unanswerable question. Before "Written History as an Act of Faith"—also before Carl Becker's presidential address of 1931, "Everyman His Own Historian" offered its relativism to the AHA—Mary Beard had perceived and asserted, in *On Understanding Women,* that "everything seems to depend upon the historian—his locus in time and space, the mere detail of birth, affiliations of class, and the predilections of sheer uncritical emotions." There she reviewed how partisan, rather than disinterested, were historians from Herodotus, Tacitus and Polybius on through Gibbon, Ranke, and Treitschke. She pointed out the political leanings of each one. Similarly, Charles Beard would a few years later focus on the political interests of Ranke, in order to burst the illusion of the objective and neutral historian. He seemed to echo his wife in retorting to a critic, "Is it possible for men to divest themselves of all race, sex, class, political, social and regional predilections and tell the truth of history as it actually was?" He had also, however, presaged the specific themes of his 1933 speech earlier: in a 1926 address he noted that historians' selectivity with their facts always constituted interpretation and in a 1930 speech posited the existence of "history as actuality," something external to the historian, the recording of which was to be sought.[76]

In considering the historian's subjectivity, both Beards were apparently influenced by intellectual currents in science and historiography. Croce's *History, Its Theory and Practice* (1923) stood out for both. Mary Beard listed the book in the bibliography of *On Understanding Women* in 1931 and mentioned the author in *American Through Women's Eyes;* Charles Beard frequently quoted Croce in the 1930s, and as president of the American Historical Association invited him (unsuccessfully) to attend the group's annual convention. Croce's position that "all history is contemporary history"—that, in other words, written history was inevitably "contemporary thought about the past"—powerfully appealed to both Beards. His underlying supposition that "only an interest in the life of the present can move one to investigate the past" expressed both of their predispositions. Croce was a more thoroughgoing relativist than either Beard, however—doubting that there was a distinction between facts and ideas, and pursuing the conviction that facts exist only in the consciousness of the observer to the conclusion that individual consciousness was the only reality.[77]

For Mary Beard, finding the facts of women's history was a life work. Both Beards stopped short of Croce's total subjectivism or solipsism, by retaining a conviction of the *actuality* of history—what was out there in the past, separate from the observer, real though not perfectly known. The relativism that Charles Beard enunciated in the 1930s was not anti-scientific or antiempirical but in tune with contemporary science: he drew on the thinking of scientists and philosophers of science, such as Alfred North Whitehead and Arthur Eddington, who tried to project the meaning of the new science of relativity for humanistic inquiry. The two Beards together and separately employed both the concept of actuality and the term *frame of reference* during the 1930s to describe the history writing at which they aimed, adapting these from the words of contemporary scientists, philosophers, and social scientists about the sociological implications of discoveries in non-Euclidean geometry and non-Newtonian physics. Both pursued their historical work of the late 1930s and the 1940s believing in the objective existence of "history as actuality," the wholeness of which the historian tried to grasp. Mary Beard's premise that "everything is related to everything else" in the "wide course of civilization" was akin to Charles Beard's claim that history as actuality would unite "all that has been done, said, felt and thought by human beings on this planet since humanity began its long career."[78]

To Mary Beard, the concept of history as actuality was not merely an instrumental but a necessary abstraction, crucial to her task of recovering women's history. In her actuality, women played full part. As she asserted in *On Understanding Women,* if women "dropped out of the pen portraits" drawn by historians in the service of states, kings, priests, or noble classes, they nonetheless "remained in the actuality."[79] Her perception of the disparity between past actuality and the fragmentary and tendentious historical record motivated her work.

Beard saw in fuller portrayal of women's history the antidote to women's underestimation of their own efficacy and the corrective to career-minded women's blithe dismissal of the relevance of gender. In the crisis of the 1930s, she was looking for a common and empowering consciousness among women that was not a sense of subjection or victimization. She was hoping for a shared consciousness among women that led not toward individualism but toward a movement for distributive justice of the most inclusive sort.[80] A unique vehicle for this appeared when Hungarian-born feminist-pacifist Rosika Schwimmer came to Beard with the idea to create an archive in which the documents of women active in the suffrage and peace movements of the early twentieth century would be preserved. As Beard initially saw the plan it represented a "way to recapture the imaginative zest of women for public life." "To recapture that zest I believe that some dramatisation of the woman's culture is necessary, is imperative," she wrote to a possible supporter. "It is perilous for society if they retreat to private interests to the exclusion of interests in the common life represented by the State."[81]

The story of the World Center for Women's Archives from its origins in 1935 to its collapse in 1940 is well told in Beard's letters. From Schwimmer's initiative, Beard developed a much more wide-ranging (and for a while, it seemed, quite successful and well-publicized) project to collect and house documents of women of all sorts. It involved dozens of sponsors and donors and served as the matrix of later major collections, including the current Sophia Smith Collection at Smith College and the Schlesinger Library at Radcliffe College. Beard conceived of it not as an antiquarian or curatorial project but as a political venture, the basis for an educational revolution, and the site from which women's public protests and social leadership might emanate.

Beard chose as the motto of the World Center for Women's Archives a phrase attributed to the French historian Fustel de Coulanges, "No documents, no history." It suited her purposes; yet her husband in the 1930s cited the positivist de Coulanges as a foil, a shorthand reference to a vision of history uncongenial to his own. "Where the records pertaining to a small segment of history are known," Charles Beard conceded in his AHA address, "the historian may produce a fragment having an aspect of completeness, as, for example, some pieces by Fustel de Coulanges; but the completeness is one of documentation, not of history."[82] Did Mary Beard choose "No documents, no history" with sharp irony, knowing that interpretation, point of view, the historian's conviction, mattered at least as much as the documents? Or did she mean to imply that documentation of and by women had unique quality in a history usually seen through men's eyes? The latter seems more likely. To sustain her conception of actuality, documents were the only proof. Because it was impossible to observe the past as a chemist sees test tubes on a table, Charles Beard once wrote, "The historian must 'see' the actuality of history through the medium of documentation. That is his sole recourse." In Mary Beard's aim to widen the frames of history to see women as they were in past actuality, documents were her eyepiece; only on documents could a new vision rest. She wrote with feeling to Dorothy Porter, the librarian at Howard University whom she enlisted to collect black women's papers for the Women's Archives project, "Papers. Records. These we must have. Without documents; no history. Without history; no memory. Without memory; no greatness. Without greatness; no development among women."[83]

Having gained what seemed to be a height of promise in 1938, the World Center for Women's Archives traveled a rocky road of factional disputes and failing financial support over the next two years. This was during the same period that public sentiment in the United States gradually moved from neutrality toward increasing acceptance of the possibility of war against fascism in Europe. Mary Beard related the two. That is, she hoped to acquaint women better with their historic role of building civilization in order to anchor them as opposers of war. "If we are ever to keep women from ganging up with men for war, we've got to give 'em a substitute in idealism meaning something to them personally," she noted to a colleague. At this time she was as much involved with her husband in the—as it turned out—futile effort to prevent the United States from joining the European war as she was with the archives. But by the late 1930s her reason and observation had crushed whatever hopeful belief she had held (if any) that women could be expected to show a pacific bent. *America in Midpassage,* for example, rejected the generalization that women tended to oppose war more emphatically—or more "naturally"—than men. It noted that the "white glare" of history showed women "as warlords of the most intransigent type at points in historic time when they ruled States or sought to rule States." In a full paragraph it recited women's methods of goading and supporting men in battle during the Great War. Yet Mary Beard (presumably she) could not resist following that recital with the claim that "in the main, fighting was man's business in history and women had been primarily engaged in the arts of peace, the making of civil society." She aimed her archives efforts to shore up that latter tradition, in which she did believe despite examples to the contrary. Neither Mary nor Charles Beard thought it impossible that "the cult of the irrational, exalting man's fighting above humanity's peace" might spread in America as it had in Germany and Italy. Their horror of involvement in the European war was in part a horror of that happening, thereby transforming the American tradition of civilian over military supremacy in the state, and also overthrowing women's constructive tradition.[84]

The edifice of Mary Beard's hopes for the Women's Archives came

crashing down around her in 1940, at the same time that American war
sentiment came to seem inevitable and Charles Beard's vociferous opinions to the contrary made him a pariah in the very circles where he had
been lionized. Officially, the closing of the archives was attributed to the
diversion of women's interests and funds to the European theater. Although Beard considered the leadership's internal weaknesses and disputes to be controlling reasons also, she did connect the end of the center
with the movement toward war in a profound sense. Both showed her
failure to get women to heed her clarion.

By 1940 Mary Beard must have felt doubly, triply rejected. Women
whom she had seemed able to marshall now betrayed their civilizing role
to march to the war drummer; feminists seemed more concerned to insist
that "there can be no true equality until a woman becomes a Major General or Field Marshal" than to oppose American involvement in the war.
Her depression-era vision that women would awaken to "cosmic consciousness" was blotted out. Her plans for an institution to document
women's lives were erased, half-realized; and her husband was increasingly excoriated in the press and in person for views that she wholly
shared with him.[85] At the peak of their influence on public opinion a few
years earlier, both Beards had been pushed to the margin by 1940. To add
insult to injury, the publisher of *On Understanding Women,* having
agreed to bring out a new edition, refused to publish the revised version
that Mary Beard submitted under a new title, *Woman: Co-Maker of History.* She blamed the rejection on the publisher's unwillingness to accept
a new preface in which she dismissed fond beliefs of women's innocence
of war-making and criticized Carrie Chapman Catt for naive denials of
women's complicity in war.[86]

The writing of *The American Spirit,* the Beards' next volume and the
only one thought by some critics to be more the wife's than the husband's
work, must have been a supreme act of will, defying pessimism and de-
featism as the United States entered the war. The book set out to trace
American uses of the concept of civilization and, more than that, to show
that the United States was uniquely situated to advance the concept. It
was more purely intellectual history than its predecessors in their American civilization series, consisting of quotation and examination of one
writer and thinker after another. Taking a cue from Henry Adams' admonition that one needs a polestar for guidance, the book re-viewed the
American experience so that civilization, rather than individualism, became its driving concept. The idea of civilization was, as the Beards wrote
it, a social principle, antithetical to individualism.

The American Spirit can be seen as an attempt to wrestle with the contradictions aroused in Mary Beard's mind by the entry to war. She had
developed and clung to the conviction that civilization—the move toward
individual and social perfection—did inhere in history and that women
were central to its making. The descent to war, even more directly than
the depression and the rise of European fascism preceding it, battered her
theoretical balance. How could she hold to her conviction during World
War II? Not only did civilization seem at risk, but women's instrumentality in bringing it to the brink seemed obvious to her. Time and again
she pointed to the women leaders and disciples of Nazism, for example,
as well as to the way that Nazism crushed the very aspirations that
women in the United States cherished. The resolution in *The American
Spirit* was that it was "sufficient for inspiration and guidance in conquer-
ing the forces of disorder and opposition and bringing the real closer to
the ideal" if "ideals and illustrations of the true, the good, the beautiful,
the social, the useful had existed in human experience from the beginning
of recorded time."

The volume provided such illustrations—among them, the efforts of
participants in the nineteenth-century woman movement. The book especially highlighted the ideas of Lucretia Mott and Elizabeth Cady Stanton,
arguing that they both worked for civilization not as narrow-minded
feminists but in a multifaceted way—"taking the full range of social
issues into the scope of their thought and argument." In a treatment curiously at odds with most of Mary Beard's earlier and later pronouncements about the women of 1848, *The American Spirit* judged that "rights
always remained, for the philosophers of the woman movement, only one
interest among many—fundamental, it is true, but never all-inclusive respecting the purpose of the movement." Beard had already shown her admiration for Mott's social contributions in *America Through Women's
Eyes*. *America in Midpassage* also made Stanton important among the
"host of men and women" in the mid-nineteenth century who "undertook to make America conscious of human values, alive to the dangers of
a purely acquisitive economy, and willing to carry out programs of reform." Had Beard extended that appreciative analysis, her later work in
women's history would have looked very different.[87]

The Beards plucked the idea of civilization out of the burning, avoiding pure idealization or pure determinism, by contending that "the progressive realization of reason and good is *in* history, though not the sum
of history." They thus achieved a dialectical view, emphasizing the human "struggle against the forces of barbarism and pessimism wrestling

for the possession of the human spirit" while admitting that the latter—barbarism and pessimism—were also human features. They did not purport to offer an explanation of the universe or the "whole truth of history" (which Charles Beard, especially, had acknowledged was impossible) but "a construct, or view of life, summational and relative." And they offered it intentionally to combat pessimism, in the moderated conviction that humans inhabited "a partially open and dynamic world in which creative intelligence can and does work." Averring that "individual and collective efforts . . . can make the good, the true, and the beautiful prevail more widely, advancing civilization," they closed the book with a supremely ironic twist. War was the one invariable in human history, itself proving—since it depended upon some degree of civilization—that "the future of civilization in the United States has at least this much assurance." [88]

Thus, by effort of will (and absorption in research and writing), Mary Beard propped up her belief in the advance of civilization and women's role in it during the early years of the war. Her next project showed the bloom still coloring the rose of her creativity. Invited to submit revisions for the *Encyclopaedia Britannica* with respect to its treatment of women, she seized the chance. Selectively lashing male predecessors, she criticized the *Britannica*'s entry on the "American Frontier" for its ignorance of women's civilizing roles and of "mutual aid in community life, the co-operative enterprises which elevated the individualistic will to social prowess." She called the treatment "extremely narrow and bigoted" for following Frederick Jackson Turner too closely: "The tight little, provincial little, masculine thesis of F. J. Turner has had a death-like grip on the historical guild and has induced . . . historical writing by laymen . . . which has made [the frontier] barbarous—and made it men without women." With insight and constructive genius, she suggested several dozen new entries on topics including air-conditioning, bathing, bread making, women's colleges, cooking, domestic relations courts, etiquette, goddesses, Hull House, hunger, laundrying, matriarchy, militarism, non-resistance, patriarchy, priestesses, revolution, social implements (as a counterpoint to weapons), women, and war. [89] Her commentaries and revisions were probably much too radical for the *Britannica* to swallow. After she had done her work and enlisted more female talent to provide biographical sketches of notable women, the editor's interest fizzled.

By early 1944, after the Beards had completed their last (and best-selling) collaborative work, *A Basic History of the United States,* Mary was involved in a new writing project of her own. She finished the manuscript of *Woman as Force in History* in June 1945, although it was not published until the following spring. It went beyond *On Understanding Women,* not only criticizing male historians' neglect and showing women's public presence and participation throughout history but also making direct assault on the "dogma" of woman's subjection to man and on the corresponding feminist goal of equality with men. More decisively than ever before Beard indicted nineteenth-century advocates of women's rights and their successors for adopting the "subjection theory." She traced their mistake to the influence of Blackstone, in whose commentaries on the common law the legal position of the married woman was presented as wholly dependent on (absorbed into) that of her husband. Beard devoted much of her book to arguing the didacticism and partiality of Blackstone's view, because it neglected the equity courts. Under equity jurisdiction, Beard argued, women gained more leverage for their own interests than under the common law and did not suffer the "disabilities" that nineteenth-century women's rights' advocates stressed. Beard's reasoning about equity repeated the same flaw that her essays since the late 1920s had shown, for she assumed from the evidence of a handful of women using equity that their escape from the iron hand of the common law was typical or available to women in general. She was proud of her findings about equity, which were significant and thought-provoking if not conclusive.[90]

If women had always exerted force, what accounted for the widespread perception of female inferiority and male privilege? *Woman as Force* implicitly addressed this objection and answered that the feminist version of history was a prime cause. By adopting a Blackstonian view of their own "nothingness," Beard contended, women had taken a disastrously wrongheaded approach to their own rights and their own history; women themselves (as well as male historians) had hidden the truth of women's force. She thus resolved the contradiction between women's accomplishments in actuality and their apparent suppression by blaming women themselves, as if they had the power to have created an alternative outcome. Beard's woman-blaming was in accord with with her insistence on woman's force; it preserved her frame of reference whole. She roundly criticized male recorders *of* history but gave no room to men's resentment or subordination of women *in* history.

It is hard to measure the influence of her partnership with her husband on her mature view, in which she blamed women as much and perhaps more than men for past mistakes; but such an influence must have been exerted. The Beards' collaborative relationship may have provided the unconscious model and conscious corroboration for her thinking about women and men in long history. Her assumption that women's historic role of care-giving was consistent with their shaping of history in its largest aspects paralleled her own combination of family and public role. Her stress on partnership between men and women as the norm, sex antagonism as its distortion, paralleled her own harmonious relationship. The lack of acknowledgement she received for their joint work kept her from being complacent. She was constantly goaded into awareness that women's values and accomplishments remained underappreciated—but her own accomplishments, in her view, were undervalued by women as much as by men, and more gallingly so.

By the time Beard wrote *Woman as Force* she had a lifetime of collaboration with her husband and a dozen or so years of disappointments with women behind her. In comparison to her earlier work, in which she acknowledged the "legitimate grievances" and "honourable battles" of feminism, here she reduced the scope of women's historic demands to a partial and mistaken monotone on subjection. She construed the meaning of feminism narrowly, equating it with sex antagonism, atomistic individualism, and a misreading of history. Beard was very hard on men in the book, too. She used corrosive sarcasm against historians, social scientists, and men of letters for their misuse of the generic *man* and for their omissions and distortions of the record of women. But she blamed women as keenly for accepting the limited sense of themselves that men purveyed and for refusing to learn otherwise.

Beard knew the book would be controversial. She presented it polemically, announcing that "the dogma of women's complete historic subjection to man must be rated as one of the most fantastic myths ever created by the human mind." Reviewers picked up wildly divergent messages from her presentation. One male reviewer read her argument as vindicating men's behavior toward women, on the whole. He suggested that Beard's method could be used "against any other lurid caricatures of history. Wage slavery never was so abysmal as it appears from the soap-box. Not all overseers were Simon Legrees." A female reviewer wondered, on the other hand, "Why is Mrs. Beard so angry? For very early in this book you raise your hands and cry 'O.K.' Men have treated women shabbily throughout history."[91]

Neither of these responses was the result Beard intended. She meant to correct counterproductive interpretations of the past, to inspire women to meet the challenge of their social responsibilities not by imitating men but by working in tandem with them. The tone of the book predominantly reflected her wartime frustration and bitterness, however. The accomplishments of women during World War II, paraded before her as she wrote the book, presented a real dilemma for her thinking. The accelerated entry of women into men's industrial occupations and the integration of women into the armed services and into government posts and professions all served as good examples of Beard's claim that women were at the center of the common life, "equally directing" social forces. But the evidence that women were joining with men in the military machine, following men's model rather than providing a social leadership particularly their own, wreaked havoc on her faith that women's civilizing presence was worth affirming. Women's visibility in publicly supporting during the war threatened Beard's dearest convictions at the same time that it confirmed her basic thesis. Believing that women had chosen during the war to follow men's models and values, she thereafter felt freer than ever before to emphasize that women *had* freedom of choice and that the notion of women's subjection to men was "fantastic," a fiction. In letters of 1947 and 1948 Beard blamed sex inequities on individual women's indolence, childishness, lazy-mindedness, weakness, or elevation of men's knowledge above their own "by choice."[92]

In response to a male friend's praise of *Woman as Force*, accompanied by his assertion that he had always been a feminist, but not in the "opprobrious" sense she employed, Mary Beard wrote, "Whether I am a feminist or not depends of course on a definition and I am not bothering about this at all."[93] It is certainly possible, and in a narrow sense accurate, to call her culminating book antifeminist. In view of her life's aims that would be a great mistake—and yet the historical context of the book makes its antifeminism more important to notice. In a sense, *Woman as Force* was more in tune with its times than any other of her works, for a rash of antifeminist pronouncements during the war and postwar years sought to pin social malaise on women's betrayal of their familiar domestic roles. The brief against equal-rights feminism in *Woman as Force* anticipated the parallel critique in the most popular of the postwar diatribes, *Modern Woman: The Lost Sex,* by Ferdinand Lundberg and Marynia Farnham. Beard's book shared with Lundberg and Farnham's the glib description of feminism as a sex antagonism that complained of subjection and proposed only equal rights and women's imitation of men. Both books pronounced that the feminist tradition ever since the eighteenth century had grossly misled women by inducing them to follow men's model instead of their own destinies.

Where the two books differed—crucially—was on the question of des-

Undated portrait of Mary Ritter Beard, probably in her fifties.

tinies. Beard found women's historic mission in world-building, and Lundberg and Farnham found it in mothering. The audience and attention gained by *Modern Woman: The Lost Sex* infuriated Beard; she raged against its pseudopsychiatric analysis of the world and women's needs and saw the book as an overt antagonist in her battle to influence minds. "Naturally I am drawn into the contest for the capture of youthful thinking," she wrote to the president of Radcliffe College. "BUT I HAVE LITTLE DOUBT THAT THE PSYCHIATRISTS AND SEXOLOGISTS WILL BE THE VICTORS." To a friend she named Lundberg and Farnham's work the "nastiest book of this year (1947)." She was no friendlier to other postwar commentators who advocated refocusing women's sights on the domestic hearth.[94] Seeing only the conflict between her own and Lundberg and Farnham's aims, she probably did not recognize and certainly did not admit that their caricature of equal-rights feminism mirrored hers.

More than one commentator has noticed a tension in *Woman as Force in History* between Beard's emphasis on women as civilization builders and her alternative theme that women have been both creative *and* destructive, as good and evil as the best and worst men.[95] That dynamic tension playing through Beard's work matched her doubled vision of her subject both as Woman—a singular abstraction—and as women, diverse individuals. Advancing beyond the typically monolithic interpretations of Woman offered by predecessors (and by contemporaries such as Lundberg and Farnham), her doubled outlook was accounted for in part by her historical location. Beard's intellectual activism overlapped two generations. The organized women of her youth, in the late nineteenth century, believed in the coherence, the nurturance, and the constructive character of the group called Woman. Further inspired by her readings in late-Victorian anthropology, which stressed women's contributions to primitive civilization, Beard had a longing to retain that view of woman's role. But she also fully participated, in the 1910s and 1920s, in the emergent, self-named feminist generation's desire to get rid of Woman with the capital W, to revolt against formalism and enable women to choose their own destinies, in all their variety. Beard had both a political and historical commitment to see women as variety rather than one.[96]

Beard's uniting vision of women's past can be seen as her attempt to reconcile these two competing—and in her mind, equally true—frameworks, the first presenting women as one group, and a constructive one; the other presenting woman as many, as diverse, and as risky a population as men. Perhaps her historical vision did as good a job of reconciliation as possible, by finding variety and individuality in women's past, consistent with the overriding theme of women's work for civilization. Beard's vision of women as force in civilization was a consciousness-raising conception, intended to enable women to see themselves as a heterogeneous yet coherent group. Toward the end of her life, in a letter to an old friend, she summed up her life's effort to restore women to history: "What I have been trying to do for years is to awaken women to the reality of their historic power . . . to incite women to realize who and what they have been, with a view to their realizing better who they are and what they are now doing."[97] More than liberal feminism steeped in individualism, her vision had potential appeal for women across ethnic lines because of its basis in women's communal strivings. Yet where Beard wanted to eliminate one myth—that of women's subjection—she substituted another. In *Woman as Force in History* that tendency was visibly exaggerated. Offering women the strength of a vital shared history at the center, she granted no legitimacy to women's collective sense of grievance at exclusion or relegation to the margins. In her effort to redirect attention to women in history, she minimized and distorted the historical tradition of feminist protest.

In a fitting summary to Beard's work, both the strengths and the weaknesses of *Woman as Force in History* stemmed largely from her concentration on women in the public realm. As her earliest article had predicted, she remained interested in woman as "world-servant" rather than "house-servant." Although she saw women's care-giving in the familial context as archetypical of their civilizing role, she never attempted to plumb the historical depths of women's roles in marriage, for instance, or child rearing. When, in her early reform days, Beard preferred to regard women as political rather than as moral beings, that was not simply her secular voice speaking (although she was entirely secular)—it was her conception of the political as participation of the public community. She put the political first and judged morality by its social or political results—its collective or communal results. Similarly, her attachment to the concept of civilization (and her insistence on including women in it) relied on its origin in the Latin *civis*, which signified to her "the life, rights, duties, and moderation of citizenship—a care for public affairs." The Beards discussed that etymological origin in *The American Spirit*, where they distinguished *civis* from *cultus*, the root of the word *culture*, and linked concerns of the home and care of children and other private matters to culture, not to the category of civilization.[98]

Exactly why Beard stuck to the public aspects of women's presence in history is difficult to say. Possibly the interests and life work of her husband greatly influenced her. He, her collaborator, kept his sights on politics, economics, and international affairs and the gravity of his force perhaps kept her more centered on questions of public rule (the law, the state) and political economy than she otherwise might have been. Her emphasis may also have had much to do with her substantial dependence on secondary sources for her investigation of women in long history. Except for her reading of nineteenth-century women's manuscripts in the Library of Congress and her reading of *published* primary sources, she relied on other scholars' works—and those works largely concentrated on public figures.[99] Whether it occurred by intent or in effect, Mary Beard's attention to women in the public arena may be criticized as a capitulation to traditional historical priorities. One might even charge that as a result she failed to heed her own adage. For in looking at women on men's ground—as the public or political realm was ideologically construed to be—was she not taking man as the measure, the very method she reprobated? Her anthology *America Through Women's Eyes* risked that reading, and certainly her accounts of women as rulers and warriors could be read as such.

Yet Beard also testily criticized the traditional limitations of history to kings, wars, nations, and states. She intended to widen that framework. Her focus on the public should more justly be seen as a utopian leap. By emphasizing that what women did was political and social, she intended to eliminate the equation between the male and the public, to reinvent a conception of the public as a communal arena in which women as well as men acted. Whether or not Beard herself would have conceded it, she shared that perspective with her forebears, the mid-nineteenth-century pioneers of women's rights who wished to assert themselves as public actors and individuals, neither dependent on or represented by men nor confined to private influence only. Most nineteenth-century women who sought greater equality with men in education and legal status and in the professions and occupations—knowing well that their private characterization as sexual beings, mothers, wives, and lovers cut short their opportunities—stressed the civic side of their characters just as Beard did in her history. Beard differed in claiming that communal responsibility belonged to women in long history; she refused to see women as prevented from such exercise until the rise of feminism. She differed from some, too, in denying that individuality in itself was a sufficient goal and in always advocating instead a social outcome for women's self-representation. None-

Charles and Mary Beard in a snapshot taken at New Milford, probably about 1940.

theless, her emphasis on the public personae and public responsibilities of women in history followed the path laid out by nineteenth-century insurgents who burst the strictures of the so-called separate sphere.

Mary Beard went so far toward expanding the boundaries of the public as to shrink the importance of the private realm. Evidence for this comes up in unexpected places—for instance, in her adamant opposition to home economics in the collegiate curriculum. Beard consistently maintained that "at college women like men should start their thinking and training with the subject of political economy as applicable to each [sex] and both together." She considered "training for home-making" a form of vocational education that belonged to technical schools. In a letter of 1936, she expressed concern that "admitting the claims of home economics to place beside public work" manifested a dangerous, even "fascist" tendency "to revert from full opportunity for women in public life." Going beyond the view of some feminist-minded pioneers of higher education for women, who believed that collegiate experience should provide an education as good as—by which they meant the same as—that available to men, Beard simply dispensed with the question of domesticity's claims on college-educated women. She wrote brusquely to a close associate who felt differently, "I have told you face to face and by letter that I do not regard the study of women's state of mind respecting domesticity and a career or their problems of domesticity itself as a proper phase of collegiate education." Although many women intellectuals and professionals who were her contemporaries acknowledged that modern women faced conflicting demands if they wished to pursue "full opportunity in public life" while also being wives and mothers, Beard looked away from this problem; she emphasized instead "the total economy in which women like men must function—whether at home or outside." [100]

Beard's position can be seen as a radical one. To an extent she was challenging the nineteenth-century ideological division of life into public and private spheres; certainly she was challenging the assignment of women to the latter only. As her claim that "everything is related to everything else" suggested, she wanted to merge the private into the public as she wanted to merge women's history into men's. But she was more comfortable and persuasive asserting women's civilizing power—placing women at the center—in reference to societies in which notions of public and private were not elaborately developed. In describing ancient or simple societies, she could speak of women's nurturance or domestic arts and feel sure that those accomplishments were recognized as both distinctly women's and distinctly public or communal, for the common good. She

Mary Beard in her study in the early 1950s, in a snapshot taken by a Japanese visitor. (Photograph courtesy of DePauw University archives.)

suggested *Encyclopedia Britannica* entries on baking and laundering, for example, but never addressed modern women's involvement in these activities. Intending to correct the typical treatment of women as private subjects in recorded history, she emphasized the public world even at the expense of examining the significance, historicity, or gender dynamics of intimate interactions. She turned a blind eye to the private realm rather than undertaking a political analysis of its construction. She never alluded to the separation of public from private in complex, modern, industrial society, unless her writings of the 1930s on feminism as a phase of historical development can be understood as implicitly recognizing that ideological development. To have explored that separation would have clouded her vision of women as world builders.

If Beard resisted historical investigation into private life because it would risk defining women in history as principally engaged in that realm, she had more complicated motivations also. She wanted to mark out an enclave of personal life that would not be subject to history—certainly not in her own case. Perhaps the tremendous irony that the archive-minded Mary Ritter Beard did not preserve her own papers can be understood in this context. Refusing to permit Merle Curti to publish her husband's private letters, she assured him that "as far as lies in my power . . . I shall see that his life as a public person is depicted in documents"—but no more than his life as a public person.[101] Her protection of the letters, like the Beards' refusal to discuss their collaboration with historians or journalists, manifested her defense of an inner sanctum beyond the historian's privilege. If the inner sanctum was, by the same token, not "in the common life," not revelatory of history, then her challenge to the bifurcation between public and private was not heartfelt. But her refusal to place gender-restrictive labels on any realm was genuine.

Beard spent most of her life reclaiming women's history as a necessary underpinning of the self-knowledge that would enable women to seize social leadership. If her coauthorship with her husband merits more attention than it has been given, her creativity in women's history was yet more farseeing; it most distinguished her and also set her apart from her contemporaries. Her major concerns and accomplishments were ahead of their time. No audience was fully ready to hear her unique message that the frames of written history had to be widened to encompass women's past. She affirmed women's agency in creating their own history and created the experimental vision that history looks different through women's eyes. Her insistence that women have always been central to history-making helped bring to life our current understanding of gender as a category of historical analysis.[102] Her deep-dyed conviction that women need their history in order to change their future is a most appealing part of her legacy. Given the boost of a vibrant women's movement and the welcome of an expanded and diversified scene of higher education, women's history has developed in the past two decades into a significant field—but neither of these circumstances surrounded her ventures of the 1930s and 1940s. And if women's history at present is still the "other," not the mainstream history despite its vital supports and the tremendous energy of its practitioners, how much more risky at her time—though crucial to ours—must we acknowledge the efforts of Mary Ritter Beard to have been? The full realization of her best insights and the practice of social justice that she did not call feminism (but we might) still lies ahead of us.

1 The Suffrage Years

Though she may have been active even earlier, Mary Beard's involvement in municipal politics in New York City on behalf of labor reform and woman suffrage becomes traceable beginning about 1909. Beard's real love and aim in the suffrage movement at this time was to involve working-class and wage-earning women, and in this venture she helped to organize a section of the Woman Suffrage Party called the Wage-Earners Suffrage League, in which the fiery trade-unionist Leonora O'Reilly was a leader.[1] It is probably a constitution for that section that she mentions in the letter below. Beard eagerly sought O'Reilly's views on the meaning of the ballot to publish in *The Woman Voter* alongside those of Columbia professor Henry Rogers Seager (a prominent member of American Association for Labor Legislation)—a presentation of "the working girl and the professorial views together," illustrating her lifelong tendency to rate academic knowledge no higher than grassroots wisdom.[2]

The letter below shows Beard in the midst of suffrage organizing with O'Reilly, preparing, among other things, a benefit performance of a play to be put on by working women. She expended as much time, money, and effort as she could muster. "If the [working] girls would only begin to wake up, it would be worth my life," she wrote to O'Reilly.[3] Like O'Reilly, the women mentioned in the letter—garment worker Clara Lemlich (whose words are credited with precipitating the garment strikes of 1909 in New York City) and social investigator Helen Marot—were both major movers in the Women's Trade Union League, a group that brought sympathetic middle-class or wealthy "allies" together with wage-earning women to foster the latter's education and unionization.

1. TO LEONORA O'REILLY

> The Woman Voter
> Mrs. Mary R. Beard, Editor
> January 1st, 1912.

Dear sister L. O. R.,

The enclosed constitution is what I got out of our conference that day. In this shape you can improve it as you see fit ready for its submission.

Where shall we meet next Monday night? Perhaps we had better meet at our headquarters in the hope that certain girls may turn up who have had handbills.

I was so absolutely worn out for a week that I had to drop all the threads and with you ill too we have not got very far perhaps; but I have had a rest of two days (only had to make the boy some suits—no suffrage) and feel ready for a fray again. However I hated to ask people to go to the trouble of rehearsing for the play for the 13th when there was no time for us to work up a crowd. When we suggested that night we forgot that holidays would interfere with meetings and then I have not known whether we could get the League [building] for $5 or whether we must pay $10. One week later we could have a well-attended performance and the girls would be able to help it go which is our reason for existence, isn't it?

I sent Clara [Lemlich] to call upon our suffrage leaders in several distinctly labor regions to see what they had done toward getting hold of working women, whether they had any meeting room where we might hold a meeting and whether they could give us names of girls. That was all right was it not for the time you were laid up? The child was nearly frantic with desire to work which especially interests me for the reason that Helen Marot said she did not believe we could get her to work. She seems to me to be keen about it and does everything that is suggested and does it well, I think. Of course we don't want to spoil her. She can help so much now with the New Year.

I shall be in to see you on Friday and if in the meantime you want me for anything, drop me a card or telephone at 4887 Morningside or 5860 Gramercy.

Yours as ever, Mary Beard.

❦

The Woman Suffrage Party was working at the state level, trying to get the New York legislature to put a referendum on the ballot to enfranchise women. In that effort, Mary Beard negotiated cooperation between the educated and prosperous women in the College Equal Suffrage League and the trade unionists in the Wage-Earners Suffrage League. This was made more feasible by the membership of both kinds of women (the former as allies, the latter as workers) in the Women's Trade Union League. All the women mentioned below—Marion Cothren, a 1900 Vassar graduate, lawyer, and reformer; shirtwaist-makers Clara Lemlich and Mollie Schepps; and hat-trimmer Melinda Scott—were activists in the

N. Y. Women's Trade Union League. The Wage-Earners' Suffrage League did sponsor a mass meeting to respond to the legislators' antisuffrage remarks and published their speakers' addresses in a pamphlet, *Senators vs. Working Women* (1912).

2. TO LEONORA O'REILLY

> Woman Suffrage Party of the
> City of New York
> Friday—[April 1912]

Dear sister L. O'R.

The College League has taken Cooper Union for April 22 for working up the wage-earners' section in the parade. I suggested to them that they get working women to answer the Senators and assemblymen who made such terrible statements in the debates on suffrage. If the bill comes up again to-day there will be more to answer. They absolutely ignored the workers—saying they "must defer to the *ladies* until they were ready for it"; they wanted "to relieve women of all burdens and responsibilities"; "suffrage would destroy the incentive to motherhood", etc. etc. *Now* if at this coming meeting you could ask "What is the incentive to motherhood to-day among the working women?" and Melinda Scott and perhaps Mollie Schepps and Clara Lemlich and a laundry worker could all go after these men with "hob-nailed" boots, we might interest the girls and have a terribly lively meeting. I have been instructed by the College League to work with Mrs. Cothren in getting speakers and have therefore left a note for Melinda, who made a fine speech at the New Jersey hearing, asking her to speak.

We had to get busy and I went ahead not knowing you were back. Am so happy to learn you are "home." Will you speak and act as chairman—April 22d then? Whom else do you suggest? Can you persuade Mollie Schepps?

Do tell me you like this idea for I am thrilled by it. We want to get out our announcements just as early as possible. We thought it might be good to give out tickets for the meeting to the union girls and girls at the lunch and other clubs around town.

We wish your mother would speak. Wouldn't she?

Here are two tickets for you and for her if you care to use them. If you can't, please let me have them again. They were given to me for you.

Love and a heart full of hope.

> Mary Beard.

•←┬

Mary Beard recalled for a friend who was pursuing the ballot for women in Japan after World War II the "devices for getting out the vote" that she and her suffrage colleagues had used decades before: "mass meetings with stirring speakers; use of the press daily with news of *events* devised for the sake of this attention-calling; street corner meetings as well as rallies in halls; booths on sidewalks, made attractive with posters and literature, where women invited passersby to hear how, where, and why to vote; parades—what parades—at night with lanterns and by day with banners—'an army with banners!' and the very fact that women would parade unashamed for the 'cause'—a way of proclaiming its urgency; bands for the parading to enliven interest and help the marchers to stay in line."

Besides writing and organizing and raising money, Beard herself canvased door to door, especially in tenement districts. She recalled:

I did a lot of this kind of canvasing for the enfranchisement of women and of course ran into every sort of attitude and reasons offered for them. When a woman replied to my appeal for help in this campaign that she would not give it because the Mother of God did not vote, then slammed her door against further annoyance, I was for a moment too paralyzed to ring more door bells. But our women who agreed to work this way also agreed to report to district headquarters at the end of every canvas and we all wanted to make the fullest reports we could, which meant speaking to as many housewives as we could.

In some cases this door to door canvasing may have been somewhat or really dangerous but I never knew of any injury to any woman's body. Perhaps the instructions which were given to the canvassers helped to make the business orderly; such as, refraining from quarreling, behaving with good manners, leaving literature and in such a way, if possible, that at least the paper would be accepted, and be careful to remain outside the door and talk there if the place seemed otherwise risky. The real danger to many of us was that our legs would give away with exhaustion from the countless flights of stairs we had to climb in the workers' quarters.[4]

During this period the Beards lived on the Upper West Side in New York City, because Charles Beard was employed as a professor at Columbia University. In 1909, however, they bought an old farmhouse in New Milford, Connecticut, where they soon began spending summers with their two children. Mary Beard's life of reform then had a seasonal cycle, in which she spent summers "in the country . . . for the family's sake."

3. TO LEONORA O'REILLY

[May 1912]
New Milford, Conn.

Dear Leonora—

I am sorry to have had to leave the fight so early but I am not so essential to it as I was earlier. There ought to be enough people interested in the Wage-Earners side of it now to make it go. The fact that such an army of tenement mothers and working women marched with Mrs. Belmont ought to stir the sluggish to action.

Though I must be in the country now for the family's sake, I am getting busy on a campaign Hand Book full of facts to be ready by autumn. So few speakers have facts and illustrative material.

I wanted to tell you goodbye. If, at any time, I can help at this distance, call on me. I wish you and your mother could have come up for a rest. My love to the girls in the W[age] E[arners] S[uffrage] L[eague] and to *you*.

Mary Beard.

Through her work on the Woman Suffrage Party of New York Beard was nominally affiliated with the National American Woman Suffrage Association—since the state work was carried on under the aegis of the national organization—but she, like others in similar local groups, was not working directly for national enfranchisement of women. That changed when in 1912 or early 1913 she came to the attention of Alice Paul and Lucy Burns, two young women recently returned from participation in the militant suffrage movement in England. Paul and Burns had in mind to reinvigorate the campaign to gain the ballot for all American women at once by means of constitutional amendment, an approach that had been dormant since the 1880s. They managed to be appointed to, and to revive, the virtually defunct Congressional Committee of the National American Woman Suffrage Association, which was supposed to deal with the federal route to suffrage. One of the first women whom they sought to join them was Mary Beard. They must have valued her not only for her reputation for effective work and connections with the labor movement but also for her husband's name. (Charles Beard published *An Economic Interpretation of the Constitution of the United States* in 1913, bringing himself even more publicity than he already had as a popular professor, municipal expert, and author of widespread articles, reviews, books, and textbooks on American government and politics). The Congressional Committee immediately began working up a huge parade to take place in Washington, D.C., on March 3, 1913, to upstage Woodrow Wilson's inaugural. Paul and Burns intended to pressure the president and Congress to make a constitutional amendment for woman suffrage a reality. They did, shortly thereafter, take up Beard's suggestion (below) to publish a national paper. A weekly, it was called *The Suffragist,* and Beard was listed on the editorial board.

4. TO ALICE PAUL

New Milford, Conn.
Sunday [early 1913]

Dear Miss Paul,

I am rather overcome by your own and the National [American Woman Suffrage Assocation]'s appreciation of me although I am very happy to be a part of the Congressional Committee.

The only hesitation I feel about marching in so prominent a place is lest the Washington women who are coming for the parade and who really have worked far harder than I—many of them—may think I am in this thing for personal notoriety. It is very comical to me to picture myself in that light but I would not do anything in the world to hurt the feelings of a single Washington woman when they all have been so fine about the movement there.

I have accepted the National's election and I shall do everything I can to help you. If you are sure there is no tactical objection to my carrying the banner, I'll be with you.

Leonora O'Reilly has had another change of heart apparently for she is circularising the trade union girls very hard for the parade. I wrote her a very long and very earnest letter pointing out what seemed to me the blind folly of ignoring political action.

The main thing I believe I can do for you will be to help start the national paper. That seems to me an absolute essential. If you are in Washington long enough, try to see Elinor Byrns about it as she will be greatly interested I know and would help solicit funds. I shall try to see her also. I am going to draw up the best scheme I can devise for my idea of the funds and organisation and send it on to you soon.

It will be good to see you on Saturday.

Cordially, Mary Beard

•←~

Participants in the demonstration planned for inaugural day were self-sponsored, so to speak: women were organized in state and occupational delegations, which had to cover their own expenses. A divisive issue emerged when a group of black women from Howard University offered to march in the college delegation; in response, several white women (it is not clear who) threatened to withdraw. The racist atmosphere and practices of the nation's capital at this time invited a segregated march. Alice Paul initially favored that resolution, but black suffragists did not give up their dignity so easily. Fortunately several white suffragists, including Mary Beard and the New York delegation, were resolute about finding a way to have an integrated march. W. E. B. Du Bois, a leader in the National Association for the Advancement of Colored People (founded a few years earlier) and editor of its monthly organ *The Crisis*, reported what happened this way:

> The woman's suffrage party had a hard time settling the status of Negroes in the Washington parade. At first Negro callers were received coolly at headquarters. Then they were told to register, but found that the registry clerks were usually out. Finally an order went out to segregate them in the parade, but telegrams and protests poured in and eventually the colored women marched according to their State and occupation without let or hindrance.

His assessment must have been based on black women suffragists' reports of their interaction with Alice Paul and the other leaders in the Congressional Committee. Du Bois affirmed that "after the matter was settled the treatment of colored participants was exceptional."[5] There must also have been a section principally made up of black women, for Mary Beard recalled decades later to her son: "I was marshal for that event of a section of the parade in which Negro women marched. I had insisted that they be permitted to participate and, since I was one of the first women to support Alice Paul and Lucy Burns, . . . my insistence that Negro women join in the parade was effective. But the fear that the hordes of people from Maryland, etc., who would come to Washington to see the parade, would be so furious to see Negro women in it, that they would resort to violence was so strong that I said I would get some men to assist me in marshaling that section. . . . I headed that division dressed in a Green Cape and some sort of cap. The men took positions at the sides of the Negro marchers—tall, impressive fellows. AND THERE WAS NOT A SIGN OF TROUBLE ANYWHERE ALONG THE LINE."[6]

The undated letter below, which must have been written shortly before the march was to take place, shows Beard's intention to resolve the racial issue to the satisfaction of the black protesters. The whole Beard family marched in the parade—Charles in the men's section, the children on horse-drawn floats.[7]

5. TO ALICE PAUL

[late February 1913]

Dear Miss Paul,

Here is a faithful report of the colored meeting. It was a small meeting but an exciting one. Three factions were represented:

1. Those who hesitated to make any demands which would possibly hurt the cause of suffrage. This position was taken by Miss Atweed of Wellesley who however wants to march with the college section if she marches at all. She is inclined to think it wise not to march.

2. Those who accepted the invitation from New York which I tried to convey to them as cordially as it had been expressed to me by Mrs. [Harriet Burton] Laidlaw. Mrs. [Mary Church] Terrell who was deemed in the early days a great acquisition to the suffrage ranks settled her attitude on the colored question by deciding positively to march with New York.

3. Those who were determined to put up a fight by marching where they belonged, they said, and not just where some women were willing they should march. These persons were certain that a southern minority was terrorising the northern majority and they felt it to be their duty now to take a stand for their own people. They are very indignant over the situation. Mrs. [Ella Rush] Murray, whose husband is a prominent man some way at the Congressional Library while she is a college graduate, represents this faction.

After a very heated discussion, I proposed that each woman sign her name on a paper saying where she wanted to march and that a committee representing all three factions take this paper to you to-day. You may not approve my action but I do want, if possible, to prevent trouble on parade day. Faction no. 3 will take the story to the antis and give it to the press, they said out and out, if satisfaction is not obtained at once.

Personally I am sick too of southern hold-ups and I do not believe that the political situation requires it for I do believe that we shall lose more in the north than we shall be able to offset by southern complacence if we have a row on parade day.

In conclusion I just want to say that Miss Hunt has not been able to stir up the colored women, had she desired, for she has not been well for weeks. The situation is entirely due to colored opinion itself and neither Miss Hunt nor I who were both present at this colored meeting could have made these women all of one mind had we so desired. They could hardly wait until I had finished telling them of the plan to put them with New York, etc., to rise and object.

We ought to be intelligent enough to avoid a race war. That is a perfect nightmare to me.

Yours, Mary Beard.

By April 1913 the suffragists following Paul's and Burns's leadership had founded a suffrage group separate from the National American Woman Suffrage Association (NAWSA), which they called the Congressional Union for Woman Suffrage. At the end of that year, relations between leading women in this group and their former colleagues in NAWSA were decidedly acrimonious. Mary Beard, as the letter below suggests, believed or hoped that the two suffrage groups could work separately without conflict, but her optimism was not justified.

The Congressional Union (CU) declared its sole goal to be achieving the vote through constitutional amendment and immediately began lobbying congressmen and attempting to send deputations of women—working women, Democratic women, women from various states—to see President Wilson. Mary Beard worked energetically on these early schemes. The letter below refers to plans for a delegation of women wage earners to see the president. Beard's connections with the New York Women's Trade Union League equipped her to aid the effort. The delegation, four hundred strong, arrived at the White House on February 2, 1914, although only twenty-five of the working women were allowed in to see Wilson.[8]

The CU was unique in seeing suffrage as a "party measure"—that is, in laying the onus on the Democratic party, which was in control of the White House and Congress. As early as 1914, the CU decided to marshal the votes of women in the ten Western states where they were enfranchised to threaten the Democratic party at the polls if gains toward a constitutional amendment for woman suffrage were not made. Mary Beard was wholeheartedly in favor of this strategy. Her speech at the hearing referred to below—before the Committee on Rules of the U.S. House of Representatives, where both NAWSA and CU suffragists testified in December 1913 in an effort to have a Committee on Woman Suffrage established—included a sophisticated analysis of the Democratic party's national electoral strength in the South as compared to the West. Beard argued that the party could not retain its power in the next national election unless it endorsed woman suffrage and thus ensured Western women voters' support. Her speech was well received by other suffragists, although Hull House leader Jane Addams reportedly thought she "hit the Democrats a little too hard." The hearing did not accomplish its object, however, for the House did not establish a Committee on Woman Suffrage until September 24, 1917, after several more years of suffragists' efforts.[9]

The great bulk of suffragists stuck with their local organizations affiliated with the NAWSA and felt either puzzled by or hostile to the aggressive new tactics of the CU. Early on the CU attracted mainly radical women and feminists, like Crystal Eastman (a lawyer, social investigator, and thoroughgoing socialist activist) and, on the other hand, some imperious elite members of the social register. The most famous of the latter was twice-widowed Alva Belmont, who had inherited great wealth from railroad magnate Cornelius Vanderbilt and industrialist O. H. P. Belmont. Beard (who was almost ten years older than Alice Paul but more than twenty years younger than Belmont) probably felt more at home with the younger radical women, but as the letter below suggests, she welcomed the reputedly cantankerous Belmont into the CU. In another letter of January 1914 she wrote to Burns, "Mrs. Belmont is justified in not wanting to be considered merely a money bag; but she says she does not intend to interfere with you—only she wants to be asked for her opinion now and then just to be a human being."[10] Beard also retained a certain distance from Alice Paul, unlike many of the suffragists magnetized by her leadership; her letters reflect what seems to be more ease and intimacy with Lucy Burns than with Paul.

6. TO LUCY BURNS

400 West 118th. St., New York
January 18 [1914]

Dear Lucy Burns,

The deputation goes on apace. Mrs. Belmont is going to pay for five women and I have promises for five more with expectations of others.

I'll send you names and pictures and speakers by the last of this week. We are planning to escort them to the station for a press story and to show them how we feel. We'll try to take working women with us on this occasion to make it seem that it is a spontaneous uprising of the proletariat. Will you be able to get hospitality for these women? . . .

Mrs. Belmont is very anxious to see you or Alice Paul. She is really very keen about the [Congressional] Union and its political acumen. I had a long talk with her this afternoon and if we treat her as a being capable of thought she will be a valuable ally, without interfering unduly too.

As for your attitude about putting it up to the Democratic party as a party measure, I am entirely with you. The other position seems to me messy and un-political. If we can just go on refraining from talking about the National [American Woman Suffrage Association] and do our job, the country is ours in a little while.

I dare say Alice Paul does not need to be warned against betraying any feeling about the National but if she has had so much that she does, you might say that she will keep her position by entering into no personal controversy of any kind. Let them say what they please and let us work. Mrs. Belmont is appealed to for instance tremendously by that policy. She never replies to any criticisms about herself, I believe.

I have some good people working on the congressmen and hope for reports soon.

Tell me what you know about the report of our hearing. They say it was lost or stolen, do they now? Do you think my talk is worth printing as a campaign document in case the committee fails to make good to-morrow in reversing that decision against us?

Yours as ever, Mary Beard

•┅

Sending a deputation of working women to see the president meant raising the money to finance their transportation and accommodation during the trip; Mary Beard was intensely involved in the details of nickels, dimes, and dollars required to accomplish this, taking responsibility for thirty delegates from Connecticut and eight from New York. Raising money through the Women's Trade Union League was less feasible than ever before, because most of its wealthy allies in New York, being NAWSA loyalists, did not wish to aid a CU venture. Beard was apologetic that she could not give more because she was "just so horribly poor."[11] Costly in time and effort, the delegation paid off handsomely, if not in President Wilson's conversion, at least in attention and adherents for the CU. At this point Harriot Stanton Blatch, daughter of Elizabeth Cady Stanton and leader of an independent New York City suffrage organization, the Women's Political Union, which had been concentrating on the vote at the state level, became quite interested in the national effort of the CU, especially with Mary Beard's coaxing. So did Emily Pierson, a leader in the Connecticut suffrage movement, several of her closest colleagues, and some possible new donors. Mary Beard continued to cultivate Mrs. Belmont, who not only promised financial support but brought into the CU's publicity limelight her daughter, Consuela Vanderbilt, who had married the duke of Marlborough and become a duchess.

7. TO ALICE PAUL

400 West 118—New York.
Feb. 4 [1914]

Dear Miss Paul—

I hope you are not very "mad" at me for not coming when you telegraphed for I was nearly dead I was so tired. Let me know sometime why you wanted me so much.

I have some good things to report:

1. Keen interest on all sides in the national situation. The working deputation thrilled every one. The press was splendid and is hungry for follow ups.

2. Persons coming over who were opposed or indifferent: (a) Mrs. Blatch who asked me to-day to come on the W[omen's] P[olitical] U[nion] Board and said the W.P.U. would try to push the parade for May 2d. Wouldn't that "jar" you? (b) Miss Symons of The Tribune now a keen friend—whole spirit changed.

Mrs. Blatch told me she would help in a campaign. She and Mrs. Belmont are working for the parade.

3. Money in sight. I went on a hunt for Mr. G. W. Perkins to-day but learned he is close to the McCormicks in the Harvester Trust so will have

to count him out perhaps for a little while but Mrs. Belmont was out all afternoon seeing men to get money from them. One she is to ask for $5000; two others $1000 each.

4. Chances that we can profit by putting Mrs. Belmont on the committee at once. Miss Reilly [Belmont's secretary] is very level-headed and she tells me how to manage things. This is confidential, of course. Mrs. B— loves the lime light as her social training was all along the line of rivalry for leadership. As she is always a good press story up and down the land, we can view her as business men would say as "a risk worth taking." She can now come to Washington and hold a suffrage meeting at a Mrs. Townsend's (biggest house in Washington?) to which every swell in town will be pleased to come. Our committee can't reach that element as she can and we need its money and support. She can preside at that meeting and have what speakers she likes and if she takes a collection or gets money, she'll turn it in to us. Miss Reilly will go along to handle the press side tactfully and she has a keen knowledge of the psychology of it all as well as a deep admiration for the Union.

Again—the Duchess of Marlborough is coming to visit Mrs. Belmont in July at Newport and Mrs. Belmont will make this play into our coffers and press.

She will give largely if she comes on the [Executive] Committee.

She can get us fine press notices if we could have meetings in the South and West where she might be present. Boston made big money out of her visit there. The national work will give her wider outlet so she may not tire as soon as she does locally.

The above are assets. The liabilities are possible inconstancy, break-out in the press, or promise without fulfillment. If Miss Reilly stays by her side we are secure and she will for a time. If Miss Reilly leaves, and trouble occurs, would we really suffer?

It is a gamble but I am a sport and I vote "take it" and do it quickly. It means money and press notices and big meetings and interest. All we need is to understand the psychology of the lady, I *hope*.

5. Emily Pierson was completely won over to the [Congressional] Union's policy and her delegates went home wild with enthusiasm.

6. Expect to have a good story in the Herald tomorrow on our policy.

7. I hope to find a contribution this week to pay for the $85 you sent me [to cover the costs of the delegation]. It is really $95 because Mrs. Nathan's check came back too. I had to use it all because I had the Conn. women on my hands. Emily Pierson could only get car fare and they had no money themselves. It was so important to see that the expedition did

not do more harm than good. Women simply would not give them hospitality and I took them to so cheap a hotel that we had to take in the Ball too. The New York delegates are pretty spoiled—some of them—and they wouldn't have gone or would have been crosser than usual if they hadn't been given money for meals on train. I felt nothing must be allowed to spoil the deputation and I would have gone right on and spent my own money if some had not come from the Union. Please tell Miss [Doris] Stevens this so she won't think it a hold up or strike. I intend to get it out of some one now.

Emily Pierson spend loads of money herself and she is grand to have won over.

I believe Melinda Scott's stories of hardships of hospitality are temperamental. Maggie Hinchey seems to have been comfortable at the place of which Melinda complained.

I hope everything went off well from your standpoint. Things are clearing up even in New York for the May demonstration and meanwhile I'll finish my reports on congressmen and try for money. *Can you* send me lists of coming congressional elections next autumn?

Hope you are not entirely used up.

Yours, Mary Beard.

Along with fund-raising and organizing, Beard continued to write articles and to testify on behalf of the CU's position—although she did not travel to the Western states to campaign, as childless organizers for the CU did. The hearing that she discusses below was held before the Committee on the Judiciary of the U.S. House of Representatives early in March 1914 to consider the woman suffrage amendment proposed to the U.S. Constitution. This was shortly after the Democratic caucus of the House had voted overwhelmingly to accept an Alabama member's resolution that suffrage was a states' rights and not a federal issue. Beard's address was a reasoned and historical attack on the Democratic leadership's position that granting of suffrage was a matter for the states to decide. Her concluding point—in an address that reached back to the Constitutional Convention and the Louisiana Purchase—was to accuse the Democrats of hypocrisy for their stand that woman suffrage was a matter for state action, at the same time that they were proposing a national presidential primary law.[12] The letter's account of the rudeness of grande dame Elizabeth Glendower Evans—a patrician radical the age of Alva Belmont—may suggest, perhaps, an exaggerated sensitivity on Beard's part.

Following this hearing, at which both NAWSA and CU suffragists testified, not the House but the Senate voted on a federal woman suffrage amendment for the first time in twenty-seven years. A bare majority in favor of the measure was achieved, far short of the two-thirds vote necessary for passage.

Undoubtedly Charles Beard's hand helped to craft Mary Beard's argument. He fully supported the CU's political approach as against the nonpartisan approach of the NAWSA. Indeed, in February 1914 the two Beards devised the idea, which Mary Beard wrote to Alice Paul, to establish in states where women did not have the vote "a democratic women's suffrage organization which would establish headquarters and watch every congressional primary to defeat in the primary every democrat who did not give a written pledge to support suffrage."[13] The CU did not adopt the plan, however, being sufficiently swamped with the effort to campaign among women voters in the West.

8. TO ALICE PAUL

400 West 118th Street
March 5th [1914]

Dear Miss Paul,

It is wholly impossible for me to go west at this time. I should like to help in that way but I am not the only one who can do so. I hope Crystal [Eastman Benedict] will be able to go.

The Hearing on Tuesday was certainly a strange one and I was very much disgusted at first. After thinking it over however I believe that there stood out very clearly (1) the fact that the Congressional Union was determined and would leave no stone unturned to reduce the Democratic majority and (2) the fact that there were two distinct types of women working for suffrage. Even if it was evident that we did not all agree, the Judiciary committee saw that one set was politically-minded and politically determined. They tried to bring out the question of our membership then to get an idea of our size. Mrs. [Ruth Hanna] McCormick called to the Union to answer and I popped up and said that our paid membership was no indication whatever of our strength; that our power lay in the appeal we had to the women voters and the financial responses we were meeting. That seemed to convince them that we were not insignificant.

As for my speech which Charles and I had worked on for two days as a complete answer to states' rights, I had to fight to get ten minutes in which to give it. When I arrived, Mrs. [Elizabeth Glendower] Evans said

"You can't possibly have more than five minutes and you must cut it to three if possible. Mrs. [Crystal Eastman] Benedict has ten and our time is short." I appealed to the committee for five more and they gladly granted it but Mrs. Evans clearly did not want me to say a word and under such circumstances my apparent desire to speak and the kind of a [speech] I had prepared under such necessity of showing up states' rights as I had deemed imperative, put me in a most outrageous position. It was the worst experience I ever had. Mrs. Evans treated me dreadfully afterwards. When Mrs. [Jessie Hardy] Stubbs insisted on the speakers having their pictures taken afterwards, Mrs. Evans pushed me from her side whither I had most casually and innocently strayed and grabbed Mrs. Benedict. The whole trouble as I analyse it is that Mrs. Evans was furious with me for wanting to show up the Democrats. She was always cordial to the extreme last winter and spring. She knew Mrs. Benedict would talk generalities and not go into their record perhaps. You have doubtless been told of how Mrs. Evans expatiated on her democratic devotion and loyalty and admiration for the President. It was terrible.

If any speaker had answered the states' rights thing which is all Congressmen talk, practically, I should have been only too satisfied but there was no comprehension on the part of Mrs. Evans that such a slogan should be met. It is because she is first of all a Democrat.

Still the Committee saw that we did not back up Mrs. Evans and so her position was weakened. Everyone will think I was just mad to hear myself talk.

I would not write you thus frankly but I know [that] you are able to work some and you will be anxious to know what everybody thinks of the hearing. We shall indeed rejoice when you are better and we all pray that you may improve rapidly.

Cordially, Mary Beard.

Although Mary Beard was certain that suffragists ought to encourage Alva Belmont's support, she wanted to keep her own distance from all that Belmont stood for. As the two letters below reveal, Beard declined to attend a strategy meeting of the CU purposely held at Marble House, Belmont's mansion in the upper-crust resort of Newport, Rhode Island. Doris Stevens, mentioned below, was one of the small group of young women who were paid organizers for the CU; she soon joined the Executive Committee also.

9. TO ALICE PAUL

New Milford, Ct.
Aug. 15 [1914]

Dear Miss Paul—

I can't do the Newport stunt. I shall probably be the only one who, for labor attachments, feels that participation in the Newport plans is inadvisable. I do feel that way and that I would lose more than I would help by coming myself. But your arrangements there are most important and I wish them every success.

If you are thoroughly disgusted and want some one in my place on the Board, act accordingly. I can't help seeing my problems in this way. Doris Stevens ought to be an official instead of me anyway.

I'll help in the autumn in other ways if possible at all for my loyalty to the Union is steadfast. Service for it is not as simple for me, unfortunately.

Best wishes for the Conference.

Yours, Mary Beard.

Alice Paul tried to coax Beard to change her mind, citing the willingness of capmaker Rose Schneiderman, a leader in the Women's Trade Union League, to be seen at Marble House—but to no avail. Beard's independence on this matter suggests, in addition to her commitment to "labor attachments," how far she staked out her own path, combining her several interests in social reform rather than following exactly where the CU led. (Child's Restaurant, which she mentions, was one of the first inexpensive "chain" eateries; there were several in New York City at this time.)

10. TO ALICE PAUL

New Milford, Conn.
August 21 [1914]

Dear Miss Paul,

The Newport arrangements are far simpler than I had imagined but as a matter of fact Newport and money stand in the popular mind for one and the same thing and you might just as well play them up together in the press reports of the conference and get all the help possible from the combination. There is no advantage in having congressmen against

whom we propose to wage war get an impression that we went into Newport and ate in Child's Restaurant and brought away no money. Let them
think we invaded the seats of the mighty and brought away a war chest.

I just don't feel like making that play, invaluable to success and a
speedy success as it is, especially since so many of you are brave enough
to do it well alone. I think I am a pure coward in this.

Rose Schneiderman did go to Marble House but there is an inner history in the labor movement among women here which I can't discuss on
paper. I ought to be interested in suffrage first and labor second but I am
frankly not. They are inseparable in my interest and I do not feel that on
this occasion you have to have me while I do realise to the full that the
Union doubtless does have to have Newport.

I hope you will understand and I wish you a victory there that will
speed the fight splendidly this autumn.

                                        Cordially, Mary Beard.

In the fall of 1914 Mary Beard was despondent about her lack of success
in raising money for the CU's campaign among Western women voters to
defeat Democrats running for seats in the U.S. Congress. She lamented
her own inability to give, writing Alice Paul, "I haven't a cent myself this
autumn but necessary car fare," and she seemed to feel inadequate to the
tasks before her.[14] She was also furiously disappointed with the NAWSA
suffragists, who, following the lead of Ruth Hanna McCormick, had introduced into Congress an alternative constitutional amendment on
woman suffrage. This Shafroth-Palmer amendment stipulated that if
eight percent of the voters in a state signed an initiative petition for a referendum on woman suffrage, the state would be required to hold such a
referendum.[15] The emphasis of this amendment on states' rights was directly opposed to all the CU was attempting, and to all of Mary Beard's
political convictions. "I'm so mad I can't think of anything else," she
wrote to Alice Paul in reference to the NAWSA convention of November
1914. "Surely it is time for that group to get down and out of the way of
suffrage. All of us become a laughing-stock through their action." At a
slighter later date she was so enraged by the NAWSA suffragists' "re-
pudiating us and blaming us," she wrote to CU organizer Doris Stevens,
that "I felt like resigning from every association with womankind I now
have and forevermore—but," she continued, "I recovered and feel quite
hopeful of the human race again tonight."[16]

Although Beard hoped that the CU and NAWSA leaderships could avoid confrontation, her emotions about the other suffragists remained volatile; indeed, so did her feelings about continuing with the cu. Her proposal to exit from the cu's inner circle in the following letter was not taken up immediately but she acted on it about six months later. The letter was written in the wake of the Congressional elections of 1914, during which the cu brought the federal approach to woman suffrage to national and congressional attention, although succeeding only partially in their electoral efforts. Only twenty-three of the forty-three Democrats against whom the cu campaigned were defeated, usually for reasons extraneous to the suffrage issue.

11. TO ALICE PAUL

400 W. 118. New York City
Nov. 7 [1914]

Dear Miss Paul,

I do not wonder at the exhaustion of the campaigners or at the exhaustion of the Washington workers. I seem to do nothing in comparison but almost no other worker has young children and no money like me. If I overwork, my children suffer and I can't go away because I have no competent person to take care of them. I probably can get some one for any big emergency but it is not a simple thing to do. I wish to God I could do more but I don't see how I can.

Do get some one in my place on the Executive Committee [of the Congressional Union] for it is useless to carry dead wood and this would be a good time to make this change. I shall continue to help whenever I can and in every way I can.

Faithfully yours, Mary Beard.

Fortunately Mary Beard could rely not only on moral support but also on material and intellectual aid from her husband in devising arguments and making contacts to further the movement begun by the cu. Charles Beard saw in the history of American political practice strong justification for the cu's attempt to make a minority group—that is, the voting women of the West—the "swing" voters who could decide the fate of a party and an election. His article in the new journal the *New Republic*, mentioned in the letter below, was the first of four he would publish there from 1914 to 1916 on the subject of suffrage strategy, all supporting cu policy rather than the state-by-state approach still taken by the NAWSA.[17]

12. TO ALICE PAUL

                                     400 West 118th St., New York.
                                     November 30 [1914]

Dear Alice Paul,

   That ten dollars I promised eludes me all the time. If I can ever get hold
of it or keep hold of it long enough I shall surely help but I am always so
hard up.

   I am trying to help however in some way. The New Republic has been
so hostile that Charles went down to see the editors whom we know
rather well and he explained and argued until they admitted that they had
been blind and foolish. Charles will have a reply in this next number.
Some member of the Union had a good letter in reply but it may be over-
looked so far toward the end of the paper so that Charles will help too by
an article farther toward the front. I knew that one signed by him would
carry more weight than one by me as a member of the [Executive]
Committee.

   I am serious about wanting to help financially but can't seem to make
good there.

                                     Yours, Mary Beard

Late in 1914 the New York legislature approved a referendum on woman
suffrage to come before the state's voters in November 1915, and as a
consequence the friction between NAWSA suffragists and CU suffragists
in New York City mounted dramatically. The CU was considering opening a headquarters in New York City. NAWSA suffragists working on the
state campaign were sure that the CU's federal emphasis and attack on
Democrats would harm the local efforts. Many CU advocates, especially
New Yorkers like Mary Beard, saw tremendous advantage to their cause
in bringing a populous state such as New York, with all of its congressmen and electoral votes, into the "suffrage column." They thought it
appropriate to wait until after the November 1915 referendum to open
CU headquarters in New York City. As earlier, Mary Beard in the following letter suggests a path that will conciliate suffragists outside the CU.
On December 19, 1914, however, the majority of the CU's Executive
Committee voted to open headquarters in New York.[18] That decision set
Alice Paul on a permanent collision course with Carrie Chapman Catt,
who was leading the New York State suffrage effort and would be, a year
later, president of the NAWSA.

The first paragraph refers to the news that the Rules Committee of the U.S. House of Representatives would report favorably on the resolution for a woman suffrage amendment, which meant that the House would actually debate and vote on the issue.

13. TO ALICE PAUL

400 West 118th. St., New York.
December 14 [1914]

Dear Miss Paul,

We are all delighted with the notice that the Rules Committee had to take even if it thinks it has played us a trick. I do not know of course what you hope to see done on December 23d. The House might vote to reject the motion of the Rules Committee and so let the Democratic Party slide from under all responsibility. I am terribly interested and anxious.

The sentiment of opposition to the opening of Congressional Union headquarters here [in N.Y.C.] grows among our friends. I have come to believe that it is a bad move for us to make right now for the reason that we could not open headquarters here without lambasting the democrats and we have far more to hope from them in this state next autumn than from the republicans, after all. Congress may adjourn about the time you would open here and it would not meet again until after our vote here next November. During that time while the campaign is on here you would be alienating, I fear, all the women and we should get no money, many more enemies, and be widely (instead of futilely as now) charged with having lost the state.

The day after election; that is, the first week in November however I am highly in favor of a move here if we get nowhere with the amendment this session.

I do not write this because I waver one iota from interest in the federal work or belief in your policy. I think we must work here among the women and on the congressmen but not through flaunting headquarters right now. Doris Stevens ought to come for a while and raise money quietly. She can do it I believe even better in that way and thus we shall keep the many friends we have and are steadily making.

I have come to believe too that it is a tactical blunder to open up with Mrs. Belmont. I can easily see that a refusal to do so will be difficult but on the ground that it is untimely to open any headquarters here that blunder can be avoided.

I can't very well write all I know and feel but I have been influenced by the great state of excitement over the situation that friends, and those valuable friends like Florence Kelley, seem to be in. She says she will resign at once if we take this step at this time though she is anxious to have us come a little later.

I think we shall be able to send a very splendid Democratic deputation on January 6th if the excuse for it then remains. Mrs. Robert Adamson is thinking of going (though you must not say so yet) and she is working it up among all the leading Democratic women. Mrs. Adamson and some of our common friends and people whom we are interested in making more intelligent about the Union want very much to see you and Lucy Burns and as many of the other members of the committee as possible while you are here. Can you stay over on Saturday night and spend that evening at Mrs. Adamson's for that purpose? Please let me know by special [delivery or] by telegram so we can ask people to come to meet you. I wish I could invite you here for the week-end but I haven't a single bed.

The Suffragist is a grand little paper. Here is my long delayed subscription. Am looking forward most eagerly to seeing you again and hearing everything.

Yours as ever, Mary Beard

With the following letter, Mary Beard began her withdrawal from the CU's Executive Committee. She felt unable to give the group its due, but that feeling must have resulted from her own setting of priorities. Besides the demands of her family, during the time of her greatest involvement with the CU she was also busy with a writing project of her own. Her book *Women's Work in Municipalities,* which required a great deal of research into the activities of women's clubs and associations across the nation, was published in 1915. Although Beard does not mention it in the following letter, the suffrage campaign in New York, leading up to the referendum of 1915, was also commanding much of her attention.

14. TO ALICE PAUL

400 West 118th. St., New York
May 15 [1915]

Dear Miss Paul,

Crystal Eastman was to arrange with Mrs. Belmont for the conference on Monday if possible and I was to reserve any time and place up to Thursday, when I go to the country, that suited them. Crystal couldn't tell whether she would be able to get to Mrs. Belmont's for the meeting or whether we should all have to go down to her home but I have been waiting myself to hear definite plans before answering your letter. Crystal went to the country for a couple of days and has had to stay longer, it seems. She is not in a fit condition to do one thing and I don't see how she can assume responsibilities for some months to come.

As for me I must go to the country and I can't help one bit more or I shall break down too. I hate to have so little strength but there seems to be no choice between being a hermit and overdoing and I shall have to fluctuate between the two performances. I must consider my young children at times and they get no attention whatever during the winter.

You must find some one to take my place on the [executive] committee and others can do the work so much better than I because they have more time, leisure, money and wisdom. I shall be glad to meet the committee on Monday for I admire you and all in the same whole hearted way. It is only that I have reached the limit for the time being—for months—of assistance to you. I shall telegraph you to-night or to-morrow where we can all meet if I can get into touch with Crystal by that time.

Cordially, Mary Beard.

[P.S.] I read your letter again and I see the date of the conference is May 25. I *can't* come back for it but I think it a good thing for you to have it and I hope you will be able to decide on some excellent person for the New York work.

●←

Mary Beard resigned from the CU Executive Committee in the last week of May 1915. The letter below suggests the mix of motives that led her to withdraw from the inner circle. Among these was her sense of inadequacy in fund-raising—an activity that she considered an obligation, even though it went against her "instinctive scruples." Notwithstanding her husband's support of her activities, she had little money to give. A few months earlier she had written to Doris Stevens that "my husband and I have a joint bank book and this winter I can't afford to get him in too deep."[19] Her unusual thought in this letter of getting a job shows how deeply she felt her lack of autonomy in spending.

At the time, Carrie Chapman Catt was accusing Alice Paul of having broken her promise not to open CU headquarters in New York; the accusation was specious, according to other CU members, for Paul had made no such promise. Beard believed Paul's account yet at the same time seemed relieved to be departing from the autocratically run CU

Executive Committee. Nor had her scorn for the tactics of the NAWSA in any way diminished. As in the letter below, through her whole life Beard frankly criticized—even despaired at—the choices and tactics of various groups of women, even while she cheered on women's achievements.

15. TO LUCY BURNS

New Milford, Conn.
June 8 [1915]

Dear Miss Burns,

I felt sure that Miss Paul had given no pledge to keep out of New York even before your letter came stating that she had not. I understand the whole spirit of your letter and share it. My resignation from the Executive Board was not due to condemnation of the C.U. but to the desire to enable a capable worker with more leisure to receive the recognition of committed membership and the stimulus that comes from such membership. It seemed the only fair thing to do. As for the Advisory Council, I'd rather not be on that now because it will only be a source of annoyance to me since I shall be called up constantly or visited by those who regard that body as advisory in character and want me to interfere with the acts of the [Executive] Committee. I leave you freer by staying off of it for outside I can abstain from interference and that is a comfort all round. Of course there will be no publicity on my action. I have tried to do the right thing and so quietly that only good will result.

I couldn't go to Hartford to-day but I sent my good husband and thereby endorse the C.U. very publicly and effectively. I think I shall get a remunerative job this winter and have some money at least to contribute to the Union. That will help more than anything and without such a job, I have no money to give as the children will both have to go to expensive schools this winter and part of our income has to be laid up for a rainy day.

I am sorry women of this country are giving such a lamentable demonstration of their political ignorance. Just as is the enfranchisement of our sex and necessary as it is, I find it very hard to be as absorbed in suffrage as I am in the labor struggles just because nearly all suffragists seem so hopeless. Our C.U. is at a critical stage of its existence perhaps but it has always been. Money is so essential that in declining to be the backbone of the support of the New York headquarters I felt it was better to make money-raising a real chore to be performed by one on the spot and more capable. I can do that but poorly when in town and not at all when out of town.

What a pity that all the National [American Woman Suffrage Association] suffragists can see is attacking other suffragists. They are in a mess about their old Shafroth amendment and I believe that is why they are so hot on our trail because they know they got in bad with that proposal everywhere. I was told that [Connecticut suffragist] Miss Ruutz-Rees said the other day she didn't care much for it now. They say through Connecticut that we declared war on the National with the leaflet "Which Amendment will You Support" and that war must be answered by war. Of course we did but they haven't sense enough to see that the c.u. has driven them into any sensible action they may now prove themselves capable of. Will it be sensible? I feel it can't be.

Yours as ever. Mary Beard

In spite of her resignation Mary Beard remained committed to the CU federal approach; at the same time she believed in the importance of working to gain suffrage in New York state. Her letter below to Carrie Chapman Catt, while personally deferential, forthrightly explains her political position and the sources of her frustration with NAWSA policies (and with certain NAWSA officials, such as Gertrude Foster Brown and Harriet Burton Laidlaw). It shows Beard's astuteness in recognizing the increased power of the executive branch in twentieth-century politics.

In 1915, state referenda on woman suffrage were pending not only in New York but also in Pennsylvania, New Jersey (the home state of President Woodrow Wilson), and Massachusetts. Throughout her letter to Catt, Beard implies the reasonableness and compatibility of working for suffrage at both the state level and the national level simultaneously. This would, in fact, be the policy the NAWSA adopted under Catt's leadership in 1916.

16. TO CARRIE CHAPMAN CATT

New Milford, Conn.
June 8th [1915]

Dear Mrs. Catt,

Some time ago I received your circular letter to the members of the Executive Committee of the Congressional Union. I have delayed replying because my personal deep admiration for you and my keen interest in the campaign you are leading so well made it hard for me to seem to have to answer except in hearty agreement with your point of view.

The more I think over the point at issue the more I deem it necessary however to explain my position in order that you may see how one whom you deem misguided does justify her position, in order that you may help to guide her out of her morass of political thinking if you deem her worth the trouble. I have always considered you so big because you have not considered those who differed with you as necessarily beneath contempt. Mrs. [Gertrude Foster] Brown has treated me that way. You, I know, will at least give me credit for honest intent if not for good sense.

Here are a few points then I wish to present.

First, granted that the [Congressional Union's] annoyance of the President seemed an importation of English militancy and a grievous mistake, what seemed an evil might possibly have been turned into great good by all of you who protested publicly if you had stated to the President that you regretted the incident *while* lamenting his stand on suffrage. That note was not sounded as far as I know.

Second, in your letter to the papers you stated your recognition of the fact that the federal amendment is solely in the hands of Congress and the state legislatures. Since we learned that technical fact as school girls however the power of the executive in state and federal government has so grown that it is the most striking thing in American political life to-day. One always has to take into consideration both the technical requirement and the facts of practical politics which are unwritten. President Wilson lashed Congress into every step it took and the chances are he will be still more a dominating figure in the year to come. At the hearing before Governor [Charles] Whitman [of New York] this past winter when we asked him to endorse suffrage in his message, I called his attention to the basis of our appeal to him in the increased power and influence of the executive. He listened very much interested to that point of view. We may not approve of usurpation by the executive but the fact remains.

Third, the President is interfering in state campaigns when he recognises with public effort the aliens who will vote against us in a state like Pennsylvania and when, in telling them everything else they need to know, he neglects to tell them to extend to American women in November the liberty that is freely and with glad ceremonies extended to them.

Fourth, his silence in his own state at the present is having a bad effect on his state. He should come out not against us but for us since he has stated that it is a matter to be decided by the voters of a state and in every issue in his own state before he has taken a hand by letter and by visit from the White House.

Fifth, the interests of the Congressional Union and of the state are compatible if followed along the lines which Marion May has probably presented to you. She and I have talked it over as individuals, not as members of any organisations especially, but as pure, politically sound, suffrage tactics. I believe that nothing would help New York like such leaflets and such type of work.

Sixth, while Senator [James] O'Gorman [of New York] took a stand against suffrage, his statement has been made in time for us to be able to make converts that count, by showing how a blind position like his will hurt his party incalculably and at once, owing to the close approach of the presidential convention and the keen interest that women voters are taking in the attitude of Eastern politicians toward the enfranchisement of their sisters. Not only can his statements be answered seriatim in speeches to the voters—who prefer to hear about politicians to hearing about the home and babies and justice unfortunately—but all politicians might pass the word down to the boys in time to help us if they felt we understood politics and proposed to use now what political power we do have.

I do not want to trespass upon your very busy life by writing at too great length but . . . I wish we might agree on the value of political work as well as educational work, on the power of the President, and on the advisability of always attacking the enemy rather than on laying defeat to women. When the Shafroth amendment, for example, came up in Congress, the Congressional Union in every public statement, I believe, and in every word to Congressmen and Senators refused to place the blame for the weakened hold the other amendment thereby had because of the machinations or blindness of suffragists but insisted that legislators must themselves be sincere in their desire to grant the essence of right and not the shadow.

I have long wanted to argue these matters with those of you whom I respect so much. I have never been able to achieve that victory of a calm argument of any kind with Mrs. [Harriet Burton] Laidlaw and Mrs. Brown has been inclined to insult me without a hearing of any kind. At least I know your spirit is bigger and if I seem hopeless in my attitude of mind I shall greatly appreciate your telling me so and why.

Sincerely, Mary Beard

P.S. I should be throwing my energies now into the state campaign if I could throw them anywhere outside the home. I can't afford to pay the

right person to take care of my children in the country and they mustn't
be in town this summer. I shall give with whole hearted devotion however
the last two months to the state provided you all are not terrified at my
cooperation. I shall not talk politics though then unless previous political
plans have been made and you approve that.

•←

The suffrage referenda in New York and the three other eastern industrial
states were defeated in November 1915. From outside the inner circle
Mary Beard continued working on behalf of the CU's effort to pass the
Susan B. Anthony amendment, as the constitutional amendment for
woman suffrage was now called, and its intention to campaign against
Democrats again in the 1916 elections. Likewise she continued devoting
attention to the Women's Trade Union League and organized labor, trying to include working-class women and their interests in the plans of the
suffragists. Her suggestion for the CU to sponsor a benefit performance
on behalf of the Women's Trade Union League was but one of her ideas to
make the suffrage movement an inclusive and "real woman's movement."
She believed Mrs. Belmont would support such an effort because Belmont
had earlier helped garment workers on strike. Unfortunately it is not possible to trace whether Beard's suggestion was acted upon.

17. TO ALICE PAUL

400 West 118th. St/. New York
February 21 [1916]

Dear Miss Paul,

I have been thinking out some way to line up the organised labor movement behind the Susan B. [Anthony amendment] and there is a way I believe. The enclosed leaflet will show you a bit of the history of the relation
of the A[merican] F[ederation] of L[abor] toward us. Having stood for
the thing once, if feebly, perhaps we can make it stand for it again and
strongly.

My idea is this. In the state campaign here the suffragists were always
calling on the organised working women to help and playing up to the
full every tiny bit of help. They did not reciprocate with any support of
working women in their own efforts to organise and the union women
have been talking it over since the defeat on November 2d. The Suffragists are trying to get them to agree to a long hard campaign. The labor
men I hear are quietly working against the suffrage all the time. Now it

would be wonderful as you know if the Women's Trade Union League here would send a public letter to all the organised groups of women in the suffrage states calling upon them to use their power and spare this league and others in eastern states from the necessity of the expensive and humiliating referendum again. The League is not at all keen about another referendum but as yet it is not with us keenly either. It is rather sick of mere suffrage talk and will slump in this work altogether possibly.

But—we could make it keen and get the letter to the west I believe if we could do something to indicate our support of a woman's movement that is big enough to include the efforts of women to organise in the industrial field. If we gave any open demonstration of this support too it would impress Mr. Gompers and the A.F. of L.

Mrs. Belmont is always ready to support labor organisation for women and so I have thought that if she would try to get those who gave "Melinda and Her Sisters" to give another performance at popular prices for the benefit of the organised working women united in the Women's Trade Union League here, that it would be one of the most wonderful things that could happen. Mr. Walsh and all good labor people would be proud of the Congressional Union for this stand and it couldn't hurt us any way. That is the advantage of the federal way of securing enfranchisement and the political way, that the labor sympathy is a real power. This would give organized labor faith in us and we would deserve the faith.

You may think me simple minded in this. If you don't, are you willing to put it up to Mrs. Belmont? If she would ask me to bring Melinda Scott to talk about it with her it could be put through beautifully. I would work on the ticket selling with might and main. The performers might take a fancy themselves to the idea of doing it for working women. It would not necessitate further work on the part of Mrs. Belmont and the players except for the settling of a date.

Let me know, will you, soon at any rate? This is the second big and glorious link in the Congressional Union's role of a real woman's movement if we can mold the link.

I shall write the Clayton Act article to-morrow.

Cordially, Mary Beard

◆━━

During 1916, having withdrawn from the national leadership of the CU, Beard became more active in its New York State organization. New York suffragists decided to go for a second try at a state referendum, to be held in 1917. Meanwhile, to foster its work among women voters in the West, the CU there renamed itself the Woman's Party, with Nevada historian and suffragist Anne Martin as president. Against Woodrow Wilson's stand that woman suffrage was a matter for the states to decide, the Woman's Party sought a statement from likely Republican presidential candidate Charles Evans Hughes in favor of the federal route to woman suffrage. (Hughes did endorse a constitutional amendment, on August 1, 1916.)[20] The following letter from Beard to a colleague in the New York branch of the Woman's Party indicates some of the stresses of operating at the federal and state levels at the same time.

18. TO JANE NORMAN SMITH

New Milford, Conn.
June 23, 1916

Dear Mrs. Smith,

What fun to be going to Wyoming during the throes of the campaign! You will have much to tell us when you return and you must let us know it all.

I did not come down for the [Charles Evans] Hughes interview for I had a telegram from Miss Burns, in reply to mine, that Miss [Anne] Martin and Mrs. [Abby Scott] Baker could take care of it. I am waiting anxiously the result. Wilson seems yesterday again to have declared for the state method and so it looks like a campaign against his party positively.

. . . As for our [N.Y.] organisation and keeping open the rest of the summer, my feeling about it changed when I learned that Mrs. Belmont had pledged such a large sum for the Woman's Party. Her pledge frees our own money for local needs more and we therefore could keep open, I suppose, although I do not know how much there is in the treasury now. I think our chief value for the summer would be in answering inquiries and helping district chairmen to maintain interest in the federal way—the necessity of making the government recognise women. I really want to see the office kept open tremendously. . . .

I think there should be a meeting next week and that the point should be insisted upon of keeping open. If I was not in favor of it last week it was because I thought every cent would be needed for the West. It will look as if we had lost all hope if we close. Personally it does not seem to me that the Democrats are going to pass the amendment but that is no reason why we should not concentrate upon the federal amendment and try putting them out of office and giving another party a chance. I believe absolutely in the political way which is the only dignified way and in making the government enfranchise us. So if it takes us longer than we hoped, the state method takes an eternity and we have chosen the better way. We must maintain that point of view—those of us who have it strongly—and WE MUST KEEP OPEN to do it.

Do insist that the meeting be called and try to persuade the women that this course is best. The up-state chairmen as well as the local chairmen need to understand our point of view and if any one is discouraged like Mrs. Blauvelt, the office secretary should try to encourage her by telling her the whole situation and urge upon the chairman personal initiative. . . .

I wish I could be down more but the work I do in the winter is only possible because of my summer change. I have to catch up with the children and many other things which I wholly neglect when I am in town. I hope I shall hear that you have met and decided generously in the matter anyway.

Cordially, Mary Beard.

The CU, or Woman's Party, gained more adherents in 1916, especially after defeats of major state referenda made more women see the virtue of a constitutional amendment. As in 1914, Mary Beard did not campaign in the West but provided articles and arguments—historical arguments—for the group.[21] For Beard as for radicals and socialists who supported the cause, it was difficult to swallow the fact that their anti-Democratic strategy benefitted the Republican presidential candidate Hughes, for he was more conservative than Wilson with respect to most domestic social policies. Yet Beard and others swallowed it, perhaps because they judged that Hughes had little chance of being elected, while their pressure was their only hope to make the Democratic party reassess its suffrage views. Beard had little appreciation for President Wilson. At the time of writing the letter below, she was angry because Wilson had made a special appearance to urge the Senate to act immediately and favorably on a child labor bill passed by the House; as a result, the Senate in caucus overcame Southern senators' resistance and announced that the bill would shortly pass. All the while, the president insisted to suffragists that he could not influence congressional committees and actions.[22] Happy with the result for child labor, Beard was nonetheless furious at Wilson's hypocrisy in dealing with suffragists.

19. TO ALICE PAUL

New Milford, Conn.
July 26, 1916

Dear Miss Paul,

Here's my hat off to you for your mastery of the situation when I was so annoyed at [Charles Evans] Hughes last Wednesday! You were true blue in pulling that kind of a statement out of the melee. I can do much better when I stay in the daily fight than when I get away for a time and look at things with a more distant perspective. I am so much more radical than either of the old political parties that, when I get off and think, I lose my whole absorption in the one fight for enfranchisement. I keep that absorption in town when I am at the office every day and have responsibilities that are heavy. The Socialists as individuals are usually pathetic and I remember that when I am working day and night for the cu because I am thinking solely of women but I can't keep away from wider surveys when I start to read and think along other lines in the summer too.

You see it is bad for me to come away. I have to though on account of the children. This summer it would be most impossible to keep them in town.

The kind of publicity that you are giving out about Hughes is perfect psychologically, I am sure. He told me he wanted what he said to come out as if it were perfectly natural. It will seem so when the way is paved as it is being paved by the activities of the women of the Hughes alliance and the confidence expressed by Miss Todd and others that he will speak up.

I have regained my balance since Wilson has behaved in such a hypocritical and insulting way about the child labor bill and the amendment. I do believe that instead of taking the Child Labor Bill as a sop, tremendously attractive as it is, women will be enraged by the President's insult to their intelligence. I believe his action will afford the very most powerful material for the campaign and that women will not yield the fight because he has put through the one thing and left undone the more fundamental thing. I could campaign with spirit now against him whereas I have had moments when I was very glad other women had to do the campaigning—moments when I have remembered [William Howard] Taft would go upon the Supreme Bench if Hughes wins, etc.

Mrs. Adamson has written you and me about letting Mr. Wilson off with endorsement of presidential suffrage. Of course I have told her that would never do in my opinion. It is her Democratic husband and own reactions getting in some work.

I have just sent an article to the Suffragist which will supply some more campaign material. It shows that Congress itself practically established manhood suffrage in the Mississippi region and the southwest and on to the Pacific. I hope to help in such ways as that.

Are you getting any more of that money from Mrs. Belmont? If you are not, I will send out a hundred letters to women I know who may be willing to give something more. If we can get our City Committee together by the first of August and reorganise we ought to be able to raise some more money very soon. Did you get the money from Mrs. Deane? I telegraphed and then wrote. I shall have to tell the women that the $500,000 is not coming in if I persuade them to contribute for they are very decided in their feelings about that. It ought not to be so, as all should play their part and the more money the better but they feel Mrs. Belmont has got so much credit for so little work in comparison with what they put in and get in return that they harbor the common standards of humans in this matter. It all seems pathetic and petty to me for I am always so glad when some other woman can be put into the headlines instead of myself as I hate so much to have to devote my life to this stupid fight which ought to have been settled years ago that I am terribly pleased we have the lady to use. She can say things I couldn't without losing all the radical friends I sympathise with and I grow more and more to thank heaven for her existence. But you see when Mrs. Deane admires Mr. Hughes so much and some other woman is keen about Mr. Wilson and they would one and all be very glad to be on the firing line of political committees or quoted as approving this and that, there are emotions which they have and we just have to understand their psychology and get what we can out of them.

I'll push the reorganisation so we can garner in all the women now who may have been impressed by recent events and achievements of the c.u.

Yours always, Mary Beard.

In spite of her recurrent doubts about the sufficiency and meaning of suffrage campaigning, Mary Beard worked hard to reorganize the New York branch of the cu.[23] By the end of 1916 her mood was one of frustration again, however, especially concerning fund-raising. She refers in the following letter to efforts to raise money to honor the memory of Inez Milholland, an eye-catching and news-making feminist and suffragist who died tragically in November 1916 during a speaking tour on the West Coast—not yet thirty, she was stricken by pernicious anemia. It is not clear to what, exactly, the opening line in the following letter refers, but it may be a temper tantrum of Beard's when asked to raise money.

20. TO ALICE PAUL

340 West 118th St., N.Y.
December 21, 1916

Dear Miss Paul,

I was a sickening disappointment to you last week, I know. I have been thinking much about it because temper—just plain temper—is a surprise to me and not a thing I shall let go any farther. I have been crushed to the earth and therefore physically tired by a conviction that the federal way even is interminable. You all feel the other way and I know the [New York State] referendum people have equal faith and so I allowed my zeal to slump. However I do want this question settled even as you do and I know it comes first in the revolutions I desire and the c.u. is wisest and most admirable, even if I do think it sometimes a bit confused in its statements.

I shall therefore atone for my temper by going to the Lewissohns and appealing with all by soul for a big gift. I am at this hour trying to make the appointment to see them and nothing shall prevent my making good on this. This was my first refusal to do any thing I really could do but the one thing I find harder than any thing else is to ask individually for money. I shall do it positively however and I have hopes that the Inez Memorial will catch their sense of beauty and idealism which they have in unusual degree.

While I have heaviest home responsibilities and must help swell rather than deplete the family income I shall rouse myself from lethargy and cynicism and plan to utilize every possible hour for c.u. work from now on.

Yours sincerely, Mary Beard

Early in 1917 the cu joined with its Western wing into the renamed National Woman's Party (nwp) and embarked on a new tactic of picketing the White House with signs and banners. "Mr. President, how long must women wait for liberty?" and similar slogans festooned the demonstrations. A few fragments of evidence indicate that Mary Beard approved of this new tactic, as she had approved of the group's earlier flamboyant actions. "You know I am never afraid of that kind of thing myself," she wrote to Alice Paul when she conveyed Florence Kelley's discomfort with the practice of heckling. Even after the United States entered the world war in April 1917 and the picketing was deplored by observers as traitorous to the nation and the war effort, Beard endorsed it. She wrote to Jane Norman Smith that in spite of virtual riots caused by the picketing, "it has done more than almost anything else could as matters stand at this moment."[24] By July and August the picketers were being arrested on charges of obstructing traffic. Refusing to pay fines, they were incarcerated; in jail, refusing to eat, they were force-fed. The ensuing publicity momentarily riveted national attention on the National Woman's Party.

In the first week of November 1917, the New York referendum to enfranchise women succeeded. Immediately Mary Beard and others organized a group called the Committee of One Thousand, made up mainly of working women, to protest the jailing of suffragists at the nation's capital and the conditions in the workhouse in which they were held. After a rally in New York, she and a few others carried a petition of the group of newly enfranchised citizens directly to Washington to President Wilson, asking him to endorse the federal suffrage amendment and to release the imprisoned pickets.[25]

Perhaps that trip to the national capital—perhaps a view of the actual picketing, which Beard had not witnessed before—led to the change of heart expressed in the letter below, written only five days later. Otherwise the cause for it remains mysterious. Beard despised the way that the NAWSA had jumped into war work in an effort to gain congressional approval of the vote for women; but she no longer approved of the National Woman's Party's tactics either.[26]

21. TO ELIZABETH ROGERS

430 West 116
November 17, 1917

Dear Mrs. Rogers—

I am slow to answer your letter as Chairman of the Advisory Council of the National Woman's Party. I am slow to answer because, while I have seen myself steadily pushed toward withdrawal from the Council, I have been so sorry to withdraw.

I can't fight the battle the picketting way even to win any more than I can use war work as a cudgel even to win. So please, let me depart quietly. Just omit my name in any publicity about the conference of advisors at Washington and omit it from the stationery hereafter.

I am willing to say no more and not even this much publicly for I have no desire to injure in any way.

We must each follow the light we have. In my case, it may be very dim. Best wishes to you!

Cordially, Mary Beard.

Apparently, Mary Beard took no part in activity on behalf of the National Woman's Party after November 1917. From the tone of the following letter, it seems plausible that she grew increasingly disaffected during the winter of 1918–19, because of the group's shock tactics, which included burning "watchfires" in front of the White House when Wilson went to Versailles, and setting his "fine words" on democracy aflame when these were announced from the peace conference.

22. TO ELIZABETH KALB, BUSINESS MANAGER OF THE *SUFFRAGIST*

336 West 95, New York City
April 9, 1919

My dear Miss Kalb,

Will you be good enough to tell me by what right my name appears as associate editor of the Suffragist?

I am well aware that the National Woman's Party calls one merely doctrinaire who cares about means to the end and that I am anathema because I do. I do object to this use of my name as if I sanctioned all the means used by the organization of which I am no longer even a member.

Sincerely, Mary Beard

2 The Activist Intellectual Emerges

During the suffrage years, Mary Beard had struggled to concentrate solely on the vote, preferring a more inclusive approach to reform. In ensuing years the National Woman's Party kept its single-issue focus, replacing the goal of a constitutional amendment for suffrage with the goal of a constitutional amendment for equal rights, while Beard's principles and inclinations led her elsewhere. A trip to postwar Europe in 1920–21 seems to have affected her greatly, leaving her more impressed than ever with the paltriness and futility of articulating a goal of sex equality apart from wider aims of social renovation. The trip fostered her anti-war feelings. If making women equal to men was not an appealing goal to her, that was in part because she saw the image of woman conscripted for war as the logical outcome—or epitome—of that goal.

In the following letter—one of a mere handful available from the 1920s—Beard gives her views of several NWP drafts of equal rights amendments intended to eliminate sex discrimination. Elsie Hill, a Vassar graduate of 1906 and daughter of a longtime congressman from Connecticut, had been one of the earliest organizers hired by the CU and was named chairman of the National Woman's Party reconstituted in 1921; a venturesome sort, who ran (unsuccessfully) as a Farmer-Labor candidate for secretary of state in Connecticut in 1920, she was someone to whom Beard could write frankly and fully. Beard's principal objection in the letter is the same one raised by most women who initially opposed the ERA: the amendment's likely impact on the laws regulating women's hours, conditions of work, and wages for which trade-union women and others had fought for two decades. Beard is prescient in seeing deficiencies in the Wisconsin bill, which became the first state equal rights law in the nation. Unfortunately it is impossible to identify from the many early drafts of the ERA the language of the "third suggestion" to which Beard responds more positively, although it may have been one of the lengthier drafts in which areas of rights (such as jury service, child custody, citizenship) were specified.[1]

Beard's opening remark about "our" series foreshadows her major occupation during the 1920s: writing history books in tandem with Charles Beard. After her husband resigned from Columbia University in 1917, the Beards kept only a pied-à-terre in New York City and made New Milford, Connecticut, their year-round residence and the seat of their collaboration. Their *History of the United States,* a high school text, was published in 1921. Although she speaks of "our" series in the letter, her name was not attached to *Our Old World Background,* published in 1922 under the names of Charles Beard and William Bagley, who were also co-authors on two previously published elementary U.S. history texts.

23. TO ELSIE HILL

New Milford, Conn.
July 10, 1921

Dear Elsie,

I am surprising both you and myself by my instant reply to your letter. I can't possibly get down to Washington for I am working hard this summer again on the last book in our school series—the European Background of American History. But of course I am always ready to comment even at a distance on so lively a subject as your proposed new amendment, etc.

As for the federal amendment, it seems to me it would overthrow all protective industrial legislation for women and I can't see why it wouldn't also do things like conscript women for war. If "equal opportunists to the bitter end" want that result, the amendment seems to hit the mark. I am not one of that party especially since my return from this last trip abroad where there is so much industrial equality that women sweep the streets and till the land while men drink in the cafes. I believe that women will be conscripted for war in the future and the essence of democracy is that the whole nation fights as the king and barons and mercenaries once fought. Women have rushed to recruit in Silesia and there will be battalions of death outside Russia; but I am not interested one bit if that is all democracy has to offer. So much for the amendment as far as I am concerned.

As for the Wisconsin bill, it is so general in its scope that it seems to me it throws the whole matter of protective legislation into the courts, as well as all other special prohibitions because of the phrase "which they now enjoy for the general welfare". Any lawyer can argue and any judge can declare that all discriminatory legislation is for the general welfare. I don't see that the bill therefore gets anywhere in fact.

The third suggestion for a state bill I like better. It is specific, except for the final "Or in any other respect". It gets rid of the undisputed sex disabilities while leaving room for protective industrial legislation for those who believe in that. I am perfectly aware of the factions that rally around that policy. I am not an ultra feminist on that point because in my mind children do add a complexity to women that they cannot add to men and I see no way of removing it entirely for the best interests of both sexes as well as the children. {Then too women have little sense of humour about the actions and works of men. Half the goals they set are ridiculous and pure imitation is both infantile and unintelligent. A! Ha!}*

It is awfully good of you to keep me in touch with these doings and I would enjoy a talk about it all. Later perhaps we can have it for you can surely come here even if I can't come to you.

I saw Doris [Stevens] on the street in Florence one day. She looked so thin and white that she simply broke my heart. Do you still plan to go over this autumn? I want to talk with you about women in Europe as well as here—how they love war and mourning and sorrow and suffering; and how bourgeois our whole suffrage and equal opportunity movement is. Women have been having that equality in the fields of Europe since the days of the Roman Empire, for example. Of course real equality would have transferred the whip to her hands and let her hitch her husband and an ass together to the plow instead of having the sexes reversed; but is that the final answer?

You sound as if you were having big times in discussion with worth while folks. It will be nice to get their points of view through you. Best wishes to my erstwhile pals and please tell them that I am working as hard as they in the way that seems to open best for me.

Affectionately, Mary Beard

After travel to Japan in 1922 and 1923, the Beards occupied much of the mid-1920s with conceiving and writing the two volumes of *The Rise of American Civilization*, published in 1927, the most famous and admired of their joint works. Mary Beard fell so out of touch with Elsie Hill that in 1927, when Hill wrote to compliment her on *The Rise* (and to beg use of the Beards' town apartment), Beard received her note "like a voice from an unknown world" and admitted she had not for many years "seen so much as a mutual friend."[2] This suggests how far she had turned her back on her former associates, immersing herself in American history.

The following brief letter, apparently written just after *The Rise* was

---

* Lines within braces were added by hand to typed letter.

completed, gives on-the-spot evidence of Mary Beard's concern and perhaps responsibility for the cultural content of that work. Charles Beard
carried on most of the general correspondence with Macmillan publishers, so it is notable that Mary Beard sent this query. Perhaps it also
indicates the relative weight of work and holiday in the Beard household
that the note was written on Christmas day! Which work by Canby—
presumably Henry Seidel Canby—she is referring to remains a mystery,
since he published no book in 1927.

24. TO CURTICE HITCHCOCK, THE MACMILLAN CO.
(PUBLISHERS)

27 West 67, City
December 25, 1926

Dear Mr. Hitchcock:

Charles and I are decidedly shocked to read the enclosed sample of a
forthcoming book by Canby for this bit so closely parallels our treatment
of Irving that we are afraid Canby will steal our literary thunder. Have
you any idea when his book is to appear and whether it is to do what we
have also tried to do, namely relate the literature to the economics and
politics? If Canby comes out first, he might think we had plagiarised and
so it seems important for you to have our statement today that our work
is alike on Irving at this moment and threatens to run along the same path
for other writers if his book carries on as he seems to have begun.

We only hope we shall appear first and we stand ready to push as fast
as we can on the proof when it arrives.

Cordially, Mary Beard

•❦—

The following letter is the only contemporary evidence from Mary
Beard's hand of the extent of her contribution to *The Rise of American
Civilization*. Florence Cross Kitchelt, the friend to whose compliment
Beard was responding, was a social worker, suffragist, and labor reformer in the 1910s and became a leader in the peace movement in Connecticut in the interwar period, while she continued to be involved in
women's issues. It was probably because of Kitchelt's work for peace that
Beard asked her opinion of the Kellogg-Briand pact, the treaty to re-
nounce war that the U.S. Senate approved in 1928 after nationwide lobbying by women's groups and others.

The letter also reflects on the Beards' trip in 1927–28 to Yugoslavia, where Charles Beard was invited to consult on urban and governmental problems. During her months in the Balkans Mary Beard was very much impressed by the strength and vitality of peasant women living close to the land. Her interest in and acquaintance with peasants had been stimulated by the lengthy stay in Japan in 1922–23. Her research on American farm production during the writing of the *Rise* "especially excited" her, she later recounted.[3]

25. TO FLORENCE CROSS KITCHELT

New Milford, Conn.
May 18th [1928]

Dear Florence,

Can it be eighteen years since first we met! Like the ideal of good-will among men, our friendship thus deepens and intensifies with time. I am very proud of your contributions toward a richer social consciousness and you are certainly generous toward my feeble efforts to do a bit in that direction.

Another bond. We too have now sat on the Pynx (do you enjoy Gertrude Atherton's Immortal Marriage?) and we too have talked with M. Grouitch et al on the subject of minorities. Don't forget your promise to drop in on us here this summer—you and the good Richard—for a talk on our hill of the world and its affairs, including the ways of Macedonia, Bulgaria, and what-not. What a freak of Fate is the Bulgarian earthquake evoking friendliness in Jugoslavia and drawing the two peoples a little closer together. I was especially interested in the political game which France and England are still playing in the Balkans. Charles is preparing a book on Jugoslavia and one unique feature will be the comment by the young King on the Crown itself following the submission of the chapter on the Crown to the King for his criticism. But my good husband did not go on behest of the government as New Milfordites seem to think. He went for the American-Jugoslav Society to make a survey along the general line of his report on Tokyo.

We motored through Montenegro, among other adventures, and I am still dazed by the insight into the life of mountaineers which I got. Water gypsies had been my greatest previous surprise. And the sublimity of landscapes will be abiding joys!

Your excellent report on your activities in Connecticut I have filed away for use later in revision of books which demand being up-to-date. It is good to note the inroads you are making on the psychology of the children for that is the hope. How do you interpret the Kellogg peace move? Do you think it positively and indubitably a throw-out to the women voters this year? I met real Amazons this winter—women who had fought and truly found glory in war—but they were one of the minorities luckily.

The Rise of Am. Civ. is deficient all along the line, we know but it was the best we could do at that time. Now we think we could improve it one hundred per cent. Reviewers often imply that the whole product is C. A.'s in spite of the fact that he had never written on cultural themes before and so I appreciate your willingness to count me in, in view of the way I drudged on the work for three years and especially since cultural side was my hunch—not just women. We hope to improve it in a revision one of these days.

We shall hope to see you ere long. Better let us know in advance when you think you can come over so we shall surely be at home. May the common shelter for you two splendid people materialise yet and soon.

Affectionately, Mary Beard

No letters of any substance written by Mary Beard between 1928 and 1933 can be found. She wrote a few articles during this time, however, all in accord with the tone of her 1921 letter to Elsie Hill. She seemed impressed with what she called in a brief essay published in June 1929 the feminist progression, "the large measure of civil and political equality actually established after the long era in which it had been only a dream." But she seemed equally, or more, disturbed about the goal in view. "What is this equal opportunity in fact and in import?" she continued. "Is it the mere chance to prove fitness and adaptability to a tooth-and-claw economic struggle reflecting the greed and destructive propensities of the traditional pacer . . . or does it signify the power to lead as well as follow?" She was deeply concerned and dissatisfied with women settling for "sheer imitation" of men.

As the Great Depression broke, Beard was finishing her first major historical work, *On Understanding Women* (1931), attempting to show what women had done and been as women, not as imitators of men, throughout history. Her mood was very critical indeed; she blamed emulators of men for failing to foresee that by coveting equality rather than giving their attention to "the broad study of life," they would attain—in veiled reference to the economic depression—"equality in disaster."[4] Yet her outlook was less defeatist than hortatory; she chastised her contemporaries because she felt they were capable of better things, if they turned their minds from imitating men to conceiving original schemes for national economic and social recovery.

Although Beard was highly skeptical about the merits of clubwomen's activities in the 1920s and 1930s, she did appear to invest considerable hope in a grand international meeting of clubwomen in Chicago in 1933, convened to mark the fortieth anniversary of a similar congress held at the World's Columbian Exposition of 1893. The National Council of Women of the United States, an umbrella group in which a score of organizations representing at least five million women participated, hosted the meeting. Its president at the time was Lena Madesin Phillips. A consummate organization woman who became one of Mary Beard's closest allies and confidantes during the 1930s, Phillips was a Kentuckian who had learned law at the knee of her father (a judge), and then had come North during World War I as secretary of the national board of the Young Women's Christian Association (YWCA). She stayed to turn the YWCA Businesswomen's Council into the National Federation of Business and Professional Women (NFBPW), becoming its first executive secretary, then president, then lifelong honorary president. Devoted to women and to women's causes—she lived in intimate relationship with Marjorie Lacey Baker all her adult life—Phillips passed the New York Bar in 1924 and practiced law in New York City, meanwhile founding and leading the International Federation of Business and Professional Women's Clubs. During the late 1930s she was associate editor of the *Pictorial Review,* a popular magazine mainly directed toward women. During the same years she was instrumental in getting the NFBPW to endorse the ERA.

Just how much influence Mary Beard had in shaping the theme of the congress of 1933 is not clear, but its overall title, "Our Common Cause—Civilization," sounds suspiciously Beardian, and she gave one of the opening speeches, which she called "Struggling Towards Civilization." In a post-conference letter to Dorothy Detzer, the executive secretary of the Women's International League for Peace and Freedom, Beard took credit for putting the subject of munitions—a personal concern—on the agenda, thus giving speaking room to peace activists Detzer and Florence Brewer Boeckel, a former Woman's Party suffragist who at the time was educational director of the National Council for Prevention of War.[5] Beard also chaired the Manifesto Committee, which was supposed to produce a document expressing the spirit of the conference. From a sur-

viving letter written by Beard to Maud Wood Park, formerly Carrie
Chapman Catt's lieutenant in the NAWSA and the first president of the
League of Women Voters, it appears that Beard, Park, and Harriot Stanton Blatch were to compose the Manifesto Committee as of March 1933;
but when the congress took place, in July, of the three only Beard remained on the committee, and the document was written at the meeting
itself, as the letter below indicates.[6]

The manifesto, certainly by Beard's hand, displayed in brief her depression-era convictions that centralized national planning was essential to
recovery and that feminism had to be linked to broader social vision in
order to be credible and meaningful in the crisis. She meant the pronoun-
cement to succeed the Declaration of Sentiments written by Elizabeth
Cady Stanton in 1848. In it she proposed the start of a *new* women's
movement, dedicated not only to the winning of equal citizenship for
women but also to "the winning of security and opportunity for all humankind." It continued:

> We believe that every person, to whatever sex, race or nationality,
> or creed she or he may belong, is entitled to security of life, work,
> the reward of labor, health, and education; to protection against
> war and crime, and to opportunity for self-expression. Yet, even in
> parts of the world where feminism has made its largest gains, these
> fundamentals of security and the good life are sadly lacking. Hence
> it is against social systems, not men, that we launch our second
> woman movement. We enter now a social-planning era following
> the harsh experiment with *laissez faire* and national aggressions,
> with a World War, and its horrible aftermath in the economic col-
> lapse. All civilization is at stake and the condition of society cannot
> be ignored. . . .
>
> The care and protection of all life is peculiarly in woman's keeping
> and thus at one of the most tragic hours in the world's history, we
> pledge ourselves to assume this responsibility boldly and whole-
> heartedly.
>
> Where the feminist movement is fundamental in any country, we
> call upon the women of the world to give it their loyalty. Where the
> social planning movement is imperative, we call upon the women of
> the world to join us in carrying it forward.[7]

The manifesto was adopted unanimously, although not without be-
hind-the-scenes maneuvering, including overriding a version written by a

former president of the National Council of Women, Amy Wood. As the letter below indicates, Beard relied here, as she would later in the Women's Archives venture, on the support of Emily Newell Blair, a Democratic Party activist who was concerned with women's voice in electoral politics. Beard's relief at achieving assent from Florence Bayard Hilles, a longtime adherent to the National Woman's Party, is also interesting, because it indicates not only the party's reputation for non-cooperation but also Beard's continuing notice of her old friends' politics. Beard left the congress buoyed up. Through the mid-1930s, she alternated between hope and despair about the likelihood of a new women's movement.

26. TO LENA MADESIN PHILLIPS, PRESIDENT OF NATIONAL COUNCIL OF WOMEN

New Milford, Connecticut
August 3, 1933

Dear Chief,

I am considerably perturbed in spite of your generous telegram over the possibility that I gummed your works, at the end. The Times report of Mrs. [Emily Newell] Blair's gallant fight for the scheme and the Manifesto cheered me immensely but of course I don't know the inner history of your contest with your Board [of the National Council of Women]. Clearly it thought the Manifesto weak. Maybe it was and is. Amy Wood preferred the one she had drafted late in the preceding afternoon but I think I did not prefer my later one just because it was mine. The whole thing was steam-rollered as I well know. But I couldn't see anything else to do in all the circumstances.

So by making the point of a planned society stand in juxtaposition or contradiction to the old individualist ideal, I hope to throw out a concept big enough to cover all the particular whereas-es which Mrs. Parsons or anybody else might have wanted to enumerate. And name it emphatically. For planning is the only means of subduing warfare and all else that we hate. The papers seemed to think that the Manifesto had punch if your Board didn't. But I try to look at the matter objectively, fully aware of my own mental anaemia. I pulled out at noon on Friday, as I did, because Mrs. Sternberger had greeted me in the lobby graciously and assured me that there would be no contest over the matter in the open. As I had been asked by you to meet the Board at the close of the morning session, I had murmured to Mrs. Blair at the door of the assembly hall that my head was probably coming off. She saw a dramatic and important opportunity to save the day and apparently did her big bit handsomely. I am told she has saved situations before!

But what is your status with the Board, if I may ask so personal a question? You are so far ahead of its members intellectually and spiritually that I have relied on superior force to win. Am I right? You won't want to put anything on paper but an "Oh yeah" would be enough for me.

The women can make the N[ational] Re[covery] A[dministration] work as no one else can and apparently they have already set about to do so, judging from the news about their pressure on chain stores in Washington, etc. But in the social planning they must also contribute creative ideas and work with their social perspective in mind.

I was thrilled by Mrs. [Florence Bayard] Hilles' seconding of the motion to adopt the Manifesto, for that prevents Woman's Party opposition and what is more—wins its recognition that social systems affect the status of women and (as in the case of German fascism) may destroy equality, once gained, by a single decree. I had talked with her at lunch about this matter when she was inclined to condemn the whole Congress for its "innocuous—ness". And she seemed impressed but I was amazed when she accepted the Manifesto so publicly. I thought that a great gain.

I would ask you to come up here for a visit at once or soon to talk everything over. But I can't do that right now. Yesterday there came a message from Roosevelt "drafting" Charles into service without pay in connection with the administration of the NRA. He is put on a board of seven members to guard it for the New York, New Jersey and western Connecticut district—the hardest in the country presumably. His instructions are to follow. Just what this may mean as to time and abode we do not yet know. If he has to be in New York for continuous work we shall take a little place there together and come "home" only for such free time as he may have, if any. So I have to leave all invitations to that home hanging. I should be able to see you in town at any rate. And maybe here.

You were a highly competent manager of the great show, dear Chief. And I have thought of you admiringly for countless reasons. It seemed to me too that the whole make-up of the Congress, with few exceptions, was indicative of a revolution in women's minds. It was a mad-cap adventure but under your chairmanship it did not work out meanly. On the contrary such publicity as I have chanced to see has reflected my own impression—that it marked a true advance for women.

You can be free to damn me up and down if you feel that I deserve it. I have no false confidence in my own powers. Your friend with her Thesaurus may think so but I was fishing for ideas while she hunted for words. And there was the need of both. A day longer would have helped in the discovery of course—of ideas, if not words.

> Au revoir, Chief, and
> blessings on your head.
> Mary R. Beard

Mary Beard's acquaintance with Harriot Stanton Blatch, who was twenty years her senior but had been her colleague during the suffrage years, seems to have been remade shortly before the congress of 1933. Perhaps Beard's anthology of documents published that year, *America Through Women's Eyes,* would have brought the two in touch anyway. Beard's attempt in the anthology to document major events in U.S. history through women's words and experience was unprecedented (and would not be repeated until the flourishing of academic women's history in the 1970s). The book put women's accomplishments and partnership with men, not their disabilities, in the foreground. Its concentration on social, economic, and cultural history and its virtual neglect of the suffrage campaign were remarkable. Neither Elizabeth Cady Stanton (Blatch's mother) nor suffrage was listed in the index, and Susan B. Anthony's words were recounted only in a Civil War–era speech against war and for emancipation. Stanton's voice appeared only to give a memorial for Lucretia Mott. Blatch herself was represented by an antiwar statement from her book *A Woman's Point of View: Some Roads to Peace* (Woman's Press, 1920), which she had written after a postwar trip to devastated Europe.

Blatch was infuriated by *America Through Women's Eyes.* Writing to the younger historian and feminist Alma Lutz, who was assisting her in composing her own memoirs, Blatch fumed, "Think of leaving out the whole of the story of the struggle—a unique and striking struggle of a disfranchised class forming one half the human race—for enfranchisement. If she had been taking as her title 'America From the Eyes of the Negro' would she have quoted Fred Douglas[s] only from memorial addresses? completely ignored the abolition struggle, the passage of the XIII, XIV, XV amendments, etc[?] She apparently does not see the connection between political freedom & economic opportunity." In momen-

tary venom Blatch accused Beard of becoming "a leader among the ma-
nipulators" of history.[8] It is hard to imagine that Blatch would have
hidden her feelings from Beard, but since Beard did not save her letters no
evidence of Blatch's direct criticism survives. In any case, during the ensuing years a remarkable correspondence and apparent mutual respect developed between the two women. When Blatch's memoirs were published
in 1940 (the year of her death), the volume carried an introduction by
Mary Ritter Beard.[9]

In the following letter, Beard takes note of another critic of *America
Through Women's Eyes:* Beulah Amidon, a former Congressional Union
colleague, who reviewed the book in the *New Republic.* After a few
laudatory adjectives, Amidon called the work "inevitably disappointing,"
"broken and incomplete," because it "pulled [the contributions of
women] out of their relationship to the whole" and failed to "integrate
women into the total picture." Because Beard's aim was exactly to restore
women to the total picture, she was understandably deflated. Where
Blatch wished Beard had focused more on women's self-defined eman-
cipatory movement, Amidon disliked imposing a line "to mark off
woman's part from man's in what is an essentially human record." [10]
Beard satisfied neither. She always had to struggle to convey her view of
the past to her contemporaries just as she had to struggle for their understanding of her critique of equality. The letter also suggests that Beard
was constantly weighing her own views against those she associated with
the National Woman's Party. A controversial speech that she delivered at
the NWP biennial convention on November 4, 1933, brought their differences to the fore.

In 1933 the Beards' daughter, Miriam, who had married Alfred Vagts
in Germany in 1927, returned to the United States permanently—to New
Milford—with her husband and son, Detlev, born in 1929. Because of
the Vagts' connections, the Beards were very much involved (especially
financially) in aiding German exiles and refugees from fascism during the
1930s. Miriam Beard Vagts was one of the speakers who helped to pack
Madison Square Garden for a public rally denouncing Hitlerism, sponsored by the American Jewish Congress, in March 1934.[11]

Blatch too had her daughter near her: Nora Stanton Barney (only seven
years younger than Mary Beard), a suffragist like her mother and grandmother and one of the first women in America to be trained in and practice civil engineering. The *Women's Political World* mentioned at the letter's opening was a publication of Blatch's earlier suffrage group in New
York City, the Women's Political Union.

27. TO HARRIOT STANTON BLATCH

La Posada
Winslow, Arizona
[January 1934]

Dear Harriot,

Charles and I had to work at top pressure until the very end of the old year and in the process we could hardly go through our mail. So it was days before I so much as saw your postcard telling me that you and Nora had a copy of the Women's Political World which I might get. Just as I finished helping Charles get off his last contracted-for obligation and was ready for my mail, the time arrived for us to pack up and depart for the west—the man in the case to preside over the convention of the American Historical Association of which he was president in 1933 and I to do a little needed shopping and then join him en route to the desert where we are now socially lost for a whole month recuperating from a solid year's siege of terrible tasks.

We shall be here in this high mountain sunshine until the first of February when we go to Pasadena for a month. Then we shall return to New Milford by easy stages through the south and we both hope never to drudge away in such horribly confining stretches again.

We are trying to think in this solitude—in my case probably an utterly hopeless ambition. I am afraid you agree with Beulah Amidon if you happened to see her criticism of my anthology in a late issue of the New Republic as "wordy and dull." That is far from encouraging but it seems to me that she herself was not entitled to mistake the entire purpose of that volume. And that reminds me that I had a letter from a woman member of the Dairymen's Cooperative League hoping for an added extract in the event of a second edition which will give a new agricultural perspective by women and saying meanwhile that she has particularly enjoyed the quotation from Mrs. Blatch in the present edition. So you may feel complimented anyway.

In the spring Miriam and Alfred are going to build a house for themselves on one of our farms so that they may have a home which they can afford in the future when we are no more. That will help us all to stretch out a little more in the meantime and thereby have our friends in for the night with more comfort all round. They both brought so much stuff home from Europe and need so many rooms at present for carrying on their work, that we were simply unable to have guests after their arrival. We missed you particularly, for both you and Nora in your individual ways furnish the finest kind of conversation and charm. There is little enough of either in America still after a hundred years. I am especially mindful of its lack after rereading Frances Trollope who, though British to the Nth degree in her provincialism, nevertheless did make some exceedingly pertinent remarks on the USA. The Pioneer Press is going to bring out a new edition of her Domestic Manners of the Americans [1832] in a year or so with the original illustrations and I have been asked to write an introduction. I may if I can forget Beulah Amidon long enough.

You know that I am ever solicitous about your autobiography. If you were not so interested in Charles' views of the world we should talk about that more when we are together. However, I recognize as well as you do the greater power of the man and must therefore bide my time to read what I should enjoy discussing. What I count on from you is a more trenchant comment on life than I was able to find for my anthology from other contemporary sources. Except perhaps from Ellen Glasgow. I thought that my quotation from her indicated a sharpness of mind and a breadth of vision but scantily revealed in her fiction. Whatever I did not accomplish by assembling the writings of American women about America, I find that the extracts have excited professors who are responsible for the education of young men and women. It seems all new copy for them. And that is something.

The National Woman's Party mistakes my point of view about equality and I must do something to make that position clearer. I am not against equality of course. I simply regard it as inadequate today. Men are so incompetent and ridiculous when not base that I can't stomach the idea of equality as the ultimate goal any longer. And in view of the fascist dictation to women which is setting in so strong a lot needs to be written still on the subject of women in a twentieth-century setting. You and Nora keep my faith alive in the vigor of women's minds and the reinterpretation of the old suffrage saw that "society can rise no higher than its women" makes our sex's mentality frightfully important now. If we play the game of the war band again there is no health in us.

I am so sorry, as is Charles, that Nora failed to be taken on for the Tennessee Valley enterprise. If housing proceeds in New York under La Guardia she may fare better. Tell her to use the letter Charles gave her in that connection if she thinks it would help. Best wishes for your New Year and Love to you three Stanton-Blatch representatives always,

                                        Mary R. Beard

❦

Beard's hope for a follow-up to the congress of 1933 was not fulfilled, but its momentum kept her writing and thinking about how to join feminism with goals of social planning and perhaps prompted her enthusiasm for a World Center on Women's Archives, an idea born in 1935. Beard's connection with Lena Madesin Phillips, who frequently sent her speeches and writings to criticize, also kept her more in touch with the activities of organized women than she had been since the 1910s. As shown in her recollection below of Ruth Hanna McCormick (the NAWSA suffragist who pressed for the Shafroth-Palmer alternative to the federal woman suffrage amendment), Beard never recanted on her position of the early 1910s.

28. TO LENA MADESIN PHILLIPS

February 26th [1934]

Dear Lena,

That's writing! Go to it. I had a good laugh over the humor and a fine thrill at the ideas set forth. It is this ability to adapt which marks the sheep from the goats. And I use this figure more intelligently since seeing the two animals perform out in the desert. The sheep are so stupid that herders have to keep goats among them. They (the goats) are sensitive to danger and don't crowd together so closely as to smother themselves. I had no idea that being a goat was a compliment. It seems to be.

If you decide to go to Washington, I shall see you there before I reach New York as we are returning via the capital the last of March. Your decision will be of deep interest to me like everything you do and are.

As for Ruth Hanna McCormick Simms, I shall not be at Albuquerque again though I did come through there earlier. Years ago I saw her, during a mad trial of Alice Paul, Lucy Burns and myself conducted by the older suffrage group made up of Mrs. McCormick, Anna Howard Shaw and Jane Addams. We had just launched the Congressional Union and were trying to start the political tactic of having already enfranchised women demand the enfranchisement of the rest through their political power. It was dandy tactics and had great effect when we went ahead with it. But the older suffragists loathed us for breaking into their game. Dr. Shaw was insulting until Miss Addams had to protest. But I was impressed that day by the utter coldness of the lady McCormick. And by her lack of political astuteness in spite of her training under [her father] Mark [Hanna]. . . .

The chances of a follow-up conference do not seem encouraging as you reveal the Council's attitude. But I believe it ought to occur for many reasons: the wave of Fascist psychology with respect to women surging high in this country articulate in the magazines and educational reports, etc; the bewilderment of feminists about next steps; the need of definite nation[al] planning for a long period of time, our manifesto, women's sense of the humanistic proprieties which ought to be phases of the planning; the value of tying independent women of the country together in a movement in which they can express themselves freely and catch fire from fire. If nothing happens to make the outlook for such a meet brighter in the meantime, when I chat with you in March, let us canvas the field again then.

May the Fates be good to you—
Thine, Mary R. Beard

Perhaps Harriot Stanton Blatch read in the NWP weekly, *Equal Rights,* the report of Mary Beard's "Wilmington speech" at a NWP banquet of 1933. Beard had declared herself somewhat disillusioned with equality, especially in education, and positively opposed to equality in combativeness. She was quoted as asking how it was possible to have sex equality in property rights, "when about 2000 men at the most manipulate all our property rights?" She went on to ask, "Do we want to be preachers, bankers, Babbitts, merely for the sake of equality with men? Do we want to be labor racketeers?" In the following letter to Blatch she moderated her tone.

Beard continued to think that feminists, rather than training their eyes solely on sex discrimination, ought to think more inclusively. During the mid-1930s she was especially concerned about the munitions build-up in the United States and the effects of fascism in Europe. Beard supported antimilitarist organizations and efforts during the mid-1930s, the height of the domestic peace movement. She spoke at meetings on such topics as "Can We End War?" and tried to foster the publication of works about the waste, corruption, and danger in mounting arms production. Keeping the Beards up to date in a very immediate way, a stream of international visitors flowed through the New Milford household, swelled by the Beards' Japanese connections (from their trip in the early 1920s) and by Miriam and Alfred Vagts' German friends and interests. Mary Beard was also concerned about the rearguard attack on women's employment in the precarious American economy. Yet where feminists such as Lena Madesin Phillips in response emphasized women's right to work, Beard brought in other considerations, inclining "to the view that women may have to supplement this notion of their rights and that workers may have to supplement their notions of rights in the case of either sex by considerations of their value in a planned economy." [12]

29. TO HARRIOT STANTON BLATCH

New Milford
July sixteenth [1934]

Dear Harriot—

I can catch the full flavor of that sniggling about "even such an authority as Mary Beard." Of course it's ridiculous. But for that matter all authority is somewhat ridiculous. Things are true or they are not. That is all there is to authority in any case. And what any one else says about me is not my responsibility.

As for my feeling about that review by Beulah Amidon, I respect her so much that I was only sorry to have disappointed her. I was not hurt in the sense of being wounded because she did not like my performance. I can laugh at and criticise myself even better than any one can do either to me. That is gospel truth to which Charles himself will testify I feel sure.

You and I cannot actually be "poles apart", as you say—unless you have gone in 100% for laissez faire philosophy. I can't believe you have. I haven't the ghost of an idea how my Wilmington speech has been interpreted by the National Woman's Party. It was not written out and turned in by me. Hence comments must be second hand at best. What I was claiming is too bromidic for you and me alike to have to debate—simply that the women of '48 were keyed to the opening competitive regime which seemed to offer immortality at that time—when the free land appeared inexhaustible, etc., etc., etc. You know that story well enough to be able to "sing it to a harp", as we would say here. Then I expatiated on the well-known stuff about how driving for "sheer equality" in a competitive economy had its economic, ethical, and political limitations. I wound up with the thesis that the political economy in which feminism has to function is the prime consideration. For that is what determines in large measure its history. Are we poles apart?

Maybe we are. But we shall see. Don't jump to that conclusion before we chat some more.

The household will welcome you whenever you can come across its portal. Until Friday of this week we have guests, for instance Mr. Fukuoka of the Rengo Shimbun, a truly liberal editor of a great associated press in the Far East who has just come to this country and who needs to get a clear-cut idea of where the U.S. stands in its attitude toward Tokyo. Charles has to go to New York on Friday but will be back on Saturday. If you could come up on Sunday morning and stay overnight, that would be delightful for us. Or any time next week.

Miriam and Alfred have interesting views on Germany, some of which Miriam has been printing. Have you seen them—in Today, the Nation, the Sunday Times? Alfred is putting his opus on German-American Relations through the press. It is being published in England.

I want to hear about your book. Remember, if you will, that I am counting on you to provide the criticism of your times which so few women seem able to do. I had a long evening with Doris Stevens in Washington this spring. She insisted that a feminist can and must do one thing at a time. She maintained that I should work for Communism. "But I am not a communist," said I. I'll tell you how she impressed me for perhaps she has reported how I impressed her. I believe that we have to do everything at once. Of course we can't, if we accept the dominant philosophy.

Cordially always, Mary R. Beard.

•↩-

Beard followed her first pathbreaking anthology with yet another, Laughing Their Way, a collection of women's humor—prose, poetry, and cartoons—jointly edited with Martha Bruere. If wags today still complain that feminists aren't funny, that was even more true in the 1930s, when highmindedness or glamour, never humour, exhausted the range of positive public images of women. In spite of Beard's and Bruere's creative searching, R. L. Duffus on the first page of the New York Times Book Review dismissively griped, "There is not much in this volume to shake a reader's (at least a male reader's) sides with laughter." The review as a whole was not unfavorable, but Beard was doubtless irritated too by Duffus' conclusion that "laughter for women is almost as modern an invention as equal suffrage"; that flew in the face of her convictions about women of the long past.[13] Criticism such as his she was able to deflect by sarcasm of her own, and besides, she was fired up with the idea for another book. The one that she would complete in the mid-1940s, however, differed from the plan outlined in the letter below.

30. TO HARRIOT STANTON BLATCH

New Milford
September seventh [1934]

Dear Harriot,

If you read Duffus on women's humor, you will remember that he talked about the undertow of feminine resentment at men. I thanked him for his review which interested me very much as a point of view and in his reply he enclosed the cartoon which I am sending on herewith to you as his notion of humor supreme—the "deep-bellied" kind which makes sides shake with laughter. So an uproariously funny article might be written on the ways in which different persons react to any given specimen called humorous. I am not witty enough to do the article but I am saving some reviews as the basis for it when some one else may try it. Edwin Seaver, for example, much prefers "ladies' laughter" of the Godey Book days to modern fun in the New Yorker, whereas Duffus can't abide the earlier form.

I am sending you a copy of LAUGHING THEIR WAY which will probably suggest to you countless omissions and improvements. I had not intended to do any of this book myself. I suggested it to Martha Bruere as a volume essential to my plan for a series on women and thought she was an excellent person to prepare it. But she got in a jam after she had collected a lot of the excerpts, we were under contract to turn in the manuscript, and I had to take over the job. My chief regret is, as I say on page 51, that the wit of your family and the feminists of your mother's time has not been caught and transmitted. I dare say a good deal of it could be assembled if one explored for it especially but I have another idea for the final volume on women in my scheme which *necessitates* the special study of the aforesaid women. This is to analyze the range and vigor of women thinkers and in this connection I am impressed by the early feminists' criticism of Church and State, among other things.

As I have visualized my series of books on women, this is it:

I *On Understanding Women*. Shows that women have always been at the center of thought and action throughout time.

II *America through Women's Eyes*. What they have written about the republican experiment in particular and how their own role appears in their pages.

III *Laughing their Way*. Women laugh as well as pray, etc.

IV Are Women Thinkers? I haven't the title yet for this and have done very little on it but I have in mind calling attention to such women as Rosa Luxembourg who could measure up to the best of philosophers even in abstruse logic.

My project as it works out is exceedingly sketchy but I hope it will be so suggestive that it may furnish a basis for "equal education" at last. For the present we have only education in men's history, men's ideas of their own thought and action, men's wit and humor, etc. If women turn in on themselves a little more, they may find out better what they really are. I don't know yet. The question of corollaries is a philosophic one. But if we are to *hold* any steps in equality, I have the hunch that we shall have to offer more to the community than straight "justice" and "right" since justice and right are never the basis of economic and political action. And in this connection I consider Fannina Halle's book on Women in Soviet Russia a grand thing. It shows that the spirit of the Slav woman from the age of the matriarchate to the age of Stalin has been so indomitable that the logic of contemporary equality in Russia is just the inexorable logic of her whole history. On the other hand Grace Hutchins' 1934 book on America called Women Who Work is such a ghastly picture of life and labor unrelieved by anything but a shriek for imitative communism that I wonder what is the logic of our own American life and labor really, in terms of woman's spirit in America. It would seem to me that the future of any society must bear an intimate relation to its past.

But while I work at these things I help to draw women into the common stream of American history as I did in the writing of The Rise of American Civilization and the various texts which Charles and I have circulating in the schools. The more I know about woman herself the better I can integrate her into the human story as a whole of course. And in every revision of a history text I am integrating her better I am sure. Just now CAB and I are having a try at a very thorough-going rewriting of a high school book and, as my opportunity is larger for including woman in the scene, at the same time I think I see her more clearly as germane to every step that America has taken. It will be so as we go from rugged individualism to ensuing necessities. (You know how Hitler has made German female maniacs serve himself?)

Forgive this long and rather detailed report of my half-baked efforts to think. I am not counting on a sheer epistolary discussion with you whom I hold in major regard as a thinker. Just a little later now I mean to have you for a sufficiently long visit for us to talk about this and all the other events and concepts which seem significant to you, to Charles, and to me.

In the meantime my best wishes for the rounding out of your memoir and for your good health—

Affectionately, Mary R. Beard

[P.S.] Charles is just finishing the proofs on the second and last volume in his study of National Interest—this one being called THE OPEN DOOR AT HOME. Next week we are both booked for a conference. On our return I hope to be able to invite you by giving you a choice of dates on which I may motor to Nyack for you.

Beard continued to encourage Harriot Stanton Blatch's history writing, which she saw as the complement to Blatch's historic actions. The following letter presages Beard's own intense commitment to the discovery and preservation of women's documents in the latter half of the 1930s.[14]

31. TO HARRIOT STANTON BLATCH

[New Milford, Conn.]
Sept. 22 [1934]

I wonder how you are getting on with your Memoirs. I trust you will let nothing interfere with their preparation and that, among the drawings you will make for it, you will give a rounded-out picture of the suffragists, showing their ideals and their courage, their fears and their weaknesses, the youth and old age inner contest (part and parcel of the strain and stress in India), the ordering and the obeying, and as far as possible the content of the propaganda. What did the women think they were doing in very fact? Wasn't your mother's group far more radical than the Shaw-Catt-Paul brigade? and didn't it have a much larger vision of the State?

Don't bother to answer these questions just to me. I simply present them as types of things I should love to see you cover.

Curiously and unjustly enough, unless you do set down your own relation to the public life of your time, dear Mrs. Blatch—for by that appellation your loyal army always talked of you—young men and women to come will have no way of understanding these times or your place in them. You were more of an orator than a scribe and so, while Mrs. Catt has manuscripts galore, taken to the naval conference at London as an exhibit, manuscripts which will pass into history possibly as the major record of the suffrage movement, your own glowing inspiration and wit and large-minded sweep of politics may not receive their due. You did not run to and fro across the continent, either, as I believe, and so nationally the one-night-standers or the national executives might have to crowd a tale the poorer for your exclusion. One who writes history has to have data he can put his hands on, you see.

So, you see again, I am tremendously keen on this point both for your sake and the country's. Your criticism would enrich the quality of American thinking and God knows it can bear the diet.

Yours ever, Mary Beard

During 1932 and 1933 Mary Beard made some of her most stirring and eloquent pronouncements about faults in women's higher education resulting from its imitation of men's. As a result of her address on "The College and Alumnae in Contemporary Life" given at the biennial convention of the American Association of University Women (AAUW) in 1933, she was asked by that organization to compose a syllabus on women—a set of questions and bibliography—for group study. The result was her fifty-seven page pamphlet, *A Changing Political Economy as It Affects Women,* published by the AAUW in 1934. This document—which she interestingly calls a "feminist" syllabus in the letter below—treated women's history in intimate connection with her concerns about aggressive nationalism and the relations between international trade, the search for markets, and war. (Her difficulty with contemporary syllabus of economist Dr. Harry Gideonse, "America in a World Economy," had less to do with his views of women than with his views of international trade relations. In the postwar years Gideonse became a major antagonist of Charles Beard.)

Beard's syllabus, divided into sections such as "the quest for sex equality" and "women and historic nationalism," full of encouragement to readers to uncover the women's history and activities in their local communities, was also notable for its acknowledgment of differences between women. She posed for discussion such questions as "Is race a factor in American sex discrimination?" and for close study "the inequalities which prevail as between women and women." Underlying the topics and questions in the syllabus was Beard's dialectical conviction that possibilities and prospects for women depended on the political economy in which they found themselves, while women's values and behaviors helped to create a given political economy.[15]

32. TO HARRIOT STANTON BLATCH

Carlton Hotel
Washington
Jan. 21st. 1935

Dear Harriot—

The judgment of my effort—as per the feminist syllabus—which you render sets me up indeed! But you would know better than any one what I was trying to do. I am not a little paralyzed by the fact that this thesis of mine is being distributed by the A.A.U.W. beside one by Dr. Harry Gideonse which is in complete conflict with everything for which I contend. Not only that, his syllabus is so messy in thought and logic that if he gets by, I should feel that mine must be in the same plight were it not for your commendation. I am flabby in spots no doubt and mine may not be a work of art but it is surely headed right, as you encourage me into continuing to believe. After a chat with President [William] Neilson [of Smith College] after breakfast a few days ago, I felt however like an infant crying in the night. There is just no glimmer of suspicion on the part of men or women apparently that women's education is not a perfect thing. If you missed the enclosed, you shouldn't. I'd like to have it back at your convenience.

Dr. Gideonse appears to be quite a favorite of the ladies. He is being advertised for the Cause and Cure of War program here this week, as quite a card.

January is waning and we shall be looking forward to seeing the Millers. And you.

And yours, Mary R. Beard

•⊷

The Beards spent much of the winter of 1935 in Washington, D.C., conducting research and also working avidly for neutrality legislation. As the letters below suggest, they were welcomed among the influential members of the New Deal, while keeping a critical distance. The invitation from Secretary of Agriculture Henry Wallace likely had to do with Charles Beard's book *The Open Door at Home* (1934), which argued for limitation of American exports and international trade in favor of the development of American "continentalism" and concentration on a "standard of life budget" for all at home. This thesis took issue with Wallace's brief for trade expansion. Wallace, disputing Beard on this point, published an otherwise admiring review.[16]

33. TO HARRIOT STANTON BLATCH

> Carlton Hotel
> Washington, D.C.
> January 30, 1935

Dear Harriot,

Did your ears burn a few days ago about noon? They should have if there is anything in the proverb. Charles and I had just had the wonderful experience of talking for a few moments with Justice [Oliver Wendell] Holmes and we were full of ideas about his place in America and his generation. You are a kid in point of years by comparison but we joined you two in our thought and what we said should have made your ears burn— not with anger either. We wish we could have joined the celebrants on your 79th birthday. But we can't believe your story of being 79. I have hesitated to inquire your age but now that it comes out I thrill anew at the strength of body and of spirit that is Harriot Stanton Blatch!

I see that you are announced here for the Birth Control dinner. So I shall see you then.

Don't think I minimize the radical proposition put forth in my syllabus. I merely wonder how far it will carry, naturally. We had dinner last night with Secretary [Henry] Wallace and other guests in his home, including [Attorney-General Homer] Cummings. Oh, God, Harriot I wish you were President and Cabinet all in one.

> Love to you, Mary R. Beard

[P.S.] I have just been going over the education plans of the Fathers in the 18th Century. Nearly every one was impressed by the need of rallying to the young republic the support of women and was prepared to include them in the scheme of education. The west and the machine checked realization.

❦

The letter below gives a more detailed description of the Beards' busy winter in Washington and their efforts to influence the shape of the New Deal and foreign policy. After *The Open Door at Home,* Charles Beard (with collaborator George H. E. Smith) also published *The Idea of Na-*

tional Interest: An Analytical Study of American Foreign Policy in 1934. Mary Beard declined Dorothy Detzer's suggestion that she stand for election to the national board of the Women's International League for Peace and Freedom; while deeply committed to work for peace and neutrality, she was not an organization woman and obviously preferred to work in tandem with her husband. She shared his acute critique of the American attempt to create world order through international intervention.[17]

34. TO LENA MADESIN PHILLIPS

New Milford
April 28th [1935]

Dear Lena,

It is good to hear from you and we must have a chat together soon. I must entice you here before long even if I have to devise a roulette wheel to win you. That's a great tale connecting Charles and gambling—one which he enjoyed with me to the full range of gaiety. He is pleased to have you approve his treatise on national interest. The fight over his point of view as there expounded has been a big one this winter in Washington and goes on at the conferences where internationalists foregather from time to time. Franklin D. [Roosevelt] read it from cover to cover and marked passages galore. But he wrote on the fly leaf of his copy: "This is a bad dish Beard gives us." We had lunch with H. G. Wells in Washington who, without studying the thesis, was sure it was just chauvinism, until we talked it over at length. Even then he thinks it "simpler" to establish world order than to put a nation into shape. As soon as I can see a freer calendar I shall ask you to come up and hear CAB "throw around some of those choice occasional words" you seemed to read in his treatise. But he has to go to Washington again and I have agreed to speak here, there, everywhere in May. I wonder why!

This is neglecting to tell you that we left the capital the last day of March. Thus I am denied the privilege of meeting Mrs. Wood. I should gladly call upon her or ask her to lunch if I were still there. No doubt my declaration in a winter letter to you that I am a "lone wolf" was intimidating when you thought that I might do this or that in Washington. But I must explain this better when I see you. It did not mean that I stood in proud isolation way off on the periphery of events. It just happens that I can do what I feel able to do in more curious ways than through organisation work. The winter was dynamic with all the energy I could muster but it flowed into a kind of underground enterprise such as private talks with government officers and congressmen by day and by night in small groups in our quarters or in theirs, with an occasional open speech and discussion at the Cosmos Club or somewhere. Without intending to, Charles and I in fact ran a perfect office at home—interviews piling on interviews, appointments made to speak at hearings on sedition bills and what-not, etc. without end. I never was busier in my crowded life. There were dashes to Atlantic City and elsewhere for meetings. There was movement in a definite direction. And maybe some results have come. Anyway we did our best to help the drive for civilian government as distinct from naval control, for a check on those who would clamp nasty sedition bills on the country, and for a rational attack on public misery and poverty. So forgive me if I missed chances to report on housing and other discussions and if I seemed indifferent to suggestions for work. I was not indifferent. I did in fact slip into the housing meeting but when I found that anything seemed able to go forward by its own momentum I was inclined to push something more anaemic provided it seemed to merit a thrust.

And what is more—I just have to stick pretty close to CAB and his enterprises because he is so helpless without me, being so deaf and generally so dependent on my cooperation. Even so, we generally have the same urges and points of view, if not in every instance.

I am keen to know about your winter of touring and talking across the continent. Why didn't you write me more about it? The *last week in May* perhaps you can come and tell me here. I shall hope to find that time clear for asking you.

Yours, Mary Beard

Through the mid-1930s Harriot Stanton Blatch's needling made Mary Beard formulate and reformulate, in a self-conscious fashion, her views of women and their history, as in the following letter. Indeed, in a contemporary letter to Doris Stevens, Beard wrote, "Harriot Stanton Blatch thinks me plain insane." Below, she makes the interesting mistake of attributing to Charlotte Perkins Gilman a comment made in fact by Freda Kirchwey, editor of the *Nation,* in a review of *On Understanding Women.*[18]

35. TO HARRIOT STANTON BLATCH

New Milford
[May 1935]

Dear Harriot,

Your letter arrived just as I was starting on a drive to Wells College and I am just home again. I never took so long a jaunt alone in the car but only good fortune attended me. It was a marvelous trip with the buds bursting all the way until one could imagine their making music doing it, after living in the Orient where poetry says they do. But the ghastly housing in the amazing landscape! It made me sick to the bone. Do these people on the land have to have task masters to make them repair rotting timbers and clean up their messes generally? I can't understand their sloth, for that it seems, when their houses lie far apart in fields so rich beside those which the Japanese or Montenegrins cultivate that they seem like paradise itself. They could at least have gardens but I saw only filth.

I am deeply interested in your criticism of my obsession with women. I have pondered on it myself right along—critically. But the work I have done in studying women makes me aware of the large social corollaries as I should not otherwise be. If supreme philosophy is the search for the primordial—and is it not?—that search is closely related to my quest. Charlotte Perkins Gilman said that I have "repopulated history" and if I have that was better than writing history "directly" along the line of men's partial offerings. As for the interpretation of history which is the larger idea, do you consider that it is an impersonal proceeding? Anyway, let us have a good talk about all this soon. It is a good theme. Would a trip to us early in June be too difficult for you? Where will you be then?

May is horribly crowded. I am going to Goucher College next week. Charles has had to go back to Washington. We seem to be running around to excess this month. But June will be a different story and the weather warmer, let us pray. It is frigid still up here.

Love as always, Mary R. Beard

Besides speaking and aiding her husband's testimony before Congress in 1935, Mary Beard had some other ideas for helping the peace cause, as in the letter below. She wrote in this vein—showing her awareness of the importance of popular culture—to leaders of several peace organizations and received encouraging replies about implementation. Beard was aware of a large peace demonstration to be held in Geneva in 1935, in which her old Congressional Union pal Mabel Vernon was a leader. She regretted not giving more money to this cause, but she had given priority to "help get some of the German men and women out of prison camps," according to another contemporary letter.[19]

36. TO DOROTHY DETZER, EXECUTIVE SECRETARY OF THE WOMEN'S INTERNATIONAL LEAGUE FOR PEACE AND FREEDOM

New Milford, Connecticut
August 2, 1935

Dear Miss Detzer,

As you know of course the students of this country have recently achieved some notable successes in causing the withdrawal from local houses of films and news reels clearly militaristic in design. They resorted to the boycott and used this agency of protest with considerable effect. But the strain of abstention from movies is a hard one to demand of great numbers of people, especially for any length of time. The war films will keep coming back wherever vigilance relaxes. War films still reap immense profits from the movie audiences. Night after night they fan the war spirit while lovers of peace seem helpless to meet this situation.

But is there not in fact a way for the protest to gain true strength? I have learned that while the war films are financial triumphs generally, the films with peace as their theme are financial disasters as a rule. I therefore make the suggestion to you as to other anti-militarists who direct national organisations that a serious attempt be made to reverse this patronage. Abstention from attendance at the play could thus be relieved and the pleasure of dramatic experience encouraged. Better peace films and different news reels would surely result from the larger demand. There are playwrights who are ready to risk their all on plunges into anti-war films, But should they be ruined in the process? It seems to me that no more effective work for peace could be done than to bring about the shift of patronage from the one kind of picture to the other.

How can this be done? I have secured the promise of Miss Helen Havener of the Motion Picture Producers & Distributors of America, Inc. (28 West 44th Street, New York City) that she will provide any inquiring officer or interested member of a civic organisation with the list of films founded on the peace idea and keep that information up-to-date for them. If this information could then be distributed among the membership of such societies with the advice that the members make it a practice to give their patronage to these plays, a still more notable success in driving out the war films might be achieved than can be achieved by the boycott alone.

You may be fully aware of all this and regard my letter to you as naive. But I am too convinced of the value of this procedure to hesitate to write you about it through the fear that some one may already be pushing it.

Sincerely, Mary R. Beard

3 The Women's Archives Begins

The following letter inaugurated a new era in Mary Beard's life, during which she devoted herself to the establishment of an institution that would preserve and maintain women's history through documents. The project began with a proposal by Rosika Schwimmer, a Hungarian-born feminist, pacifist, and radical reformer residing in the United States, who had been active in international woman suffrage and peace efforts since the beginning of the twentieth century. Schwimmer, one year younger than Beard, was personally acquainted with most of the leading lights of the prewar suffrage and peace movements in the United States—Carrie Chapman Catt, Jane Addams, Harriet Stanton Blatch, for instance—and she had discussed with several of them her idea to create an archive of documents reflecting those struggles. Both Harriot Stanton Blatch and Dorothy Dunbar Bromley, a columnist for the *New York World-Telegram,* suggested that Schwimmer should enlist Mary Beard's help.

In July 1935, when Schwimmer first wrote to Beard suggesting a meeting, she had in mind "an international feminist-pacifist archive," to collect and preserve documents and thus to keep alive the truths of women's international efforts and achievements for equal rights and world peace before and during the Great War. In Schwimmer's view, the postwar years had seen retrogression on both fronts, as women's rights had been compromised in many countries, the "militarization of women" was proceeding apace, and peace efforts by women were diminishing in influence. Her view of militarization in the United States was greatly affected by the refusal of her own application for American citizenship. She pursued citizenship through the 1920s all the way to the U.S. Supreme Court, which in May 1929 handed down a decision confirming her ineligibility on the grounds of her unwillingness to bear arms for her country.[1]

37. TO ROSIKA SCHWIMMER

New Milford, Connecticut
July 21, 1935

My revered Rosika Schwimmer,

Your name signed to a letter to me fills me with infinite delight. It leads me to venture to ask you whether you could come to see us in the country and talk over the archive of documents here. I rarely go to town in the summer but I shall do so if that is the only way or the best way to have the talk with you. Any time that you might set for a visit here before August first, when my house will be fuller for a week or so, would bring rejoicing to all the Beards.

As for your project it has my fullest sympathy. I think it imperative to put this material together. No doubt we have many of the same reasons for seeing it that way but it does me great good to learn that one so competent as you stands ready to assume the task. I shall be only too happy to tell you how I visualise the thing, parts of which I have longed to tackle myself but have not done and see no way to do myself. I look forward with the keenest enjoyment to meeting you—a privilege far too long denied me.

Cordially, Mary R. Beard

Beard visited the residence of the sisters Franciska and Rosika Schwimmer (leaving behind her handkerchief by accident). It was "a memorable day," Schwimmer wrote to Beard: "It was quite rejuvenating to meet again someone who possesses a fiery spirit and intellectual superiority,— something that has become so rare in the ranks of feminists."[2] As the letter suggests, Beard immediately set about collecting supporters for the project.

38. TO ROSIKA SCHWIMMER

New Milford, Connecticut
August 6, 1935

Dear Mme. Schwimmer,

Your generous words about my personality convince me that I caught fire in your presence. But who wouldn't? I am an intellectual babe who should stay in the woods but who is delighted beyond words when you help me pretend that I am growing up. It was wonderful to have the chance to commune with you and your sister! I hesitate to risk spoiling another by sending you a copy of one of my books but I hope that you will see in it the raw material of a great book when some one more gifted than I writes it on some such basis. I have asked my publisher to mail a copy to you.

Now that your plan has arrived for the Archive, I shall proceed at once to push for its execution. Your statement is so completely convincing that I must believe that the scheme will capture the imagination and appeal to the practical sense of American women in a position to carry it out. I shall make copies tomorrow and send them to such persons as Marguerite Wells of the League of Women Voters whom I know to be vitally peaceful in intention, Mrs. Geline MacDonald Bowman of the [National] Federation of Business and Professional Women, and Dr. [Kathryn] McHale of the [American Association of] University Women. It is possible however that there will be delay on account of vacations. I will let you know what response I get without delay. I am writing Mrs. [Eleanor] Roosevelt and Ellen Glasgow too. Each and everyone whom I suspect of being capable of intelligence I shall ask to consider this proposition for, conceivably, such a dramatisation of feminism and the woman's angle on life might even do something now to halt the backward movement which you so graphically picture.

The last of this month when some of my husband's engagements have been filled and I can be sure of his being at home, I shall try to lure you and your sister here by motor, sending my car for you.

Thank you so much for my five cent handkerchief so beautifully laundered that it looks expensive.

Cordially, Mary R. Beard

The women whom Beard initially contacted to support the archives project were of several sorts: old friends from suffragist days who had continued in anti-militarist efforts, obvious big names in women's organizations, potential sympathizers who had risen to importance in the New Deal, and women with money. Florence Brewer Boeckel had been a Woman's Party campaigner and editor of *The Suffragist;* after the Nineteenth Amendment was passed she became educational director of the National Council for Prevention of War, an anti-militarist organization of men and women.

Beard's fury at Harry Elmer Barnes' *History of Western Civilization* (New York, 1935) and Will Durant's *The Story of Civilization* (vol. 1, *Our Oriental Heritage* [New York, 1935]) was neither the first nor last of her trumpets against male historians of civilization for leaving out women's part.

39. TO FLORENCE BREWER BOECKEL

New Milford, Connecticut
August 10, 1935

Dear Mrs. Boeckel:

Here I am at it again! The enclosed [description of the Archives plan] is self-explanatory and I am behind it one hundred percent. I saw Mme. Schwimmer the other day in town and found her having to decide at last about her own archives. I hate as much as she does to see them boxed or burned.

Beside I am enraged by the new books on civilization—Will Durant's and H. E. Barnes'. They just know nothing whatever of the woman in any case. It is our fault I think. And in our fault all men and women are at fault.

I think that if we could dramatise the woman's culture as this Plan suggests, we might recapture the feminine imagination for a woman movement on a grander design, revive some of the old indomitable spirit which centered around the old Cause, and regain a united front directed toward peace and creative enterprise. It is worth trying, isn't it? Do you believe so? . . .

It is proposed (by me) to collect a group of women in New York soon after Labor Day to discuss the matter and get a sponsoring committee. Can you come?

Love and best wishes, Mary Beard

Another correspondent of Mary Beard's during the 1930s was a woman exactly her age who had been campaigning, ever since the design of Mt. Rushmore by sculptor Gutzum Borglum in the 1920s, to have Susan B. Anthony's head carved there along with the four presidents honored. Beard's letter to Powell brings out her particular interest in women's contribution to *public* life; it is also worth noting that she invents the phrase "woman's culture" to use in these recruitment letters.

40. TO ROSE ARNOLD POWELL

New Milford, Connecticut
August 10, 1935

Dear Mrs. Powell,

Your familiarity with Susan B. Anthony's passion for preserving her

own and Mrs. Stanton's archives—meaning more than the personal interest of course—will make you receptive of course to this broad plan for a
great international feminist archive which Rosika Schwimmer has drawn
up. I don't know where you stand on the issue of war and peace but I
entertain, as one of my feminist props, the belief that time and again in
history women have had to take over men's bankrupt societies and that
the Schwimmer-Addams' and other feminists' attempts to take charge of
the western world in 1915 was a great outburst of the same sort of responsibility. All the correspondence and the interviewing connected with
that drive for peace are in Mme. Schwimmer's keeping. But she is getting
on in years and is by no means well. Nor can she afford to house this
archive any longer. It is good feminist material and should not be lost by
burning or by boxing for no one to read. In my opinion.

What is even more on my mind in championing the enclosed Plan is
some way to recapture the imaginative zest of women for public life. It is
perilous for society if they retreat to private interests to the exclusion of
interests in the common life represented by the State. To recapture that zest
I believe that some dramatisation of the woman's culture is necessary, is imperative. And this seems to me the way. Reverencing our pioneers is important. But work in our own time for our own time is equally vital, is it not?

Let me know your reaction to this Plan anyway?

                                        Cordially, Mary R. Beard

Not surprisingly, Beard called upon Lena Madesin Phillips' support for
the archives effort. As noted in the letter below, she initially imagined that
a woman's college might be connected with the archives to offer an alternative education grounded in understanding of women's contributions to
world history. Beard's critiques of existing structures of higher education
in the early 1930s resulted not only in utopian visions but also in a tendency to blame women for not knowing, or for willfully ignoring, their
own history.

41. TO LENA MADESIN PHILLIPS

                                        New Milford
                                        August 20th [1935]
Dear Chief,

I have not bothered you for ages, have I, with a fantastic scheme of my
own? But you have been thrusting out in new lines while I have been in-

cubating for new thrusts too. I long for a chat about yours and mine for maybe we have both got a new lease of life. If the meeting which the enclosed proposes comes off soon after Labor Day, I'll stay over in town for a chat and a bat if you are "agreeable." In the meantime I have got to bow down night and day to the revision of a High School book on American history with blood in my eye for more material on woman for one thing, but not everything.

I hope you will be enthusiastic about the enclosed Plan. You may or may not think highly of Rosika Schwimmer. That, I think, does not matter. Her suggestion is enormously important. I see in it, beside what is set forth by her, the nucleus of a true Woman's College. We could have seminars at the Archive Centers and talks by competent persons on the role of women in society. No writer or orator or "statesman" should be able after this gets going to publish a tome, deliver a speech, or plot a national program without an apprenticeship to this institution. I feel enraged for instance over the just published History of Western Civilization by Harry Elmer Barnes which takes no account really of women as involved in the story. It is overwhelmingly masculine and consequently unenlightened about how civilisations are made. But I think his fault is women's fault in knowing nothing of themselves.

Will you come to a meeting at Mme. Schwimmer's soon after Labor Day to consider the Plan and a sponsoring committee? Have you a choice of dates to propose?

> Best wishes and love,
> Mary R. Beard

❦

The first meeting on behalf of the archives project was set for Tuesday, September 10, 1935. It did not include Alice Paul, mentioned in the letter below, although she became a sponsor. The national chairman (so called) chosen a few months later was a National Woman's Party figure, Inez Haynes Irwin. A successful author of fiction and journalism, Irwin had narrated *The Story of the Woman's Party* (New York, 1921) and had also published, in conjunction with the international congress of women in 1933, a popular history of women, *Angels and Amazons* (Garden City, 1934). The organizational structure for the World Center for Women's Archives (WCWA), as the project was shortly to be called, with a national board and state branches, was similar to Alice Paul's structure for the National Woman's Party. But Beard constantly strove to make the membership and leadership represent and appeal to a much wider range of women.

42. TO ROSIKA SCHWIMMER

New Milford
September sixth [1935]

Dear Mme. Schwimmer,

. . . As for our joint Tuesday meeting, I . . . had urged Mrs. Blatch to interest the National Woman's Party because I thought that she might have more influence now with Alice Paul than I have. But on receiving your letter I wrote directly to Alice Paul myself. I worked very closely with her years ago. Indeed I was the first and for a long time the only backer she had in New York. But we have not seen eye to eye on post-suffrage programs. We have not disputed personally but I have seen nothing of hers for a long, long time and so I had turned to Mrs. Blatch for pressure for the Archive. I asked Mrs. Blatch also to write to Mrs. Hecker about the matter. I agree heartily with your appreciation of Mrs. Blatch's place in the movement of thought. We are close friends. She has reached an age which may make her a little forgetful and we may have to repeat the details or the spirit of our enterprise but maybe not.

. . . Don't let us worry about personalities hampering our campaign. The more diversity we have the better for the plan, it seems to me. And beside it must thrive on moral force such as you symbolize or it will not thrive at all. We'll work out all together some kind of sponsoring organization which will seem to our pooled intelligence the best way to proceed.

I sound ridiculously wise, don't I? No one was ever in fact more infantile of mind. But I have sense enough to know that I am comical. And I have at the same time the keenest desire to do what I can to push this thing along.

I am anxious that the Tuesday conference may move as swiftly as is consistent with efficiency—for the sake of you and your sister. I have some women in reserve on that account—women who are endless verbalists but who can be drawn in later to do the talking which will be necessary to achieve our goal. In the meantime my warmest regards to you and "Franciska".

Mary R. Beard

Beard's reply to Rose Arnold Powell, who had written her usual plaint concerning Mt. Rushmore, gives the flavor of her hopes and excitement about the project just after the initial supporters' meeting.

43. TO ROSE ARNOLD POWELL

New Milford, Connecticut
September 14, 1935

Dear Mrs. Powell,

Deeply moved as I was by your letter I am slow iñ replying. And the reason for the delay is that I just returned from days in New York filled with effort to launch the Archive Center about which I wrote you recently. And your letter increases my zest for this Center.

We do seem so helpless in our individual protests against the determination seemingly displayed by men to maintain the credo of the man's world. But if we make group protests, the present group set-up is marked by such special interests that protests from women's organisations savor of special interests and are limited to that extent in their social effects. So the problem of next steps and longer strides is one which lies much on my mind as on yours.

I therefore see two things in one through this Archive project: the collection in one place of the data on women, including the rich personal material such as letters, diaries, memoranda; and the using of this material right at hand by people competent to use it, with the force of the Archive Center behind them. If, for instance, from such a place could go forth the demands and the protests, issued by a watching committee with its power increased by its wealth of data at its hand, then possibly the woman's culture could be integrated into the study of culture in the large and all our common intelligence enriched. Such is my dream anyway.

The Plan of the Archive Center will be framed in concise and clear form and presented on October 17th to a large but picked group of women in New York for approval and pressure. I am not sure just where the meeting will take place but I shall let you know when I know. Do attend it if you can.

That is a wonderful quotation from Montaigne which you give in your letter: "Men are nothing until they become excited." We'll be less as women as long as we are less excited. But with excitement must go fine

reasoning and finer organisation than exists at present if we are to be
more than the excitable something.

I do value your writing me freely for that helps my understanding and
helps to keep me stirred.

Cordially, Mary R. Beard

A second, larger meeting for the archives was held in New York on October 17, 1935. There, Beard was able to confirm the sponsorship of such
women as birth control reformer Margaret Sanger, well-known physician
Dr. Florence Sabin, lawyer and pacifist Elinor Byrns, novelist Fannie
Hurst, head of the American Association of University Women Kathryn
McHale, as well as stalwarts Emily Newell Blair, Harriot Stanton Blatch
and Lena Madesin Phillips.[3] The American Woman's Association (AWA),
a New York-based club whose thousands of members included professionals and society women, loaned its Manhattan building for meetings.
In view of Beard's intense commitment to this project, her remark in the
letter below that she would soon "cease concentrating to such an extent
on women" appears to be tongue-in-cheek.

The reference below to flying from New Milford to Blatch's home in
Nyack, New York, is curious, because neither Mary nor Charles Beard
thoroughly approved of the fact that their son, Bill (then twenty-eight),
had trained as a pilot and flew a private airplane.[4]

44. TO HARRIOT STANTON BLATCH

New Milford
October 28 [1935]

Dear Harriot:

You are lenient—by letter at least—with my corrupt practice in asking
for funds in such an irregular way. I had no right to do it. I did do it
without right simply because I must get this project launched, if I am to
share in it, immediately, as I am forced to be tied up for the winter
months. It has such a momentum now that it will surely swing along at a
good pace. Denied the privilege of citizenship, Rosika Schwimmer is kept
from earning as she might otherwise do and out of the sum collected at
the AWA, the amount she had spent in trying to work for the Archives
Center can be returned and more left for the initial sponsoring.

I am unhappy because you had to go to bed after this last trip to New York. I would have asked Bill to fly me over to Nyack to tell you of this sorrow if he had been on the spot. I came home myself feeling and certainly looking bedraggled after my own two days in town. But even so, I betook myself to one of the dingiest spots known—the coal fields of Pennsylvania. The teachers of Scranton had asked me there and as I had never got off the train to mingle with a mining community, I was glad of this chance to do so. I came back sooty but I did get a feeling about life and labor in the coal field. I had lived over a volcano in Japan and caught something of the flavor of life thus lived, by the Japanese. It helped me to understand life over coal mines with the earth trembling and actually caving in on occasion. Somehow I had never realized that the carved out caverns were actually under peoples' houses; that miners who try to buy little cottages have awful damages to face from time to time; that the earth may open and swallow street car, truck, or detached humans when it feels so inclined. Yet the teachers chatted about backs or no backs in evening clothes to a degree which appalled in another form. I am back to fresh air trying to recover if not in bed.

. . . By December first I think that I am intending to follow your advice at the long last—to cease concentrating to such an extent on women. But the alternative is surely not to concentrate on man. What a mess he is! What a tragedy of life he makes for himself! Do you know the last lines of Shelley's Prometheus Unbound? About "Love from her awful throne of patient power." Love should come from woman for the healing of hate. But that takes me backward to my obsession I suppose. Anyway my true love—

I hope to enjoy the news that you are up again and refraining from town for a good while.

Mary Beard

❦

The resumption of Beard's correspondence with Doris Stevens, a former Congressional Union colleague, must have been occasioned by Stevens' request to Beard to consider another former CU suffragist, Helena Hill Weed (Elsie Hill's sister), for a job. Stevens was active in the National Woman's Party in the 1920s and 1930s, leading its international efforts to attach equal rights for women diplomatic treaties. She supported the archives effort, as did many former and current NWP members, although she did not become very actively involved. The friendships forged during the suffrage struggle lasted a long time—and even for someone like Mary

Beard, who usually looked little to it, the network of acquaintance functioned for a lifetime.[5]

45. TO DORIS STEVENS

> Hotel Syracuse
> Syracuse, New York
> November 14, 1935

Dear Doris—

Reading your vibrantly beautiful letter again today here amid our heavy-witted Club women whom for some unknown reason I had pledged myself to "address," I come again to your lines: "Often I realize how little what I do counts. Life should be lived magnificently." How my mind and my heart respond! That's why I brought your letter along—to keep me company. Instinctively I felt that I should need it.

Harriot Stanton Blatch thinks me plain insane to keep jabbering about women and this I don't understand in view of her intransigent feminism. But that probably proves that I am insane.

Let's have a two-some chat—you and I in Washington soon. I shall be there early in '36. And that's very soon.

You have married, dear Doris. I have thought of you a lot and hoped for your deep happiness—for your living magnificently. Your radiance and quick wit stirred my very soul when I got to Washington in 1915. I was clumsier than any donkey then, as I still am. You were all glow and charm. Keep all of it you can. Take time to live while you labor. One must not expect to see much of the result of the latter. But she must catch a good deal of the former to be rejuvenated for giving to the other. I can't bear to think of your strength fleeing. But I am growing very old. And these Club women age me a thousand years!!!

If we do get the money for the Archives Center I should recommend Helena Hill Weed with genuine enthusiasm for the work you suggest. We are making headway. The thing looks good. It cheers me to have your approval. But it takes time to materialize naturally. I am writing Mrs. Weed. I'll keep you in touch with "progress."

> Much love—Mary R. Beard

After the second meeting it became clear that administration of the plan for an archives center rested with Beard, who plunged into issues of organization, funding, location, and the like. She consulted frequently with Lena Madesin Phillips and also welcomed the help of Emma Hirth, a career official with the Young Women's Christian Association. Lura Beam, a researcher and writer on education and the arts who had written up studies for the National Committee on Maternal Health in the late 1920s and early 1930s, was also among the first directors. Another valuable ally was Mina Bruere, assistant secretary of the Central Hanover Bank and Trust Company in New York, one of the first women in the United States to make a successful career in finance, and president of the American Bank Women from 1928 to 1930. (Her brother Robert was married to Beard's coauthor Martha Bruere.) It is not clear exactly who Beard was referring to in her mention of the "wild women" in the letter below; she may have meant Florentine Sutro and friends. Sutro, aging widow of philanthropist Lionel Sutro, had a lifelong commitment to reform, had been president of the Manhattan division of the Women's International League for Peace and Freedom, and was close with Schwimmer, but her ideas about publicity for the archives project were not always palatable to Beard. The initial interest of the New York Public Library in collaborating with the project, mentioned in the following letter, seemed a boost in 1935, although the collaboration did not materialize. Perhaps fittingly, when the women's archives dissolved Rosika Schwimmer chose to deposit her papers there.

46. TO LENA MADESIN PHILLIPS

New Milford
Nov. 17, 1935

Dear Lena—
     . . . I had been invited to tell the heads of the NY public library about this Archives project and that I did on Friday morning. The heads of all the branch libraries were present. It was a large gathering and it became an excited gathering. The head of the organisation made it very emphatic that the library would like to take the project under its wing—put a division of the library building apart to house the documents and take care of their preparation and use. So at least we should be able to perform a true service to women and men if we went no further than to get the stuff for the library. But I did not turn over the project of course. We couldn't have the school feature and I should not like to give up that unless we had to. Anyway Mr. Lydendecker said in open meeting that the library would receive our archives as we collected them and keep them for us until we get a separate building, if we approved that offer. And it offered more

yet—this time at my suggestion. I asked whether the chief could use his staff to make a list of present library material and catalogue archives as separate from casual and usually fuzzy commentaries on the female sex; I was told that the library would be charmed to do so. There is a lot of valuable material already on its shelves of course but so jumbled as sense and nonsense that it badly needs this division. We must have a similar catalogue made up by the Congressional Library. It would be a distinguished achievement, if we found nothing more to record, to have carried the present libraries thus far in their appreciation of the woman's story. I am cheered immensely by this advance.

But, let us not give up the larger enterprise at this stage anyway. I'd prefer the library to a museum piece at the NY World's Fair but it does no harm to acquaint the city officials with their present neglect to draw any women into that Fair. . . .

There is more comfort: Mina Bruere is so enthusiastic that she is perfectly willing to be treasurer. Are you as gay over this as I am? The banking women have apparently been collecting their documents just as the medical women and others have been doing. They like the idea of a common center for many very clear reasons. So with Miss Bruere's practical financial experience and connections, it seems to me that one big problem is clarified enormously. But I'd like your opinion.

We must get back to our general assembly of sponsors with the plan of organisation, etc. at the earliest date. If we set the meeting for the first week in December—say December 3—could you and Miss Hirth and Miss Beam be ready to report? Miss Bruere might come into your committee meetings and bring some good suggestions? She is at the Hanover Trust as you no doubt know.

I have asked the AWA which offers us its gallery lounge free whether we could hold the big meeting there the evening of December 3d and if not what other nights that week we could have. Dr. Sabin and many others want to attend and can only do so at night. This date would clear us from the approaching Thanksgiving engagements and clean us up before Christmas. The question of incorporation will be one to face. No end of thanks for putting your shoulder to this wheel with me!

The matter of a budget is well-nigh insoluble now. We can go as strong as patrons will permit of course. The design of a building could take account of all sorts of things: separate rooms for the materials of separate organisations: alcoves for such individualistic documents as those of Rosika Schwimmer, etc. including a lecture hall and alcoves for student tables. The expenses of filing and cataloguing and serving could be ascertained on some ratio basis from Mr. Lydendecker of the Public Library and/or from the Special Libraries Association the woman head of which has written hoping to help us on our way. I shall look up her letter and send in her name. If Miss Bruere could get her banking group to work out a finance committee for us, what say you? . . .

IF we can—as we must—go back to the general assembly by early December with a plan of organisation, an improved prospectus, and a proposed governing board, with Miss Bruere authorised to form a finance committee perhaps, we should really be scrambling to our feet, should we not? All the sects of feminists, now including Doris Stevens, are ardent for this thing. Mrs. Catt gives her full support and cooperation. Publicity must be controlled from this day forward a good deal better. Wild women have broken in but the china shop is not wrecked, luckily. Don't breathe a word about their having been such, for they are supersensitive in that relation; they consider that they can make no mistake.

If you and Miss Hirth and Miss Beam and Miss Bruere could complete, say in a week, everything short of the governing body, notices could be sent out for the forthcoming general meeting quite some time in advance. And as for the governing body, the four of you and I might bring in our respective slates to a joint conference before the general meeting long enough in advance to be sure that the members of our agreed-upon group would consent to serve if approved. . . .

Love and best wishes   Mary Beard

By the end of 1935 administrative complications had thickened. While Mary Beard was seeking donors among the Carnegies and Rockefellers and collaboration with the Institute for Women's Professional Relations in New London, Connecticut (which focused on vocational issues), a divide among the founders was shaping up. From Beard's point of view, Rosika Schwimmer and her important supporter Florentine Sutro were more interested in publicity—including planning a site at the upcoming World's Fair to be held in Flushing, New York—than in the groundwork for the substantive collection. Beard respected and admired Schwimmer, and regarded Sutro favorably as an "activist par excellence." (As noted in the letter below, Sutro reflected on her life in an autobiography published in 1935, *My First Seventy Years* [New York, Roerick Museum Press, 1935]). But the pressure of the two for quick actions and immediate publicity made Beard uneasy.[6] Perhaps stress accounted for her unwonted and unwanted comment in the letter below about "the racial urge." This must have referred to the Jewish background that Schwimmer and Sutro had in common, although Schwimmer was the daughter of an agnostic and a freethinker, and Sutro's father was a founder of Ethical Culture.

In the nation's capital again in 1936 for midwinter, Beard was investigating the possibility of funding the archives project through the Works Progress Administration (WPA), the New Deal federal relief agency that created millions of jobs to combat unemployment. She approached Ellen Woodward, head of women's projects for the WPA, in league with Sutro and Lola Maverick Lloyd, a Chicago clubwoman who was an intimate friend and loyal supporter of Schwimmer.

47. TO LENA MADESIN PHILLIPS

The Mayflower
Jan. 23 [1936]

Dear Lena:

It was mighty good to see you and have a good chat together. The subjects under discussion will keep on brewing in my mind. And as you say to me: "We shall see what we shall see."

This particular follow-up is to state that it now seems that Mrs. Sutro will have to be put on the executive committee. She is here and she insists upon this. I suppose the racial urge is part of it. But she is also deeply interested in the Archives and has, it cannot be denied, thrown herself into its promotion with zest. She has some good points: great energy and will, time, money, wide social contacts. Her autobiography gives her more eclat. She will not be denied. If we attempt it, she will give us a black eye and we don't want that. She might very well be made responsible for some particular phase of the work. She has infinite persistence which is what promoters of a project need. If it is guided it may have infinite value.

We are making important progress here in connection with the WPA. In addition to what I put down on paper for you, it is possible that we may get a good sum of money. I may know tomorrow when I have an interview with the woman in charge of women's projects [Ellen Woodward]. I am to put up to her—encouraged by men in this division—the archives project. I was told that men and women on the inside have been as disgusted as critics on the outside over the fact that only cooking and sewing could be concocted as women's projects. So the ground seems prepared for our bold attack. I shall make it as valiantly as I can. Mrs. Lloyd and Mrs. Sutro will go with me to Mrs. Woodward. Indeed to Mrs. Lloyd and her daughter who is in the government work we owe the opportunity to come thus far and to go farther. I am jittery with excitement today.

Much love—Mary B.

Mary Beard's group meeting with Ellen Woodward and with Luther Evans, director of the Historical Records Survey under the WPA, was exciting enough to generate the heady suggestion of a "woman's Smithsonian." This gave her hope of instigating a lively group of supporters in Washington, D.C., as well as in New York.

In opening the letter below, Beard reflects on a Liberty League dinner for two thousand at which Al Smith, the unsuccessful Democratic party candidate for president in 1928, ripped into the New Deal, declaring it an un-American communistic experiment, a travesty of the party platform of 1932. In the *Washington Post* the crowd was described as "brilliant-gowned, tailcoated" and "hilarious" at Smith's oratory.[7]

48. TO LENA MADESIN PHILLIPS

The Mayflower
January 26th [1936]

Dear Lena:

The day after the Al Smith circus, my dear, writing you my daily! The enclosed report you might miss and that would surely be a loss. My sister and her husband, vice president of the American Cynamid Company, were down among the cheering plut[ocrat]s helping to roar appreciation of the thrusts at taxation for the poor. I listened in upstairs after watching the drunks prepare for the dinner below. This morning when I went down for extra copies of the Post, it was still colorful to hear the pages shouting "Mr. Du Pont?" Well, here we are.

I see in the paper too that you are to be toastmistress Thursday night for the B[usiness] & P[rofessional] W[omen]. So thought I'd write you more about the WPA. You might like to share in dramatizing us wimmen.

After arranging with Dr. L. Evans to get in on his listing of documents, printed and unprinted, as I set down on paper for you—at his suggestion, Mrs. Lloyd, Mrs. Sutro, and I went post haste to call upon Mrs. Woodward, chief of the women's division of the WPA. The interview had been arranged by Dr. Evans himself who came to it himself bringing a fellow worker and the WPA publicity woman, Miss Carol (I believe that's her name.) The upshot was that everyone called for a Hall of Women's Records comparable in dignity and importance to the Smithsonian, if you please! We three New Yorkers found ourselves expanding until we were unrecognizable to ourselves.

The Woman's Smithsonian. Well, you see the WPA can't give funds to any private institution. I had asked for money. But if we called for the making of a public institution such as the Smithsonian, we might have a standing. We'd have to get Congress to authorize it. It might authorize the whole appropriation. We were told to get busy before it is too late.

One of the men at this interview has worked years at the Smithsonian. He is keen about this newest proposal, chimed in in its support, said the government would not interfere except to accept (maybe help name) directors. Miss Carol and the women were tense with excitement. Mrs. Woodward was called away but her secretary sat at attention. The gang is coming to see me at the hotel.

Are we ganging up on a Woman's Smithsonian or something like that? Quite a step ahead to discuss with the wimmen! Why not?

Mrs. Lloyd and Mrs. Sutro then plunged over to see Dr. Charl Williams [field secretary of the National Education Association] and burst in upon her with this idea. It was surely sudden. What could she say?

So there is more to the ball we started rolling than we had any idea of in the beginning. Somehow it appears to me that we should let all the women who have sent letters in appreciation of the idea of an archives center know what the idea has produced up to date. A circular letter might be mimeographed and widely distributed? If you wanted to bring any of this into your toasting, it should bring publicity!!

                                                        Oh my dear!—Mary

Eleanor Roosevelt's announced interest in the women's archives brought a great flurry of newspaper publicity and put Beard in the limelight. The project had received some publicity when launched, mainly in the *New York World-Telegram* for which supporter Dorothy Dunbar Bromley was a columnist, but in February and March 1936, when Bess Furman, who covered Eleanor Roosevelt for the Associated Press, got into the act, articles and editorials were carried in the *New York Times,* the *Chicago Tribune,* the *Boston Traveler,* the *Washington Herald,* and newspapers as far flung as Houston, Cleveland, and Providence. Schwimmer was content to have her own role little noted, because she was aware that her radical and controversial reputation might jeopardize the gaining of sponsors.[8] As the letter below makes clear, under Mary Beard's leadership the project had expanded far beyond the collection of papers of feminists and pacifists of the prewar era, to include a broad range of women in history. Beard hoped and imagined that because of the scope of the project, women of many different ideological orientations would be willing to cooperate in supporting it. Thus her hope at the end of the letter—where she mistakes the first name of Emma Guffey Miller, a leading Democrat—for women of differing political loyalties. Beard's glee at the apparent momentum of the project in Washington was tempered only by her awareness of factional strife among the New York women involved.

49. TO ROSIKA SCHWIMMER

> Hotel Mayflower
> Washington, D.C.
> February 14, 1936.

Dear Rosika Schwimmer:

I should have made this letter arrive as your Valentine conveying to you my congratulations on the IDEA! But the best I can do is to write it on this day and mail it on the 14th of February.

The truth is that my phone bell, my door bell, and my fan mail have been so compelling since I went to Mrs. Roosevelt's press conference last Monday morning that I have had no single half hour in which to report events to you. I did hurry over a kind of report to Miss Savord thinking that a necessary thing in case you were all meeting soon again—only to learn from you today that she is no longer secretary. Well! Well! But before I comment on the inner conflict which seems to be strong in New York, I shall tell you what I see as the important items in my Washington drive.

So I begin with Bess Furman's visit induced by your and my common invitation. We had a wonderful morning together. She sent out an advance story before the meeting on Monday night which you saw—as much as we printed—in the NY Herald-Tribune but which I have not seen because I have been too rushed to look at the papers, knowing they were carrying things. Mrs. Furman is carrying on—preparing more stories, one for Sunday the 23d for instance in which she hopes to tell about such crimes and misdemeanors as the prolonged burial of the

Aletta Jacobs library in the Creerar [Library] vaults. I hope I am still right about that. If you know anything to the contrary please wire [at] my expense. It was Bess Furman who got the invitation to the White House conference. She seems to think that I did not disgrace you all there.

Immediately after appearing there, woman after woman who had been at that conference telephoned in for a longer private talk about archives. I have already filled several of these appointments—as today with Mrs. Griffin whose husband owns or operates a string of New England papers such as the Waterbury Republican and the Hartford Times. She is deeply interested and is going to write as many stories as she can, one immediately for the organ of the women Democrats. Winifred Mallon, now president of the press women who meet at lunch once a week, took charge of all the publicity for this enterprise of mine—including the night meeting. She was generous of her time and very efficient in management. Some newspaper reports were taken out of the hands of women for some reason I can't quite understand and garbled as second-hand stuff was sure to be. Thus I was made to say that Cleopatra was a Phoenician and that the women of the south were *responsible* for "reconstruction" after the civil war. Neither thing did I say of course. No woman at the conference would have been so mistaken. I did not use the word "reconstruction" at all. I did use the word "rehabilitation" which has a different meaning in that connection to every American. But never mind. I put out my neck and got a few cracks naturally. On the whole a lot was done—to the good. Kathleen McLaughlin [who] is writing a column for next Sunday's Times, sent for more copy and I gave her what I thought she might want.

The NY World-Telegram telephoned via some man on the paper that it was proposing to run six articles on New York women who ought to appear [in] works on history but don't. He asked for the names of such neglected women. I had to work fast but this is what I gave him:

Margaret Hardenbroeck of Dutch New York, sometimes called the most enterprising person, male or female, in the colony—great landlord and business woman who probably ran the first packet line between America and Europe.

The De Lancey and Livingston and Schuyler women who waged a civil war within the nationalist war for independence. Mrs. John Jay the name for the patriot leadership.

Elizabeth Cady Stanton and Susan B. Anthony—widening democracy with criticism of Church and State as thinking of high order.

Eliza Lee Schuyler, granddaughter of Alexander Hamilton, for social work. Katharine Bement Davis and social hygiene by way of good measure.

Dr. Mary Putnam Jacobi—medicine and public health

Etc....for bigger measure.

So the young man said: "The boss has given me two weeks off in which to do this series and I regard it as the best assignment during my 13 years on the paper." So I gave him bibliography.

Publishers are writing from near and far for persons to write books.

Mrs. Roosevelt really gave us a big boost. I opened my talk at her press meeting by playing with the phrases "off the record" and "on the record." I said that she had made the former famous and would probably make the latter equally so. I tried to show the relation between being off the record by self-determination, voluntarily, and being off the record involuntarily, unjustly, to the detriment of social understanding. She agreed, asked questions, commented. During the hour we all spent together, one of the journalists asked whether you were on the central committee. I was wary but I tried to be honest. I replied that you were not a citizen and so were handicapped when it came to being a committee member but that you knew about the location of many important documents and about the women abroad and in the USA whose documents should be in such a center and THAT YOUR LACK OF CITIZENSHIP IS OUR LOSS. I did not say more, being wary, I did not know the woman who put the question, you see. I did state that your loss is our loss. I hope that may do some good.

Today Gladwys Jones, executive secretary of the National Deans of Women, asked for twenty or so copies of the press releases to take with her to St. Louis to the national convention of educators which opens the 24th. She got them and will distribute them among the deans. I gave her two concise points to emphasize in talking with teachers and deans.

a. To make equality function, the intellectual climate—public opinion—must be favorable. Archives pave the way. Using the story of the Weimar constitution as an ill.

b. It is not only woman's "progress" which we have in mind to demonstrate but the progress of civilization through women too.

She had come to our AAUW meeting and got excited and thought up this way to push the cause along.

I am looking around for some faculty person to do the same for teachers.

You inquire about the resolutions passed at the evening meeting. I sent in a list of women who signified their approval by signing cards. But there were some who incline to favor the placing of the archives as collected in the Congressional Library or other general institution. I claimed that that would again take women off the record and they were open-minded. A resolution I feared would crystallize such opposition and so it was agreed that every one would clarify her mind on the point—and all those women have minds—and that we would come together soon—perhaps in a great public meeting in the ballroom of the Mayflower. That is an ambitious plan. I shall have to find someone else to swing it if it is accomplished. But it should be accomplished and I think it can. Say in two or three weeks. By that time the NY committee should be sufficiently organized for us to be able to solicit funds and members on a wholesale scale. I left the money-raising to that follow-up affair to which may be drawn the leisure class with exchequers. These women have only intelligence.

I deeply regret the appearance of factional strife in New York. I know that almost every member of the group is damned by other members, except that I have never heard Lena Phillips go after others as they go after her. I know that some have candidates for paid positions. I know that she thought Helen Havener right for publicity person. On Miss Havener I should agree. I have seen her operate for a number of years in every kind of situation. She has the selfless devotion of a saint born of intense enthusiasms. She will work till kingdom come in an emergency. She is experienced and knows the ropes. She is available. Some of the candidates I know less well and yet I know that there are and have been wheels within wheels which have led such candidates in some instances to be like enemies in the past. Even Mina Bruere is criticised by one of the women whom you would least suspect. So we have not and cannot escape factionalism it seems. I am sorry, very sorry. I hope it will wash out without delay. It is always present in the beginning of an enterprise, isn't it? I don't know. I should prefer to have pure idealists at the helm—idealists with wonderful competence. But hunting for them would consume years and possibly a life time. Meanwhile fascism might arrive.

I am glad anyway that you are to be near that gentle and loving Mrs. Lloyd in Chicago now. Do remember me to her. May the medicine of today do you worlds of good! I shall send you any news that comes my way by my own manufacture or by the work of others. I have been ghastly tired for a little while but I recuperate quickly and the breathing spell of a weekend will bring me back to the norm. I want to leave behind in Washington the strongest possible committee to work with the NY committee.

May it be strong too. Mrs. Carol Guffey Miller has asked me to lunch with her on Monday. She is on the Democratic National Committee and thrilled by the archives project. I'll get a Republican too. Maybe ranking partisans with a lot of non-partisans can form a coalition in the archives' behalf. I'll see.

[M.R.B.]

Beard's response to personal publicity shows her evenhandedness with sarcasm—pointed toward herself as well as others.

50. TO LENA MADESIN PHILLIPS

> Hotel Mayflower
> Washington, D.C.
> March the first [1936]

Dear Lena:

Thanks for the clippings. They show how badly I have been thrown to the wolves or rather how I threw myself to the wolves by meeting the people of the press. I wonder where Lem Parton got the idea that I said women were increasingly important and men were beginning to feel abased. But where does anybody get anything? Just out of his own hot air. Anyway I helped to put the archives on the map if in the process I became a cartoon. My "generous mouth" to which Parton refers has certainly wagged an awful lot. And he can testify to you and the archives committee that I have wasted no time in beauty parlors. But oh gals, I wish I could! I do need a shampoo terribly. I thought Bromley did a very neat job on her column.

It was cheering to have a chance to talk with Emma Hirth again. We had Friday evening together and I expected to see her again but lost track of her hiding-place. She reported how competent, as usual, has been your handling of difficult situations. Thus we manage to keep on our way. As I told Miss Hirth, I am going to try to raise some money here at once for the Archives.

You've been running around. I hope it has been some fun amid the physical hardship. March is here. I'll be turning back north before long and seeing you again.

Yours, Mary B.

By April of 1936 Rosika Schwimmer was very troubled by what she saw as self-seeking on the part of some women involved in the archives; she did not approve of the method used to elevate women to the national board. Mary Beard reassured her of "the amazing devotion of the committee to the project—how night after night women, responsible by day for huge tasks, tried to put weariness out of their minds and contribute their highest intelligence to the formidable work connected with organising the Archives undertaking." She attempted to mollify her: "Dear Mme. Schwimmer, you must know that we all hold you in high esteem. My interest in you and my affection for you have never changed. I have been so delighted that we could find women capable of carrying out the grand idea which you formulated for an Archives Center. I could never have helped you to get it into circulation by myself. If we had tried to perfect an organisation alone, where should we ever have got? One has to trust others if accomplishment is ever to come." In spite of these coaxings, Schwimmer formally withdrew from the project early in May, because she felt mistreated (even bullied) by some of the New York women involved, including Lena Madesin Phillips. She was dissatisfied with the publicity efforts and enraged by a contact made against her wishes with Rosa Manus, an Amsterdam woman who had plans for a similar archive in mind. In a confidential discussion among Beard, Schwimmer, and Inez Irwin, Beard too threatened to resign, but Schwimmer insisted, "You cannot do it Mrs. Beard. Without you this idea will die." Schwimmer resigned and Beard stayed on in her post as chairman of archives. Years later Beard wrote to a close friend that Schwimmer "was in many respects a very great woman but she was terribly difficult and really so self-sure that she wrecked some movements by her will to dominate."[9]

51. TO ROSIKA SCHWIMMER

New Milford, Connecticut
May 12, 1936

Dear Rosika Schwimmer:

I have thought of little else for days than our coming together over the women's archives and the ups and downs of the succeeding relationship. No doubt if mortal were more perfect, there would be no downs in mortal affairs. But such is not his or her construction. As for myself I am deeply aware of my shortcomings.

Despite all the problems, the difficulties involved in winning understanding and support for the project, and the temperamental errors which perhaps all the rest of us have made, we move forward, I believe, toward accomplishment. In going forward, perhaps we have not made irretrievable mistakes.

A strong executive board is now collected and as it takes upon its shoulders the heavy task of getting members and gifts, surely this is advancing in the best way that those of us who tried to put our strength behind this thing would make it advance. I have been unwilling to lash and browbeat the other women into going faster than the speed they thought wise. I have often talked to you about American women versus Continental ways. Maybe this is American notwithstanding the usual idea that it is a brash people. Anyway we all feel better now about first getting incorporated and then asking for papers and funds. I shall do a lot through the summer here at my home in seeking members and money, though I cannot interview many people directly.

Most of the women will be away—several in Europe. But we shall have the plan of organization, the incorporation, and the names of a committee to go out now in responsible ordering. In various ways work will go on through the intervening months until a strong drive opens up in the early autumn.

I believe you should be not-a-little content at the way I got behind your idea and then got other women behind it—women of the kind who would really push it along to realization. You and I could have spent the rest of our lives picking and choosing purely intellectual, spiritual, feminists and pacifists as the guarantee of THE IDEA in its perfection. But we should have no outcome, I fear, if we undertook that fine work of selection by elimination. As it is, a widely representative group, several with national and international reputations, representing peace, feminism, labor, the three major religions, racial and civic work and the arts, has been brought together.

You will "give me a hand" on this, can you not?

As for your invaluable documents, have you ever placed a price on their head? We must get around to that matter now as soon as we can. I can't say what luck we shall have with moneyed benefactors but we shall search them out without more delay. Indeed that quest has begun. I full realise your sitation with respect to your papers and none of us has a desire to exploit you even if we could. We were not prepared to offer your friend any sum at this moment for her letter about which you wrote. I meant to inquire however about the nature of the letter but I got worried the other day and forgot.

> Believe me as ever your friend and
> admirer—Mary R. Beard

●←—

While focusing on the establishment of a World Center for Women's Archives Mary Beard was still committed to furthering the vision, which she shared with her husband during the 1930s, of an ordered and "collectivist" civilization. Her comments on an essay on taxes drafted by Lena Madesin Phillips show her continuing concern to establish for the nation priorities other than international and military power.

52. TO LENA MADESIN PHILLIPS

> New Milford
> June 3d—1936

Dear Lena:

I have now read TAXES—a most attractively written challenge to women to think upon the subject. You know how effectively you present even complicated matters, in my opinion. And isn't it stimulating to tackle the biggest things and try to devise the armature for a piece of sculpturing? We must chisel and mold and rub though we have only typewriters as tools—terribly clumsy instruments. I said in a Washington meeting recently that I feel like a plumber with a huge monkey wrench when I try to write instead of like a skilled craftsman. A plumber was in the audience!!!! I heard a murmur about plumbers being skilled workmen!!!!!! After the meeting (one of Mary Van Kleeck's Inter-Professional affairs) the plumber himself came up and what do you suppose he said: "My dear lady, let me propose your name for membership in the plumbers' union." I told him that I would practice harder with my tool to qualify.

I have two criticisms of Taxes—probably not important.

One of these is verbal:

Page 1. Paragraph 1. Statement of fact: "the mother . . . . was always willingly chained to a fixed spot." Nay, nay, Pauline. Not *always*. Not always *willingly*.

Paragraph 2. Last line. Change "really" to "not"???? She does hate to pay taxes, does she not?

Page 4. Would cut "a municipal airport". One of the scandalous wastes is an airport in every village idea, as I see waste. But every village wants one. And many get them—at terrific expense. You would watch the cost. I would eliminate most of them.

The other is philosophical if I may be bold enough to say so.

Your point of view seems to be that of the League of Women Voters too. I sat in on a state convention of theirs at Hartford two years ago when they were going to school for a week on taxation. Officials instructed them. Expert statisticians reported to them. They gave their own views of efficiency. But there they were in the heart of a munitions-making district, where profits had been rolling up, where the inhabitants were in need of every species of social service, *concentrating* on restraint in taxation and elimination of waste in management. Now I don't uphold extravagance and I condemn mismanagement. But I would bring into review as well the idea of community planning for the meeting of community needs—real needs for a civilisation—and on that build a wise taxation to cover the cost of civilisation. That is a collectivist, or socialist, outlook less solicitous of the interests of the few.

I'll see you on Friday and try to obey the rules at the Board meeting even if I have departed from the social code herewith.

You know me—Lena.

Affectionately, Mary R. Beard

•←─

The tone of the following letter to Rose Arnold Powell (who was concerned as usual with memorializing Susan B. Anthony) suggests Beard's frustration in her efforts to make a dent in public consciousness about women in the context of world economic depression. Her comments in 1936 ran the gamut from great hopefulness to despair. To Florence Brewer Boeckel at one point in the fall she wrote, "Women are challenged as never before to work together for ends larger than self. I like to use the phrase The New Feminism, in this connection." Yet just a few weeks earlier she had written to Harriot Stanton Blatch, about her efforts to find institutional support for the archives, "I get as sick at my stomach in presenting this case as I used to do when I asked a Southern Congressman to vote for our enfranchisement. One has to start with the ABCS in just the same way. Men are just as afraid of women's discovering themselves now as they were then." [10]

Beard's brother's impeachment and conviction also affected her reading of her own political efficacy. Halstead Ritter, a federal district court judge in southern Florida, was impeached in the spring of 1936 on allegations of misconduct and corruption in office and filing false tax returns. Although the Senate acquitted him of the specific alleged statutory crimes, he was convicted of "conduct unbecoming a judge." His case set a precedent by broadening the definition of impeachable offenses in the federal judiciary. Mary Beard later said she saw the conviction as unjust, a political ploy to unseat a Coolidge appointee in a Democratic era.[11]

53. TO ROSE ARNOLD POWELL

New Milford, Connecticut
June 14, 1936

Dear Mrs. Powell:

The items you send me about memorials to "our great" and Congressional and Executive action therewith are certainly revelations of the ridiculous in economic politics to the Nth degree! It is such fantastic operation. But it is the incredible which alone seems to happen. How can I offset madness with reason? What you do expect of me!

Last week I was captioned in the press which reported my Commencement speech at the New Jersey College for Women as "Denouncing" or "Decrying" the "Dominance of Men." In fact I used no such language but your clippings make me wish I had. There scarcely seems to be enough intelligence loose to put in a thimble.

You have been notifying women's organizations of what is going on. They could make a mass protest, if they would. All I can do, if anything, is to try to work pretty much alone for a more distant future as I live far away in the hills and am but an individual with a typewriter. I keep that pounding nearly every waking moment and I shall keep on doing that at any rate. I wish it might be heard in Washington. But you see they impeached my brother this last winter in the Senate and I shall be tarred with that stick for a while. I should only hurt our Susan B. [Anthony] if I tried to befriend her on the spot. Some one deemed holier than I—the sister of the brother—will have more weight on Capitol Hill.

Cordially as ever, Mary R. Beard

Mary Beard remained closely in touch with peace and neutrality activists in the mid–1930s. Here, differing respectfully from a longtime acquaintance, the peace educator Florence Brewer Boeckel, she concurs in Charles Beard's published views on cultivating one's own national garden rather than imagining international order or looking to impose it on others. Her distaste for H. G. Wells' internationalist pronouncements was seconded by her scorn for his *Outline of History*. Simonds, mentioned below, was an expert on international war and peace who had made his name as a commentator on World War I. (He died early in 1936.) The Joad to whom Beard refers was likely the British philosopher Cyril E. M. Joad, who wrote a number of popular pacifist and agnostic works during the interwar period.

54. TO FLORENCE BREWER BOECKEL

New Milford, Connecticut
July 28, 1936

Dear Mrs. Boeckel:

We are both so happy to hear from you and we too wish that we could have a talk, ensemble, away from the madding crowd, with plenty of time to cover the ground which may only in fact seem to divide us. I feel very sure that our idealism is the same. It is the way to see more of it realised which is the point at issue. If we too were not running off for August, I should urge you to come to us for a day at least before you leave for England. Maybe you can come to us when you return. We are going to Antigonish in Nova Scotia to spend a little time in that cooperative community guided by St. Xavier College idealism. Father Coody has invited us and we both look forward to being inspired by the rare combination of dream and reality, made manifest by such intelligence as he possesses.

As for the grand world dream of [H. G.] Wells, I heard him talk about it two winters ago in Washington at Frank Simonds'. He then maintained that it would be easier to put the whole world in order than to put one's own "house", or nation. With respect to England, that is a natural view today as utopia. But what competence has England or the English displayed to warrant one's believing that that nation and its people have the wisdom for putting the world in order? They have a vast part of the world already under their control. As for tackling the grand job with our assistance, what have we to contribute? Have you seen the study of our Homestead land distribution recently reported in the July number of the American Historical Review? It seems that 3 1/2 per cent of the "people" actually got free farms under its provisions—for the reason that the government land grants to railway builders plus the speculative accumulation which had already gone on by 1862 left almost nothing for the people despite the legislation. The story of our American business men on this continent of virgin soil and free from clerical or feudal restraints is too appalling for aught but a burning sense of shame. We might start to clean up our own house and in that experience get some knowledge of how houses might be cleaned elsewhere. But until we have that inner knowledge and will to be clean, I just can't see what we can do ranging round the world with advice and good-will.

Of course if free trade seems the economic solution, then the solution is simple. But the history of the free trade idea and the condition in which it rose and flourished, then fell, must surely be taken into account when one accepts that simple solution. But here comes in our—my—mania— history. Wells, it is true, is supposed to have a flair for history. But special history must always be considered for there is every kind of the thing.

There could be no question between us as to life values vs. property values. I have no idea whether you suspect or detect a concern with the superior values in either or both Beards. It is there in both cases. That concern with life values is our supreme concern as yours. But basic human needs must be gratified somehow and that brings us down to the matter of economy whether we enjoy it or not. We can come up for air but if we live in the upper air all the time, are we not merely precious?

Personally I think that Joad has done some very silly writing and I have not an iota of confidence in Wells' common sense. I rejoice in their liberal outbursts for they set other people to feeling. But as leaders, I should regard them as hopelessly muddle-headed. I never in my whole life heard so much sheer drivel in one hour as Wells delivered at Frank Simonds winter before last. His imagination is majestic! His force lies wholly in that direction.

It would seem that a united front however is imperative among men and women who want to live the good life and see societies rest on that concept. Trying to create a decent society in the USA would be a rare laboratory experiment, would it not? You may believe, with Wells and many others, that we can't do anything here unless we try to do the world thing. But at least don't take it for granted that Charles and I, who believe we must try out our own competence here, are blind to world values of international association. Our view is not provincial. If we could believe that free trade is the right world economy for the good life for all, we would seem to you perhaps to raise no question of our provinciality. That is the crux of our difference in thought about the practice underlying life values I dare to believe. We are not anti-English or pro-American. Nor are we pro-English, for there is a danger that Americans will let the English do all their thinking for them continuously. Internationalism can so easily become just British reasoning. And it was that which helped to drive the Germans crazy and into the World War.

Do let us see you when you return from England.

With genuine admiration
for you two, Mary R. Beard

During another midwinter season in Washington, Beard was greatly enjoying reading American women's documents in the Library of Congress while plugging away at the plans for the World Center for Women's Archives. She was especially impressed with the papers of Anna Dickinson, who in the 1850s and 1860s was a much-loved orator for the cause of antislavery and the Union. The following letter indicates that she also read Gilbert Barnes' and Dwight L. Dumond's edition of the *Letters of Theodore Dwight Weld, Angelina Grimké Weld, and Sarah Grimké* (New York, 1934). The prestige of her speaking engagements seems to have been on an upswing: she was preparing the opening for the final discussion of the AAUW's convention in Savannah, Georgia, in March, the keynote speech at the one hundredth anniversary of Mt. Holyoke College in Massachusetts in May, and a speech before the general session of the National Education Association in June in Detroit.[12]

To the additional notoriety brought by the WCWA she responded ambivalently. The *Washington Post* featured her picture in an account of the *New York Sun*'s annual list of outstanding women of 1936, where she appeared with thirteen other women of the world, the "outstanding feminists" of 1936. At the top of the list were Wallis Simpson, for whose love the King of England gave up the throne, and politician Ruth Bryan Owen, daughter of William Jennings Bryan. (The latter was appointed minister plenipotentiary to Denmark by Franklin Delano Roosevelt, but because of her marriage to an aristocratic Dane in 1936 her new Danish citizenship made her unable to continue in her diplomatic post.) Mrs. Florence Kahn, whom Beard also mentions, was a six-term member of the U.S. Congress.

55. TO HARRIOT STANTON BLATCH

> Carroll Arms Hotel
> First and C Streets, N.E.
> Washington, D.C.
> January 2d [1937]

Dear Harriot:

We were on the wing—actually went to Atlantic City for a break!—at the time when other people were at their desks mailing the seasons' greetings as of course we would be, erratically. None the less we remembered the few men and women closest to our hearts and among these few you were remembered. Now belatedly we send you our love and best wishes for others' sanity in 1937, taking it for granted that you and we have it already.

Don't attribute to me the insanity which in the press blackened me with two errors this last week: one, claiming that I was coupling the World Center for Women's Archives with a proposed Woman's Charter of Rights and also approving that Charter as printed; the other, with being a "leading lady" of 1936 in the company with stars such as Wally, that depressing Ruth Bryan Owen, old Tory Mrs. Kahn, and what-not. Charles tells me not to make a mountain out of a mole hill a propos the latter but I reply that the tragedy for me is the mole hill. Anyway, it is nicer to remember friends than the press.

I have sent in your suggestion for a competent Archives secretary-promoter and the Board will be grateful for the name. I am glad to know that Miss Claghorn is interested too. The "project" has reached the stage of a drawing of the desired building with floor plans, a budget, and consideration with a view to financing on the part of a woman's Foundation. We shall know our fate in this quarter this month. Mrs. Holden has even been looking up land for the building! There is fine determination about victory.

Charles and I have tucked into a little apartment here in a very quiet part of D.C. within easy walking strides of the Congressional Library where we hope to go on working day by day until April. I came across Anna Dickinson's papers yesterday—five trunks of which were rolled into the Library in 1933. There are interesting letters—from C. D. Warner, Wendell Phillips, and others which I quickly saw. But I have not gone through the five trunks for all the treasure. She kept calling cards, theater programs, everything it seems.

In going over the letters of the Grimkés and Theodore Weld, just published a year or so ago, I found what was to me a most amusing comment
on your mother to the effect that the devout Angelina or was it Sarah?—
thought that her free mind needed subduing. What a breath of fresh wind
she must have been in those pious circles. I have laughed and laughed
over Angelina's nun-like fear that she was sinning when she fell in love
with someone not Jesus Christ. I had no idea that any of our women carried that bride of Christ idea so far. I am improving my mind at least.
Justice Holmes told us he got tired of that idea at the age of ninety. So
may I.

Come on back during the winter and we'll have a long chat, being freer
than ever before for it.

Our love to you—Mary R. Beard

[P.S.] I am so hot over the military emphasis for the Inaugural. Have
protested. But protests roll in—to no effect. "F.D.[R.] wanted this,"
Grayson says.

Mary Beard had made a particular, and she thought successful, effort in
the World Center for Women's Archives to include advocates of the equal
rights amendment as well as their opponents in such organizations as
the League of Women Voters, who favored sex-based protective legislation for women. The alliance was never entirely stable, however, and
was rocked by a brief controversy over Beard's role in the "Women's
Charter." In 1936, international social welfare worker Mary Van Kleeck
and a small group of women thought the time was ripe to speak out
firmly for labor legislation for women while also affirming equal rights in
the face of fascist and liberal attacks on women's work outside the home.
They hoped to draft a Women's Charter of basic rights and to mobilize
behind it women in both the equal rights and protective labor legislation
camps. Mary Beard was invited to participate in the initial deliberations
on the document, and did so, but she withdrew before the document was
signed because of disagreement about the language to be used. (Subsequent disagreements among the group prevented the movement from ever
becoming a reality.) Publicity about plans for the charter mentioned
Mary Beard and the name of the World Center for Women's Archives in
connection with the venture, however, raising the hackles of National
Woman's Party advocates, who were not conciliated by or satisfied with
the language of the charter. Beard's letter below to the chairman of the

NWP National Council, an archives benefactor, attempts to exculpate herself.

56. TO FLORENCE BAYARD HILLES

> Carroll Arms Hotel
> Washington, D.C.
> January 5 [1937]

Dear Mrs. Hilles:

The moment I saw in the Times the story of the Women's Charter with my name attached and the World Center for Women's Archives attached to my name as if I were representing the Archives, I telegraphed indignantly to Meg Irwin, the Chairman of the Archives Center, asking her to get a denial out to the papers at once through the publicity chairman. There was absolutely no warrant for such a use either of my name or of the Archives. I had never signed that draft of the Women's Charter which appeared in the press. Nor have I signed any other.

Last summer I was invited to a conference purely as an individual as I supposed and insisted to consider a "Charter" combining the desires of all leaders of women. I was interested in the idea—though obviously not a leader of women myself. I attended that one conference. I did not like the draft there presented and have been critical of every draft I have seen. I understood, until the press story appeared, that the whole thing was to be for a long time in the discussion stage.

It is not my fault that the World Center for Women's Archives was thus thrown to the wolves. None could have been more shocked than I was when I read the paper.

I have sent in my rectification with a statement of my own position to Dorothy Bromley of the N.Y. World Telegram in reply to her comment on me and the Charter.

I can only pray that the World Center for Women's Archives has not received a deadly blow through the irresponsibility of some news-giver unknown to me. I am trying to locate her myself.

Of the contradictory nature of the proposed Charter as printed I am fully aware and I have pointed that out myself to its sponsors. Now I refuse to have anything to do with further correspondence on it.

What a strange thing to happen, to me and my sincere loyalty to World Center for Women's Archives! I am afraid to poke my nose out of the door again.

> Cordially yours—Mary R. Beard

Historian Alma Lutz, who was assisting Harriot Stanton Blatch with her memoirs, was also a devoted member of the younger generation of the National Woman's Party who helped to keep the party journal, *Equal Rights,* alive. She asked Mary Beard to clarify her position respecting the Women's Charter. Beard's answer is a lucid and eloquent description of her own third path, resonant with her insistence on linking feminist with wider social views and her alarm about the threats to human values and women's status embodied in fascism abroad and the economic crisis at home. Grace Hutchins' *Women Who Work* (1934), mentioned by Beard, was an indictment of the system of women's double burden of home and work by a pacifist social worker of Beard's generation who joined the Communist party in 1927 and remained active in it for several decades.

57. TO ALMA LUTZ

> Carroll Arms Hotel
> First and C Streets. N.E.
> Washington, D.C.
> Jan. 29, 1937

Dear Miss Lutz:

I deeply appreciate your goodwill in inviting me to state my position with respect to the Women's Charter for the readers of Equal Rights and the members of the National Woman's Party. The National Woman's Party has offered me its floor on several important occasions to "speak my piece" and this is another evidence of its consent to hear, even though what it hears may be a variant on what it defends. In accepting another invitation, I am dividing my statement into three parts with a view to being both clear and emphatic.

1) As to the past. Up to this hour I have held aloof from the factional strife within the woman movement despite the continuous attempts that have been made to smoke me out of my "ivory tower." And I have held aloof for the reason that the two major factions—the two great parties I may say—have both seemed to me very inadequate as to program. Thus the equal rightists, I have thought, ran the risk of positively strengthening anachronistic competitive industrial processes; or supporting, if unintentionally, ruthless laissez faire; of forsaking humanism in the quest for feminism as the companion-piece of manism. The woman's bill of rights is, unhappily, long overdue. It should have run along with the rights of man in the eighteenth century. Its drag as to time of official proclamation

is a drag as to social vision. And even if equal rights were now written into the law of our land, it would be so inadequate today as a means to food, clothing and shelter for women at large that what they would still be enjoying would be equality in disaster rather than in realistic privilege. This I have said at National Woman's Party meetings and banquets, in a voice sometimes decidedly shaky because it was emotionally hard to appear to be unsympathetic with the fierce pressure for a woman's bill of rights and emotionally hard to appear critical of many women for whom I have both affection and high regard. However I could not throw my heart and energy into the mere struggle for equality on a basis of laissez faire in the twentieth century.

Nor could I throw my heart and energy into the mere struggle for a minimum wage, even for women. The protectionists satisfied me as little as the rightists, sorry as I was to be so fussy. The minimum wage implies *a* wage and leaves out of account the millions of unemployed to whom a wage at all is sheer utopia. It has seemed to me to represent too complacent, too sentimental, an acceptance of capitalism and to be too consistent with the economic rule of a plutocracy. Neither equal rights nor a minimum wage for women could make a dent on such an anti-social American labor system as that pictured, for instance, in Grace Hutchins' "Women Who Work."

In short, while I have always recognized the value and "justice" of the equal rights principle and lamented its historic lag, and while I have also recognized the value of restraining exploitation, since neither the one program nor the other struck at the issue of employment itself—that basis of all culture—I have lacked the zest for throwing myself into the fray of the factional dispute among women—until this hour.

2) As to the present. Now I am hurled into its center through no intention of my own. For that event Mary Van Kleeck gives the explanation in a letter to the New York Times. For the inaccurately bold publicity with respect to the Women's Charter, she offers the correct version. I desire therefore to call a halt, as far as I am concerned, on further ill-feeling engendered by that mistake—for the sake of the future.

3) As to the future. Being thrust into this fray and kept in this fray despite Miss Van Kleeck's publicity correction, from the necessity for revealing my attitude at last to both factions of women, I offer my challenge to both factions within the woman movement. For their common inadequacy against women's and democracy's ruthless enemies—war, fascism, ignorance, poverty, scarcity, unemployment, sadistic criminality, racial persecution, man's lust for power and woman's miserable trailing in the

shadow of his frightful ways—I offer the ideal of adequacy. No doubt we should have our woman's rights to equal opportunity but with them let us combine the demand for a decency of life and labor all round and security if possible to attain. Let us fight neither over the crumbs that fall from plutocratic tables nor over the right to be plutocrats dropping crumbs.

Let us demand, for example, a set-up in every industry which will carry with that industrial set-up a high minimum of labor reward without discrimination of sex, widening the laws which exist and creating the broad principle of the irreducible minimum from the start in the formulation of new national codes for industry now in process of revival and development. Let us go beyond equality in unemployed disaster and beyond equality in the exploitive privilege to equality in social leadership designed to win security for all. Let us even go beyond equality of leadership and be creative leaders in the vanguard, if men drag along steeped in their vested interests so heavily that they cannot see humanity for seeing money profits and dictatorial power.

If we will not so envisage our future, no Bill of Rights, man's or woman's, is worth the paper on which it is printed, for eventually, if not immediately, democracy will go down with plutocracy into militarism and the time will have passed when women can get together even to blow off steam about rights and protection—even about a Women's Charter. Men will win—the cruel types of men whom no woman should desire to equal.

Sincerely yours, Mary R. Beard

The leaven in Mary Beard's winter was her delight in reading American women's documents at the Library of Congress. "Oh the precious speeches and letters of women that nobody knows! I nearly go dotty over some of them up in the MSS division," she wrote to Madesin Phillips. "I am hunting for basic women thinkers in America and finding *some*. A lot of their stuff is not printed and has to be gone over in fading lines on yellowing paper. I had the pleasure of an admission to the five trunks of papers acquired by the Library just three years ago in which Anna Dickinson reveals herself. Who she was is shown in that 4 vol. History of Woman Suffrage which nobody knows either. She saved the Republican Party in 1872, for one thing."[13]

This reading undoubtedly confirmed and fueled her convictions about the importance of the World Center for Women's Archives. Yet, curiously and ironically, her concern did not extend to her own papers, either the ones she received or wrote. When a New Jersey supporter of the archives inquired whether Beard had any letters written by Alice Paul in her own possession, Beard promised to look but admitted, "I have never kept correspondence systematically—even important letters. It has not been concern for my own archives which has thrust me into the big archives business and in many ways this is too bad for I have had valuable letters through the years. I am a typical woman, I suppose, in my indifference in this matter as a phase of my long life." [14]

58. TO HARRIOT STANTON BLATCH

Carroll Arms Hotel
First and C Streets, N.E.
Washington
January 24 [1937]

Dear Harriot:

I have longed to rush in upon you with my excitement over your mother! And to talk more to you about the progress on your memoirs after discovering how beautifully you prepared her papers for the Congressional Library and for posterity. All your penned notations, all your ties, and folders touch me to the core. I should never have known how to prepare papers so well. You whose youth was spent among the entourage of your mother must have felt about all the records you thus handled even more sensitively than I feel, though I am honestly stirred to my deeps. Those wonderful letters from your father to your mother, even though he was "scared" to have his Liz face the hooligans at a meeting on the outbreak of civil war. Every item in those folders excites me. I have written you countless letters in my mind as I turned over the documents.

I have made a complete copy of your mother's speech on Labor which I should like to use if I can manage to get together a book on American women *thinkers*. I have assembled other types of American women for consideration, putting off to the last the more difficult task of finding thinkers if such there were. I consider your mother a basic thinker and it is genuine delight to get closer to her in the way you have made possible. I understand now how you feel about the Susan B. For Susan's birthday, I have agreed to write the script for a broadcast, spurred to do so by that indefatigable Ethel Adamson. But I am as adroitly as possible making the point clear. I shall send you the script, hoping for your partial approval at least.

Now this week I come on to your W[omen's] P[olitical] U[nion] scrap-books—looking primarily for traces of your speeches. Have you nothing in the way of record for your Socialist candidacy in N.Y? Nothing, I mean in the matter of speeches? It is very evident that you are a chip off the old block re social consciousness. That reiteration of ignorance and poverty by your mother moves me intensely. I was so ignorant that I feared I should not find the fundamental economic thought. Thank god, it is there!

My rushing in upon you is only postponed.

Affectionately, Mary R. Beard

It is likely that Doris Stevens wrote to Mary Beard about an upcoming protest at Mt. Holyoke College because its trustees had broken precedent and appointed a man—a Yale professor, Roswell Ham—to succeed long-time president Mary Woolley. Perhaps Stevens suggested that Beard re-fuse to give her slated address at the Mt. Holyoke centennial. (As it hap-pened, the alumnae raised a storm of protest about the appointment, and the college trustees proceeded as they wished nonetheless.) Beard's re-sponse to Stevens articulates crisply her insight that human experience has a gendered character. Cornelia Pinchot, mentioned as differing on this matter, was married to Gifford Pinchot, governor of Pennsylvania, and was herself a Republican politician in the 1920s and 1930s.

59. TO DORIS STEVENS

New Milford
May Day [1937]

Dear Doris:

My May Day is rendered gay by the discovery that you and I see eye to eye on the acceptance of woman as woman. I am surprised to know this but my surprise of course shows how far apart we have lived and only that. I think you are dead right about the folly of pretending to represent something as neutral as a "human being" neither man nor woman. But I did not keep sufficiently close to you to remember that you could never be anything so strange. I am so happy to have caught up with you again for in my younger life it was your very radiance as a human being which made you so enchanting for me. Now your letter will help me to shoot my bolt at Holyoke with less fear of its futility.

I shall send you copies of my two speaking efforts as soon as I can get the copies made—the AAUW speech at Savannah and this next one at South Hadley. I don't know whether the AAUW Journal will have room for all my words. You can be as critical as you like when you read them.

The household found Senora de Tejeira a grand experience. How clear her eyes are and her head! She told us as much as she could in the hours she spent here about the life and no-labor of Panama. So her visit was all to our good. There was here the same day a Brunhilde from Vienna and the contrast of these two women was dramatic but Brunhilde simply adored the Panaman[ian] and the Panaman[ian], if not a little terrified by the exuberance of the Viennese (Frau Anna Askanasy), was none the less tremendously interested in her take of life over a volcano confronted with sadistic men in arms.

As for the protest eventuating in a demand for [Roswell] Ham to resign from the presidency of Mount Holyoke, that I think I must leave to alumnae who will make it I think. But I am entirely in sympathy with your call for resignations. What is more I am sure we should all get further with everything if there were more voluntary resignations on the part of persons who find themselves blocked by Tory opposition. As Charles told several Republicans in the last campaign, it is really not imperative that Landon should win: it is even better to be in the right than to be president.

On the point of admitting oneself to be a woman and making that reality and influence count as such, I have argued often with Cornelia Pinchot. She claims that whatever she has accomplished has been because she has not agitated as a woman. The point of view is often hard to break down. I have told her that everything she may have accomplished has been because she was a woman.

Mrs. Abby Rockefeller has declared herself ready to give us a thousand dollars to open an Archives Center office, provided we can get five more women to match her thousand. I think we can. Then we shall really be in the field for a building and for documents.

My love to you—Mary R. Beard

The Beards returned to Washington in January 1938 as they had the several preceding years. The previous spring they had started work together on the successor volume to *The Rise of American Civilization*, eventually called *America in Midpassage*, published in 1939. Busy with this as well as with the WCWA Mary Beard also assisted her husband in his extensive testimony before the Committee on Naval Affairs of the U.S. House of Representatives. Charles Beard was opposing increases in naval appropriations and arguing against an American foreign policy that sought to insure *world* peace rather than simply national defense. The following two rare family letters, the first to their grandson, Detlev, and the next to their daughter and son-in-law, Miriam and Alfred Vagts, give a unique presentation of Mary Beard's view of this task.

60. TO DETLEV VAGTS

> The Mayflower
> Washington, D.C.
> January tenth [1938]

Our dear Detlev:

You are having a birthday and maybe ice cream! Remembering this great event your grandparents wanted to find some rare and beautiful or especially original object to send you as an honoring gift—for a young man who has made such good use of his eight years, I mean nine.

Three dollars can be rare and beautiful if not original. Maybe you can put them to some original use however as a birthday gift for a boy of nine. I might suggest, for instance, that you spend them to take your mother to a Saturday afternoon concert. But that is only "for instance." When we get the big navy bill outlawed, I shall look in the shops for the object, with my whole mind devoted to the quest.

You guessed that grandfather would have the taxpayers in mind in opposing the big navy bill. But I think he forgot taxpayers entirely in thinking about fine lads who should be allowed to live. We are arguing this matter with the biggest navy and army men in this country and many of them feel just as we do. Tomorrow General Rivers is to testify and it will interest you to know that he went [all] over Washington trying to buy as many globes as he could today to place before every member of the Committee, if possible, while he talks geography to them. He told me that they have used only maps (I didn't hear exactly what kind he said) (or did he say charts?). He is sure that they do not know what the seas and lands are like. He is a fine old soldier who wants to stop another *levée en masse*. I can speak French with you of course. I wish you were here and I could take you with me to listen to General Rivers.

Your school sounds most attractive. Your letters are positively attractive.

Have a happy birthday now and many many more !!!!!!!!!!!!!! without number.

Our love, The Washingtonians

61. TO MIRIAM AND ALFRED VAGTS

The Mayflower
Washington, D.C.
Thursday [early 1938]

Our beloveds:

It's like running a presidential campaign these days and nights in repre-senting the opposition to the president on his foreign policy. Only—we are candidates for jail rather than the White House.

I shall write a longer letter just as soon as the H of R Committee on Naval Affairs thinks it had better let loose of CAB. We are working some 20 hours a day and have been for quite a while. But in these nice rooms where sun enters and the air is good we are both keeping well. I sit beside CAB as he confronts those roughnecks on that Com[mittee]—and see that he gets every question. My being there he remembers not to get too angry but to take plenty of time to feed out information. And the guys today actually cried for "Light". Can you believe it true?

It's not an easy life either of us or any of us lives. I long to hear every detail of yours naturally. But you generously reported essentials and you have done better than I.

In a day or two—more from us.

Always our love—Mother

4 The Women's Archives Continues

On December 15, 1937, the World Center for Women's Archives was officially launched at a gala dinner at the Biltmore Hotel in New York City, where the charts, maps, and letters of departed aviator Amelia Earhart were donated by her husband, George Putnam. In this new stage of progress, two women became especially important to Mary Beard. One was Marjorie White, a self-styled scholar with interests similar to Beard's, who sought employment at the center and volunteered her full loyalty to the project. The second was Miriam Holden, a philanthropic New York City liberal, member of the National Woman's Party, volunteer for the NAACP and birth control movements, and an intellectual and collector of books herself.[1] Holden had volunteered on the board of the project since its early days but became at this point Beard's mainstay in New York. Holden and Beard carried on a voluminous correspondence concerning the policies and problems—especially the money problems—of the WCWA. In the letter below, Beard mentions her plan to ask for funds from the wife of Eugene Meyer, who had made a fortune in investment banking and was the owner of the *Washington Post*. (It is not clear who Mrs. Bremer was, but perhaps Edith Terry Bremer, head of social services for immigrant women within the YWCA.) Beard's testy remarks about other women in political life—including grande dame Alice Longworth, the precious only daughter of Theodore Roosevelt, and clubwoman Daisy Harriman, who had been born into wealth—suggest how frustrating it was for her to get response from women (or men) with financial resources. At the same time, Beard was pressed by her writing and political efforts with her husband.

62. TO MIRIAM HOLDEN

Mayflower Hotel
Washington, D.C.
March 12, 1938

Dear Miriam Holden:

Do by all means tell Mrs. Bremer to come to see me here. I agree that her interest harmonizes with the archives plan.

But I get no word which seems to indicate that we can do our thing. If it has to be built up any longer around me who started it, then it must mean defeat. I simply cannot at my age and with my burdens carry this one as my sole responsibility. If the Center does not grip other women as it grips me, then there is not enough belief to make it a reality. If the Board members won't even go to meetings to help make a quorum, we should at least try to get women who will do that and more. You have been splendid in every way and so this defeat, if it comes, will not have you to blame.

I am going tomorrow for the day to the Eugene Meyers camp across the Potomac. But I got the sickening feeling at their house on Thursday night where we were invited to help honor Thomas Mann that women will only play up men and not respond to appeals to explore their own social role as knowledge. They spin theories. They do not want to know. I say this because, as I watched Alice Roosevelt sweep into the room with the air of a grand duchess and look straight beyond me, though she knows me perfectly well and not long ago at Mrs. Borden Harriman's rushed up to me to ask to meet my husband (!), and move over to join Mrs. Gifford Pinchot and Mrs. Meyer, I felt my first genuine despair. "Princess Alice" has not even answered my letter asking her to let me see her a few moments. I know Cornelia Pinchot exceedingly well and she denies her interest in women and reveals the truth of that declaration constantly. I have Mrs. Meyer tomorrow but she may take the same stand as she seems to be of their breed. These three standing together and so gaily like close chums that they are represent about *eighty million dollars*, according to hearsay at least. The Spanish ambassador and Senora and I in our trio close by represent only the thought of human tragedy. In this assembly was Thomas Mann. What a strange thing life is and society!

If we do not get some money soon, we must fold up. I am sorry. There is nothing I can say to Mrs. Bremer, I fear.

                                        My love to you, Mary R. Beard
[P.S.] Your inquiry about an exhibit at the World's Fair is one I can't answer in view of the state of our project. Who can assemble the stuff? I can't.

It is useless to talk about moving the Center to Washington. I can't swing that whole thing here either. I can get a DC group of women to work intelligently but they won't want to tackle the nation as we had proposed to do. The shift would simply mean that New Yorkers wanted to escape their responsibility. I refuse to consider it.

I HAVE AS ONE OF MY IMMEDIATE OBLIGATIONS the burden of working also for an effective opposition to imperialist adventures on the high seas. Charles and I have done everything side by side as that is the only way he could accomplish as much as he has. My heart is in that cause of course but if we are ever to keep women from ganging up with men for war, we've got to give 'em a substitute in idealism meaning something to them personally.

•←

The essays Mary Beard published during the 1930s lodged in small-circulation feminist journals, such as the National Woman's Party's *Equal Rights* or the Business and Professional Women's *Independent Woman;* her occasional efforts to reach wider audiences through intellectual magazines such as *Harper's* or mass women's magazines such as the *Ladies' Home Journal* were not successful. Articles that were published to these wider audiences frequently enraged her, as witness her comments below on two articles in *Harper's,* Pearl Buck's "America's Medieval Women" of 1938 and Genevieve Parkhurst's "Is Feminism Dead?" of 1935. Best-selling author and journalist Pearl Buck, recently returned from years in China, had written a terse and casually polemical essay portraying relations between the sexes in America as utterly bowed under tradition, which demanded that women be little more than pretty, accommodating creatures at home. Only half-satirically, Buck argued that women would be more satisfied with their actual portion if they were not educated as though they had open horizons before them. Presumably Beard objected to Buck's assumption that in the past—in the tradition— women acted only at home, providing services to men, and had no wider public role. Since Beard herself frequently criticized both sexes in similarly harsh terms, it is less easy to guess her response to Buck's portrayal of American men's childishness and their hypocritical tolerance and fear of women, or to Buck's claims that American women accepted the crumbs that men left in the job market and failed to support other women's professional or artistic endeavors.[2]

This letter also reflects increasing difficulties among the New York supporters of the archives. Because the group included both employed women, who could not attend daytime meetings, and leisured women, who were accustomed only to daytime meetings for their volunteer work, even the seemingly simple matter of arranging meeting times was laden with organizational implications.

63. TO MIRIAM HOLDEN

[New Milford]
July 29 [1938]

Dear Miriam:

I am writing you right off the bat though longing to talk directly with you about that awful article by Pearl Buck. It made me sick to my marrow as it evidently did you too. We just can't let such stupidity circulate forever and I feel like hugging you for your mutual consent to fight.

After receiving your letter I dug out the article which Harper's had rejected more than two years ago. I had tried to reply to an article Harper's had just published, called Is Feminism Dead—just as absurd a thing as Pearl Buck's. But the editors would have none of mine. Probably the thing is not attractively written. Buck employs all the cheap and nasty gossip which makes a sensation. I attempt a little history but history is emphatically tabu in all the magazines.

For instance the Ladies Home Journal is trying to recover its old circulation by claiming to have aroused American women to take an interest in public affairs. To this claim Dorothy Thompson and Dorothy Bromley seem to have given loud cheers. But when I was invited to fill out one of its questionnaires about my attitude toward birth control, divorce, etc., I popped back with a comment that "women had always been interested in public affairs" and I should like to do an article proving it. The reply to me was flatly that no history was wanted.

I was thinking that perhaps Catherine Mackenzie could get in a reply to Pearl Buck when your letter came. I was about to send her the thing I had had rejected. Now however I am sending it to you so that you can better discuss the Harper attitude with [its editor, Frederick Lewis] Allen. It is really outrageous for Harper's to give women these raw deals time and again. I have forgotten who wrote the thing on Feminism and in that case perhaps the editors thought they were giving women a new deal but its total ignorance of history made the deal rotten. Anyway, I shall adore hearing what Allen has to say. My feelings do not have to be spared because I am not a prig pleased with my own composition—merely a woman cultivating the memory of women. It is silly for men to think of men's role in the world alone and sillier for women to play their game exclusively.

As for our Archives Board, I am grateful to you for letting me see Miss Brezee's letter. The problem is a real enigma. I fully agree that leisure-class women are apt neither to know what is involved in attitudes toward women nor as accustomed to accomplish hard work as women professionally employed. It will be a miracle if we get any of them to push on this job. On the other hand five o'clock is a frightful hour for meetings and it has been a major reason, I think, for our inefficiencies. Everyone has been sitting on the edge of her chair ready for a dash out of the door. The salaried women come tired. Others, except you and me, don't come at all. Miss Lewisohn is increasingly faithful and I am so very glad for she has much to give, and by that I don't merely mean money.

If we don't put salaried women on the Board, we ought to have them working on committees or in an advisory capacity, don't you agree? As for our present boss, I wish I were sure myself.

I'm delighted that you enjoy Kate [Hurd-]Mead['s *A History of Women in Medicine*]. She has had a lot of good reviews and Governor [Wilbur] Cross let me do one for the Yale Review.

Affectionately—Mary R. Beard

In spite of Mary Beard's intent to make the World Center for Women's Archives a rallying point for women of all political factions, supporters of the equal rights amendment did play a major role in it. The choice of author "Meg" Irwin as chairman—even if she was mainly a figurehead, as appears to be the case—warned off women who held a brief against the National Woman's Party. Carrie Chapman Catt, for instance, supported the archives only nominally; she wrote to Alice Stone Blackwell in 1937, "I doubt if it will succeed. It has no place in which to house the archives and no money with which to maintain it."[3] In the following, Beard tries to conciliate the aging Blackwell, who was the daughter of nineteenth-century suffragist Lucy Stone and had lifelong ties to NAWSA, which made her suspicious of any organization with strong National Woman's Party representation in it.

64. TO ALICE STONE BLACKWELL

Mary R. Beard
New Milford, Conn.
July 29, 1938

My dear Miss Blackwell:

. . . I had read your biography of your mother with deepest interest and great enthusiasm both for author and subject. The copy you sent me

I shall keep in sight all the time now and give my other one to my daughter to remind the younger generation of things it must remember. . . .

You cannot know how often your name is on my lips as I inquire from friends who have the honor of knowing you how you are these days. It has grieved me very much that the proposed World Center for Women's Archives seemed spoiled for you by the personnel in part. But the attempt had been made to make the collection of materials widely representative and it seemed wise therefore to have all groups and interests among women identified with the leadership. The chairman had to be someone who would act in that capacity—for a time at least. Now however the Board is undergoing a drastic revision with a view to getting more efficient action. I shall write you about the outcome as soon as it is known. The next elections to the Board and for its officers must wait until the autumn meeting.

It would be a very specialized set of archives if only one or a few feminine attitudes toward life and labor were assembled, you will agree I am sure. But it is equally important to have some one head this movement in whose intellectual powers enough women—all women who have such powers themselves—believe. That is our enigma but one we must solve as soon as we can.

I think you will be interested to know that we have some ten state organizations and a branch in Washington, D.C., all really exploring the region for women's documents. The Newspaper Women of Ohio had already begun this research and are about ready to publish the history of women in Ohio. Gradually therefore the total ignorance of the rising generation about women who have risen before should be alleviated.

>   With my truest respects and
>   devotion to you, Mary R. Beard

As the two letters above suggest, the board of the archives in New York was undergoing reorganization in 1938. Mary Beard had precipitated some internal dissension by her favoritism toward Marjorie White. White was very good at archival research. It was she who discovered, for instance, that Carrie Chapman Catt's gift of the NAWSA papers to the New York Public Library lay crumbling and rotting in several drawers, uncatalogued and uncared for. She was not interested in fund-raising, however, to which several board members gave higher priority. Mary Beard hired Marjorie White as executive secretary to the organization in December 1937, even though Glenna Tinnin had already been appointed to such a position. The conflict between the two appointments was temporarily resolved by the board's decision on December 19, 1938, to employ both women part-time, White tending to archives and state branches, Tinnin devoting herself to fund-raising and office management.[4]

65. TO MARJORIE WHITE

[New Milford, Conn.]
November 28, 1938

Dear Marjorie:

Hsh but it's a fact that a crisis has come in the Archives movement. I hope it can be resolved rationally and in the interest of an intelligent victory. If so resolved it will take all the skill that I can command and all the understanding that the Board as a whole possesses.

I brought it on unwittingly when I asked the Board to engage you—especially as I did not at the same time insist that Mrs. Tinnin be taken on at full time. I am now told by Mrs. Tinnin that I have broken all good budgeting practice and disrupt the credit of our organization.

Moreover she can't stand the crowded office and is generally upset.

She regards the pressure for archives themselves as unimportant at this time. Her view of the Exhibit is theatrical and nothing else counts. She is pleased to have found for the Board new members to offset the "radicals" as she calls some of us. She has an idea which must be promoted through thick and thin. She considers herself as having been very shabbily treated. Maybe she has; certainly she has been devoted and some of her own money has gone into bills she did not know how to pay otherwise.

In the circumstances, to avoid a "scandal", I must ask you to operate as if you were my private secretary only. I hate to do this for your sake but it is the only way to keep from destroying all the gains uptodate. The situation cannot be definitely defined until the Board meeting on Dec. 19th. I shall send you my check for the December 1 to December 19 salary and I am writing Mrs. Tinnin to report that. There will be an interim of but two or three days between the writing of this instruction to you and your receipt and "eviction" from the office. Those days will be included in the Archives office check to you.

Please oh please cover up everything in dealing with Miss Evresoff. Plan to see her outside the office. Don't lose her fine volunteer aid. Make excuses.

Your idea of the Exhibit is mine. The other is balloon ascension. The thing will have to be threshed out on the 19th by the Board. The worst of the business now is that it has gone so far in enlisting the interest of Miss Branch and the Grand Central Galleries and others that to fight its direction via Mrs. Tinnin may break up the whole archives "cause" in a row. I think I should not do that.

I may have to pull out of the Board to save my own mental integrity. That I shall do if need be. Quietly.

Your report which arrived this morning delights me as usual.

There is the special matter of the letters to the European women both on Miss Phillips' list and on the Schwimmer list. Proceed to get the criticisms and approval of Miss Phillips and Mme. Schwimmer quietly but hold up the letter mimeographing and mailing until after the 19th. Say nothing on the matter to Mrs. Tinnin.

Just go ahead as you have been doing. The letter to Miss Quaid is sound. Send that. Keep track of your stamp expense. From today. I shall settle that with you from now on. I am returning the Quaid letter as you may not have a copy.

If I can get down before the 19th I shall. Next Monday—a week from today, I hope to. Then we shall meet in retreat and have a good long talk. Don't quit.

My love—Mary R. Beard

Whether in spite of or because of the resolution of December 19, 1938, there was a major walkout—or "voluntary purge"—shortly thereafter by New York board members, including the executive secretary whom Mary Beard did not favor. Beard thought this "housecleaning" might be favorable to the organization. At any rate, she was glad to be free of Tinnin, whose political views were too right-wing for her taste.

In the following letter, Beard subtly encourages Holden to appreciate the political benefits of Tinnin's departure. During an earlier stage of the board's organization, she had urged Holden, "You must keep on the spot to help back up the liberal labor side of the archives collection." The first line below refers to a protest Beard had received from Florentine Sutro, about being eased out of leadership; Beard implies that Tinnin, perhaps for political reasons, had conveniently forgotten Sutro.[5] Congressman Martin Dies, Democrat of Texas, mentioned at the close, chaired the new Committee on Un-American Activities in the U.S. House of Representatives and pioneered the techniques and slogans later made famous by Senator Joseph McCarthy, charging groups and individuals with being "soft on Communism."

Beard was nonetheless reaching across the political spectrum for women's papers. The Mrs. Pratt whom she encourages Holden to interview was likely Ruth Pratt, a conservative New York state legislator who had no allegiance to feminism whatsoever. Beard was also hopeful about the archives at this point because a vigorous group of women in Washington, D.C., seemed to have taken hold of the idea, making her less reliant on New York supporters.

66. TO MIRIAM HOLDEN

> Hotel Henderson
> Aiken, S. Carolina
> February 6, 1939

Dear Miriam:

The enclosed letter from Mrs. Sutro has a good deal of justification despite the fact that she is too old to keep books now and despite her kind words about me. It is a shame that she is not on the list of sponsors. Mrs. T[innin] is alone responsible for that. You will see, won't you, that in the next printing, her name is there?

Have you heard that Washington, D.C. has waked up and is planning a big archives luncheon for February 25th? On that day the women in the government can attend and I have suggested that the women of the diplomatic corps be invited, with Doris Stevens' Latin-American friends. Every woman who attends is to be asked to bring an archive for presentation and that should bring national publicity of the right and vivid kind. I shall run up for this luncheon if the promoters insist although they can of course swing it perfectly well without me.

So we are not dead or dying. I think our purge may work to our genuine advantage, apologetic though I am if I committed any injury. . . . Surely we need a money-raiser who can answer people when they ask "What good does an archive do? And don't we know enough about women already?" The reply which Irene Wright, vice chairman of the Washington Branch makes is so direct and effective. When some of the women remarked that the documents which might be brought to the luncheon would not be important, Miss Wright replied that every one might be highly important even in its apparent littleness. And Miss Wright is so competent to say so; she was a professional archivist in Spain for the old government—having set herself up as of that profession and having got that big appointment. This was certainly a fine post. She now understands that we need to know more about Spanish women as about all the rest. Don't you want to tackle an interview with Mrs. Pratt? She might arrange for you to see her friends too???!!! Why let her drop? I should think you would be ideal for interesting her, provided you could soft-pedal on labor, etc. And you could.

I feel that in our new circumstances we can go straight ahead toward a comprehensive archive without Mrs. T[innin]'s hostility to everything liberal. She told others she was all for the Dies investigation and that was her basic inclination, as I got it.

Don't be afraid to upset my equilibrium by writing me if things look very bad. I don't believe they do.

My love—Mary R. Beard

Not a letter, the following unique manuscript was Mary Beard's response to the Camp Fire Girls' request for a relevant project to carry out. It illustrates especially well Beard's absorption of cultural anthropology and her innovative thinking about what would be called, in the 1960s, "history from the bottom up." Envisioning that some of the materials for the WCWA would be generated through oral interviews and through digging into local history, she here provided the Camp Fire Girls with guidance for producing such documentation. The organization took up the challenge, instigating an "Older Girls' Americana Project—on Women of Yesterday, Today and Tomorrow," in the spring of 1939 in Buffalo, New York; Reading, Pennsylvania; Sherman, Texas; Tulsa, Oklahoma; Des Moines, Iowa; and Columbus, Ohio. The results of the projects are unknown, however.[6]

67. PROGRAM FOR RESEARCH ACTIVITY PLANNED BY SPECIAL REQUEST OF CAMP FIRE GIRLS

Your work for soil, water, and forest conservation is something that you will want to carry on through all the years either directly or by giving support to the conservation movement.

But you will also want to work for human life. And to work well for human life, including your own lives, the lives of great women should be helpful, as examples of intelligence and heroism.

Why not begin to know your great grandmothers? That might be a delightful exploration and it could take this form:

a) What do you now know about your own grandmothers?

b) Where were they born?

c) Did they spend their whole lives in one place?

d) If they lived in more than one place, where did they go? And why?

e) How were they educated? Did they go to school? Did they learn to read and write at home?

f) Did they produce crops or other kinds of wealth, such as textile and canned goods and clothes and millinery?

g) Was life easy for them or hard, in your opinion? Why?

h) What difference do you find between your lives and theirs?

i) What do you think they might have done that they did not do?

j) What have they left behind to indicate their work, their tastes, their interests?

k) Was either of them a doctor on horseback on the frontier?

l) Are there in your family attic old letters or a diary or journal written by a grandmother? Or speeches she delivered but never printed? Or a novel she wrote but not for publication? Or poems? Or things she wrote down as just notes about life and what she saw and felt?

m) Were your grandmothers interested in community affairs? And in the larger affairs of the state and the nation?

Suggestion: If you discover interesting old papers of the kinds described, the World Center for Women's Archives (address Hotel Biltmore, New York City) would like to know about this very important discovery. It would appreciate your writing to it to make the report. Perhaps the papers thus discovered might be given to this Center so that they would become a part of a great collection of materials about women which it is trying to assemble for students and writers to read and use.

While you are becoming acquainted better with your own grandmothers, you might think about *the most interesting living women in your community*. And think about them in this way:

a) Who are the most interesting women in your opinion? Why?

b) Are they interesting to the community as well as to you? Why?

c) Have you talked with any of them? About what?

d) Could you get them to talk to your group about the work they are doing and the other things in which they are interested?

e) Could you write a sketch about any one of them, and say what they mean to you and your village or town? Try it.

f) If you do not know enough for a good sketch, perhaps the women you have in mind would let you interview them so that you could write them up. In this case, you could show them what you had written before you placed it in an album of such sketches prepared by the other girls too in your group. (Such an album would be welcome material for the World Center for Women's Archives.)

g) In your sketches, remember to put down these items:

Birthplace of the woman about whom you are writing.

If not born there, from where she came and why.

The character and size of her family, including her parents, brothers and sisters.

What she has done as work for herself and family.

What she has done for others.

What she has written or said or made as a work of art.

What kind of person you think she is.

To *widen your discovery of human life*, you might inquire whether there are any *legends* in your community about women who once lived there.

If there are such legends, try to write them down after getting all the information you can.

Are there memorials in your community to any women? If there are, find out the reasons.

To *deepen your discovery of human life*, ask yourselves whether you know about any women in *written history*.

If you do, make lists of them, for your group album with something clear written under the names about them.

If you do not know any women in written history, try to find out where you could get the "news" that women have been important persons in history.

Then to think about human life as girls, try to decide which woman or women in all this exploration you would like most to resemble.

●┉

Late in 1938, with trouble brewing in New York but hopes for a vital unit in Washington, D.C., Marjorie White attended the convention of the recently founded National Council of Negro Women (NCNW) to solicit that group's cooperation with the World Center for Women's Archives. Mary Beard had drawn up a race-inclusive collecting plan, beginning with the "aborigines"—Native Americans—and continuing to women of Spain and France who arrived on the North American continent before moving on to the English settlers in the Northeast; her interest in collecting documents of black women's history was also genuine. Mary McLeod Bethune, founder and leader of the National Council of Negro Women (and director of the division of Negro affairs within the National Youth Administration, a New Deal agency) pledged her support. Bethune named Juanita Mitchell, a young woman from St. Paul, Minnesota, who later became an important civil rights lawyer, to chair a committee on Negro women's archives to work with the WCWA.[7]

68. TO JUANITA JACKSON MITCHELL

> Hotel Henderson
> Aiken, S. Carolina
> March 1, 1939

My dear Mrs. Mitchell:

Word has come to me here where I am having a little rest that you have consented to serve as the chairman of the Negro women's archives for World Center for Women's Archives. Nothing could give me greater pleasure as general chairman of archives. And nothing will mean more to this Center than a fine record of this side of American life.

You have asked Miss White for some specific and concrete suggestions for your procedure and she modestly seeks my help in that connection. First then you yourself are on the right track in listing types of materials as essays, magazine articles, official documents, letters, and pictures. Your "etc." may properly go on to include letters, diaries, journals, even mere notes and the jottings down of memoranda, speeches, programs of organized action, unpublished manuscripts, books, honors and awards, and publicity (the latter will cover the attention paid to novelists, musicians and artists, actors, social workers and others).

Classifications may be made: i.e. women in education, in science, in businesses and professions, in the arts, in agriculture, in industry, in domestic service, etc.

Not only shall we want the documents revealing Negro women since the civil war but everything we can get pertaining to their lives and labor under slavery.

There are Negro women's national organizations whose records we should welcome. And each of these might make a list of its most distinguished personnel and ask for materials telling about them. From Dean Slowe of Howard University, about a year and a half before her death, I learned that the Negro College Clubs had a good collection of materials which they would probably like to place in this Center; unhappily for us all she died far too young and I miss more than I can tell you the opportunities to see Dean Slowe from time to time. Perhaps you can inquire about this college material.

Now and then a Negro woman has written me about her work. In this way I heard some time ago about a Miss Parkhurst (if I remember her name rightly) who went from Hampton Institute, I think, to Chicago and who was making her research an exploration of her race. If you know about her and what she has found, that would be splendid material. There are no doubt other women in the field of research who are building up the record of Negro women.

Such activists in the South as Julia Harris of Athens, Georgia, belong in the Center of course. What papers she may have I do not know but her work has been extraordinary since she left Atlanta to work with and for her own people. The Negro girls who have gone to Smith, Wellesley, and other colleges may have kept diaries. I do hope so. Years ago when the first great suffrage parade was held in Washington, I insisted until I got the consent of the promoters to have the Negroes included in that parade. Anything else would have been absurd. In that relation I met many fine residents of Washington and if a chairman for the capital could be found to work up materials there, that would be a definite service.

The Negro woman in the home as mother, wife, etc., is a story nobody really knows and one which should be known if it can be explored on paper. Her development of cookery, nursing, and all allied occupations is important to the story.

I am so deeply interested in the task of discovering the history of our Negro women that I am inclined to write you now to excess. Do feel free to ask questions at any time. All this work is new for us all and we shall have to feel our way as we go, with the road constantly widening.

Cordially yours, M.R.B.

Few moments early in 1939 were so full of triumph and promise for Mary Beard as the luncheon on behalf of the WCWA held in Washington, D.C., on March 4. The following letter, written from the Beards' Southern retreat, reflects that flush—although she was still aware that problems lurked in the wings.

69. TO MIRIAM HOLDEN

> Hotel Henderson
> Aiken [S.C.]
> March 9 [1939]

Dear Miriam:

I hoped to write you immediately about the Washington luncheon but I couldn't do it, largely for the reason that I had to follow up instantly several leads which came there and demanded quick recognition. I made a report to Miss White on several details which concerned her work especially and added some items for her to report when the Board meets on the 16th. I thought it would meet later and so I shall have to miss one more meeting but no more.

The Washington affair was a marvelous triumph I think everybody agrees. I must qualify with respect to my speech. Otherwise it was a grand victory. Nearly 500 women turned out and they were the master women, such as Mrs. Roosevelt, Miss [Frances] Perkins, Fola La Follette, Dorothy Detzer—all of whom spoke. The wives of several Supreme Court Justices were present and stayed to the very end—that is, from 1:15 to 4:15. Leading women officials came. The leading women in civic affairs were there and outstanding political women, such as Emma Guffey Miller. It was an entire afternoon party with only three or four women slipping out, and that on Saturday when week ends make their claims. Cards were passed up to me declaring pleasure at the "renaissance" of the movement, notably from Ellen Woodward and Izetta Jewell Miller. Crowds ganged up around the table at the conclusion of the meeting to talk about documents they have or want to get and to offer to work. A rich sceptic seems to be completely converted and talked later to Mrs. [Emily Newell] Blair about the money.

Mrs. Blair has written me for suggestions about further procedure and I sent Miss White a copy of the things I wrote in reply. I suggested, for one thing, that the D.C. keep the documents it collects between now and next October, safely deposited, for a grand Exhibit at the capital in the autumn which could be followed by one in New York using the same materials and things which we shall have. I hope you think that a good idea. It seems to me that it makes a clear objective for the drive from the Archives side and will produce the kind of Exhibit which you and I and all intelligent men and women can fully respect.

But I promised especially to report to you just how this luncheon was handled. Well, I couldn't get precise details and the main reply was: "It was so spontaneous we hardly know how it did happen to be such a success." The time of preparation was very short. There wasn't much advance publicity. There was no time to send tickets to individuals in advance and a tremendously long line had to wait to get in. But it did not seem angry. The idea itself may have taken fire from the President's Archive publicity and the logic of one for women.

I haven't learned about the publicity after the luncheon and can only hope that it went far and wide. Miss Beatty will be getting that information.

Mrs. Blair made a fine presiding chairman. She had a very hard task but carried it through extremely well, knowing when to stop the meeting and how to provide for various forms of interest-provoking. She omitted reading the numerous congratulatory messages and introducing all the officers to save time for the ceremony of presenting documents. This was not allowed to drag on but the documents which were presented indicated the power of the project. I was particularly touched by Frances Perkins' concluding remark to the effect that this Center with its factual information could be a place where citizen-women could justify their ways. Mrs. Roosevelt wrote out and signed that statement she made at the Youth meeting in New York as her gift and nothing could be better.

Now the Washington Unit (the name it likes) will reckon up the membership and assemble the ranks and forge ahead both for money and for papers. Oh it is so beautiful to sink roots this way!

I long to be home and near the Biltmore again. There can be no doubt that we did the right thing in checking that wild theatrical proposal and revising the management of WCWA. We were on the verge of ruining a glorious movement I firmly believe.

No one has done more or as much to save the day than/as YOU.

My love—Mary R. Beard

[P.S.] And four Negro women attended the luncheon without disrupting the affair. They came up to the table like others—enthusiastically and safely. I did wish you were there. Mrs. Jerome Frank is keen to work for Jewish records.

In the following two letters (as in others to Phillips), Beard offers her perspective on women in public life in the context of her contemporary concern with militarism, the rise of fascism in Europe, and the threat of international war. While in 1938 she was minding the vexing details of WCWA, she was also extending the wider reach to finish *America in Midpassage* with her husband. This sequel in their series on American civilization was contemporary social, political, and cultural history of the United States in the 1920s and 1930s.

70. TO LENA MADESIN PHILLIPS

> Hotel Henderson
> Aiken, S. Carolina
> March 9, 1939

Dear Lena:

I am returning the speech as you requested, following a deeply interested reading of course. I always want to keep in close touch with your thought and action and the part of your address on this occasion which appeared in the press made me want to know all the rest. But what I could not get precisely was the character of the inquest to which you addressed yourself. It comes through in part and seems to signify rather a customary academic subject for the discussion—leadership more or less in the abstract.

Your own former emphasis upon leadership as an expression of underlying popular urges and surges is, in my opinion, close to the grass roots of the business. And I can also see great value in the study of great leader-personalities set against their backgrounds. Max Lerner in the recent New Republic reviewing a set of new books on Lincoln asks very pertinent questions in this relation. I think you did well to try to shatter the concept of women's expecting something of leadership now as if leadership were a thing outside themselves. It is my contention that, if women knew their own history down through time, they would realize their own historic leadership as they do not know it today. I would play less modestly than you have done on that string, for I believe their leadership to have been exerted always in every aspect of life.

And in playing more stridently I would tell men more emphatically who and what they are as leaders, rather than presuming that they can answer any of the questions you ask, for I don't believe they can. I am so afraid that when they are not brutes seeking war, they are hopelessly childlike with respect to business and other civilian enterprises.

In the thing which I want to do in print I shall attempt an interpretation of the roles of men and women—brashly of course. As you say: "sometimes the more ignorant, the more ideas, and certainly the more feeling."

I am glad you are going to write more and on your own purposes.

The Washington luncheon appeared to be a vast success. The committee decided it was important to have Mrs. Irwin, not only because she is chairman of the Archives Board but also because she is a Republican and devoted to Hoover. There would have been an undue New Dealish or Democratic atmosphere otherwise. Fola La Follette held up the frontier-Progressivism and I the mugwumpery. But your speaking skill was missed. Nearly 500 of the outstanding women of the capital came to the lunch and stayed on lingeringly from 1:15 to nearly five. Mrs. Roosevelt of course gave distinction. She was flanked at the speakers' table by Mrs. Justice Stone and Black, Frances Perkins, Julia Peterkin, Ellen Woodward and women of that ilk. Dorothy Detzer made the final speech and it was tersely exquisite.

The ceremony of presenting documents went off effectively. It could have been carried on for a long time but variations were sustained to make the session interesting. Afterwards woman after woman came up to say that she had important papers, notably Mary Meeks Atkinson who told me she would give to the Center 1000 letters from farm women.

Maybe best of all was the conversion of a rich woman at the capital whose name I will give you when we meet next time. She told Mrs. Blair after the luncheon that she believed now in this project very strongly and thought women would offer the land (we think she may mean she will offer it) and others raise money for the building if it could rise at the capital. There is a growing interest in locating it there and perhaps none of us would object seriously if the capital could achieve land and building. But that is not a decision for this hour.

Mrs. Blair and her committee are to follow up the luncheon at once with a fine organization including a finance chairman. The thing is positively on its feet in Washington.

so you and Mrs. Holden and Bessie Beatty have not been toiling in vain in NYC. I tried to bolster up the movement to assure you on that point. Volunteers will materialize in NY this month, I have reason to believe—the reason being imparted to Marjorie White—volunteers who are college grads and capable.

On April 11th I am to speak at a banquet at Syracuse being arranged by the alumnae of that college. A huge throng of collegians is expected from Syracuse and other colleges. I am to stay over for a day or two and meet groups and out of this effort perhaps we can find a chairman for NY state; we need her very badly.

I must not scribble on and on for you have plenty of reading matter on

ommendations which Dr. [Kathryn] McHale [of the AAUW] may make will be of women who belong to a different "school" of thought about international relations from mine. I am against American intervention in foreign quarrels on the order of our excursion into a world war again, at least. So are many, perhaps most, of the women who are associated with the AAUW, League of Women Voters, and the large affiliation which composes the Cause and Cure of War annual conferences. But in my opinion the attitude they take on foreign policy is just another war risk.

IF we could really produce a grand civilization in the USA where we have every facility at hand or could get what we need by quiet decent barter with other countries, exchanging directly what we have to excess for what we need and what they may have in that line to excess, in my opinion, and my husband's, we could do more for economic world rehabilitation and decent international relations than we can ever possibly do by thundering at dictators and trying to work with nations whose own record is so horrible too.

But the other point of view can be expressed by women galore from the AAUW and other groups. The most aggressive of them now is Dr. Esther Brunauer of the AAUW who has taken the leadership in lining up her association and others behind the foreign policy known as "collective security." There are speakers galore on that—Mary E. Woolley and countless heads of groups who have been studying international relations under the guidance of a group of men among whom Prof. Shotwell, Prof. Fenwick, and Prof. Gideonse have been mainstays.

On my side an excellent speaker should be Miss Edith Abbott of Chicago University. She protested in a letter to the Times recently against the way in which the AAUW and the League of Women Voters have been veered in the interventionist direction and privately she has carried on that protest. She is, you probably know, the sister of Grace Abbott with whom she lived until Grace's death a few days ago. Edith might like intensely to go to California next season and present her view of international relations. No one should be listened to with more genuine interest on account of her record in public life. Miss Abbott might have suggestions for other speakers if you would write to her. Her side (which is mine) should be represented. We are not evangelistic but deeply concerned about the kind of a society which is developing in the USA. We can defend it, we believe, without participation in another world war. Quakers as a rule want it so defended but some of them have been caught in the idea of policing the world, I find, or avoiding the need by challenging dictators with a counter axis, or bloc.

I have heard about Mrs. Macpherson's gift of books to Scripps but I wonder whether rumor is correct in reporting that the collection is largely made up of books on queens!?

The Radio Program about Women in the Making of America has revealed a depth of ignorance of the subject which should instigate some good hard work in this connection without delay. This program I have not managed in every respect by any means. I have merely kept it within certain bounds of accuracy and knowledge. I had especial difficulty with this week's on Freedom of Education for the women in charge had supposed that women were never educated until they began to go to such little academies as Mary Lyon's or to Oberlin. If the Women's Archive can go on the air on its own next winter, it should do a much better program. This one is a beginning, however, and with the tendency all over the country to shut married women out of posts where they can earn money it is important to keep the insurgent spirit alive even if it is somewhat brash in its statements.

Of course we Beards value the memory of you Saunders and of your work. It is a gracious fate which renews our acquaintance if only by post.

Do give my warm regards to Mrs. Campbell and the women I met there—all of whom I hold in affection.

Cordially, Mary R. Beard

[P.S.] You wouldn't like to undertake together, would you, a Southern California promotion of the Archives? If you are interested in the idea, I shall tell you what the work would be and how to go at it.

❦

In the spring of 1939 Adolf Hitler's armies occupied Czechoslovakia and Mussolini's invaded Albania. Hitler and Stalin signed a German-Soviet nonaggression pact in August; by September 1 Hitler's armies were in Poland, and two days later Britain and France declared war on Germany. To permit Allied purchases of armaments in the United States, President Roosevelt called Congress into special session to ask for amendment of the Neutrality Act. The rally to which Detzer invited Mary Beard as speaker was focused on that issue. Unlike her husband, however, Mary Beard did not take her views on U.S. diplomacy to the public. Whether the reasons cited in the letter below or some other unstated reasons were the controlling ones can never be known. Public sentiment for neutrality was not strong enough, in any case, to prevent the Senate from repealing the arms embargo.

74. TO DOROTHY DETZER

[New Milford, Conn.]
September 26, 1939

Dear Dorothy Detzer:

I am pro-neutrality without reservation.

I want to speak my mind on Friday night.

But it would be a tactical mistake for me to speak on this occasion in Washington. I might be attacked by the opposition through the disgrace that came to my brother—his impeachment by Congress. The opposition could say that I belong to a family........

The opposition could also attack me as having a German name. My father's name was Ritter though my mother was a Howard—as English as that—joined to a Lockwood. My people on both sides were colonial Americans and I never knew a German in my youth. But I was stopped on the village green here a few days ago by two women who accused me of influencing Charles in his neutrality through being a German myself.

Well, I must give you no possible opening for a thrust against me as one of your speakers.

Sorry to the point of grief.

At the same time enormously honored by your invitation.

Yours as ever, Mary R. Beard

In the WCWA Beard aimed (unsuccessfully) to unite women, but she knew that on matters of international relations her own opinions aroused controversy and disagreement. This letter was written after the Soviet Union had invaded Finland but before Hitler's blitzkrieg in Europe, in the period called "the phony war" by American journalists. In the following months full-scale popular debate between noninterventionists and internationalists became acrimonious in the United States. Mary Beard's opinion remained with the former group.

75. TO DR. MINNIE L. MAFFETT, PRESIDENT OF THE NATIONAL FEDERATION OF BUSINESS AND PROFESSIONAL WOMEN

New Milford, Conn.
February 22, 1940

Dear Dr. Maffett:

I have your forceful appeal relative to "good Samaritans" and I cannot be insensitive to that ideal and practice of course. Human suffering grips the heart strings of every one who has a heart and a lot of warm blood passes through mine.

But there is an aspect of the International Federation which bothers me very much indeed. Two aspects in fact. And these I feel that I should lay before you in order that I may not seem merely indifferent if I do not continue to send in my checks.

First. If feminist philosophy calling for full equality of women with men, requires that, in the world crisis, the National Federation and its International ally must do much about, or even care much about, equal pay and equal work in the fighting forces, then my heart does turn cold and dry up. Granted that in many countries women must now actually fight, in my opinion the emphasis on rewards makes fighting too laudable an occupation and I am unable to think of it in terms of titles and pay.

I heard an American feminist declare recently that there can be no true equality until a woman becomes a Major General or Field Marshal. I replied that that was the oldest stuff in the human experience; that women were top war lords in many ancient societies; that Isabella of Spain and Jeanne D'arc of France led the troops as women on horseback. In short, lack of historical knowledge of women blows up absurd cliches of harmful social consequences, as I see them.

Second. The Good Samaritanship of the I[nternational] B[usiness] & P[rofessional] W[omen] might, conceivably, be a factor in getting the USA· into the world war. Sympathy with Finland is a sympathy no one of us can resist, naturally. But I consider extremely dangerous to American democracy and culture the kind of proposals geared to that sympathy which women seem lightly to accept. And I believe, firmly, that the apparent determination of Americans to stick their fingers again into a European "peace" is another equally dangerous thrust in the dark, based solely on sentiment. We did Europe infinite harm, as well as ourselves, in my opinion, by our performances at Versailles and I believe we have no more sagacity now than we had in 1918, as far as sense about European peace is concerned.

So, dear Dr. Maffett, I feel that I cannot just run along with any organization which may be headed toward a program which I cannot endorse. Simple incidents can drive us mad, I fear. For instance if the old King of Sweden has to abdicate and Scandinavia which we all admire so much has to fight Russia, we could forget that America confronted a fairly similar world situation in the Napoleonic era when Napoleon put one of his marshals, Bernadotte, to rule over the combined Norway and Sweden and that this King is the heir of that earlier world war.

Staying out of the Napoleonic wars was our salvation. Going into the present war or trying to help Europe solve its own continuous messes will be to jeopardize our whole economy and civilization.

And yet all the leading national women's organizations have sanctioned points of view—defined for them by men whose loyalty to their European nativities or cultures is clear-cut, if the women would only realize it, or induced by allegiance to the Vatican—which are not, in my judgment, wholesome for our America.

Moreover, I am far from happy over the strength within the National Federation of Business and Professional Women of sympathy with the operations of the Dies committee. I do not like drifting with crowds when I fear their drifting.

Yet I hate to resign and resign from women's organizations. On the other hand, I cannot be satisfied with participation in groups which my membership helps to strengthen when I doubt the wisdom of their courses.

I have written you frankly. And at length. You believe in frankness and I admire you wholeheartedly for that essential quality of high leadership.

Most cordially, Mary R. Beard

In the latter part of 1939 the WCWA risked what Mary Beard called genuine crisis because of squabbles among the office staff and the national board in New York, and lack of money to rent sufficient space or to hire adequate personnel to keep its operations going. At the same time, it had reached a certain height of accomplishments: over sixty names of distinguished sponsors graced its stationery; thirty college presidents had loaned their names to the effort; branch groups functioned not only in the nation's capital but in Michigan, New Jersey, Connecticut, Indiana, and Pennsylvania; and an impressive collection of documents had been donated and more pledged. Mary Beard was working directly, as chairman of the committee on archives, with a specialist on Indian lore, with Mrs. Jerome Frank on the collection of Jewish women's records, and with several women designated by the National Council of Negro Women. Her propensity to want to work with researchers such as Marjorie White, to discover more information and more documents, was not fully shared by other members of the national board. White felt unappreciated and snubbed by board members. "Everyone top-hats her. No one has the faintest idea of how she has slaved and what she has accomplished," Beard lamented to Lena Madesin Phillips. Miriam Holden's own interest in printed books (rather than in manuscripts) was causing some friction between her and Beard.[8]

Furthermore, while Beard was actively recruiting African-American women's archives, it appeared early in 1940 that the Washington, D.C., unit, on which she had placed so many hopes, was going to be riven with discord over race. The group of women designated by the National Council of Negro Women was busy. When Juanita Mitchell withdrew because of her distant residence, Mary Bethune appointed a Washington-based committee chaired by the experienced supervisor of the Moorland Foundation collection at Howard University, librarian Dorothy Porter. Other members were Sue Bailey Thurman, the wife of Howard's dean, and two distinguished former presidents of the National Association of Colored Women, Mary Church Terrell and Elizabeth Carter Brooks. These women were probably not aware, as Mary Beard was, that WCWA regulations required members to join a local branch, nor that the white Washington unit would not admit them because of their race.[9]

Beard's way out of this dilemma was to ask the "Negro Women's Archives" group, in February 1940, to work directly with her committee on archives, bypassing the Washington unit. The Washington unit was in some disarray anyway, because its chair had resigned—whether because of the race issue or other reasons is not clear. From the black women's perspective, it appeared no anomaly to work directly with Mary Beard on archives, and Dorothy Porter readily agreed.[10] While hoping that the Negro Women's Archives group would funnel findings into the WCWA, Beard also encouraged them to seek an exhibit of black women's documents at an exposition being planned for Chicago by Congressman Arthur Mitchell, who (after leaving the Republican party in 1930) was the first black Democrat to sit in the U.S. House of Representatives.

76. TO SUE BAILEY THURMAN

New Milford, Connecticut
March 25, 1940

Dear Mrs. Thurman:

It was such a pleasure to be received in your home last Saturday and to see there the interesting evidences of your visits to India! Of course I read the "archive," which you gave me, with genuine interest and I think I can fully appreciate what you felt in India as its esthetic charms. I have been moved myself by similar charms in the Orient. The memory of sensitive ceremonies continuously enchants my thought and imagination with the idea that our lives in America might become more beautiful and beauty-loving. You and I have one bond in our affection for the Old East.

But we are both Americans and that is another bond. We talked together on Saturday about work here and now. I am sure we both want to instill into our work here and now as much of the delicacy and sweetness of ancient societies grown old in wisdom as we possibly can.

When I spoke of the old Spanish-Portuguese culture which some New York families have inherited, I did not mean of course that this culture is to be cherished by the heirs alone. What I hope I was saying is that the rest of us can know it better if its best features can be assembled as archives in our WCWA where students and writers can learn about it as few could learn about it if the learning required close personal association with the "old" families who cherish that culture.

I find it so true that the women of those families and the women of all other cultural groups can meet socially and yet know nothing in fact of another as far as innate tastes and aspiration are concerned, that the idea of a World Center for Women's Archives is for me the idea of realistic cultural exchanges made impossible by merely formal occasions.

This underlies too my enthusiasm for a possible great participation by Negro women in the grand Exposition which the Hon. Mr. Mitchell is proposing. Such participation would be the preliminary to a grand participation by Negro women in the World Center for Women's Archives. I am seeking every archive I can get from your beloved East too. The collection of documents which Negro women would assemble for the Exposition at Chicago would come straight to WCWA for its collection I like to assume.

And so I hope that you will call upon Mr. Mitchell immediately and let me know what he is doing about women's participation in his proposed Exposition. My mind fills to the very edges with dreams of a great demonstration by Negro women there. On my way home from Washington I could think of nothing else and I am sitting down to my typewriter soon after my arrival home to ask again what you think about this great objective and the possibility that your Committee will make it theirs. Mrs. Bethune will be enthusiastic, unless I am terribly mistaken. And those fine delegates whom I saw at the convention in New York of the National Council of Negro Women will also be enthusiastic no doubt.

I can't refrain from jotting down some ideas I have by way of sugges-

tions on a separate piece of paper. As I visualize Negro women's participation in that Exposition—or failing its financial support—in one of
their own, that feature might run as I have suggested. Surely nothing
would stimulate the best culture for the Negroes—*and therefore for us
all in the USA*—like a great appraisal made visible with respect to the
cultural strife of Negro women.

Do please let me hear what your committee says on this point and what
you learn from your call upon Mr. Mitchell.

There will be objections on the part of many Negro women—perhaps
few on the part of Negro men—to a separate Exposition, and/or to
women's separate exhibition in such an exposition. But this is precisely
the objection we meet with respect to our Women's Archive. Many
women and many men deny the validity of a separate archive for women.
I maintain however that only by dramatizing women can women be recognized as equally important with men. And I now maintain that only by
dramatizing the hopes and achievements of Negro women per se can they
be recognized as equally important with Negro men. And I also maintain
that the proposed Exposition, by dramatizing an important minority of
our population, may aid in awakening a stronger realization of its cultural values. For I take for granted that the Negro women who would
have the responsibility for their division would lift the cultural values
above the cheap and purely imitative strife for acquisition and enjoyment.
This is not to say that the efforts of Negroes to enjoy food, clothing, shelter and recreation are beyond the range of cultural values.

I have chattered to excess in this long letter to you.

But the chattering helps my heart.

                                        Most cordially, [Mary R. Beard]

In the following letter Beard tries to justify her position regarding the
Negro Women's Archives group to Miriam Holden, who had for years
been involved in the cause of racial justice through the NAACP and local
efforts in Harlem. The bylaws to which Beard refers required women
joining the WCWA to affiliate with a state or local branch. The letter
makes clear both the genuineness, and the limits, of Mary Beard's inclusion of black women. She ranks the importance of the majority—
whites—in the sustenance of the project higher than justice to a minority,
yet believes she has a solution that will attain both. The black women
with whom she was working accepted her goodwill enthusiastically and
invited her to speak at the occasion launching a new publication by the

National Council of Negro Women, to be called the *Africamerican Woman's Journal*.

77. TO MIRIAM HOLDEN

New Milford, Connecticut
March 25, 1940

Dear Mrs. Holden:

The teachers whom I "addressed" in Washington seemed truly stirred by WCWA and I think we can count on their working hard for the records of their profession. This crowd belongs to the Delta Kappa Gamma Society, made up entirely of women teachers who are recognized by their profession and by their communities as outstanding for their contributions to education. They were the most intelligent crowd as a whole to whom I think I have ever talked. Handsome women with noble brows. Intelligent and active as such types must be. I felt encouraged by their response of course but how to take advantage of it?

The woman who had expressed a strong desire to aid WCWA in money raising at the NY AAUW meeting was also present at this one and seemed equally alert. You have her name, I think, via the office as one who thought she might collect a thousand dollars or so. Was it Evans? She lives in Yonkers and must be an exceptional teacher or she would not have been admitted to this Society. If you have not yet written her, you might do so now to even more advantage.

I ran again into *the* Washington problem as of WCWA. We cannot get a strong activity there for funds until we can handle this problem by our Board. There is firmness like adamant on this point. Shall we then permit the wreckage of the movement at the D.C.? I attempted to prevent it in this way:

Having heard that the Negro Congressman from Chicago, Hon. Mr. Mitchell, is proposing a great Negro Exposition to be held in Chicago and is asking for Congressional aid, I called upon Mrs. Bailey [Thurman] whom you had met in our office and who is still the chairman of the Negro Committee selected by Mary Bethune. I was most graciously received at her home and we had a nice long talk. Her husband is Dean at Howard University and they are both prominent Negroes. Again I asked whether her committee would work with my Committee on Archives directly so that we could be sure what they would do and be sure of their archives.

On my way to Mrs. Bailey [Thurman]'s I thought of this way out of the dilemma—the dilemma of a minority's possible wrecking of a majority and for what end? The way out to be a concentrated effort by Negro women throughout the USA for a woman's exhibition in the aforesaid Exposition, following which all the materials collected for that exhibition would come to WCWA. Mrs. Bailey [Thurman] had not heard about Mr. Mitchell's plan. She didn't know whether women had been or would be invited to participate. I urged her to go to see the Congressman at once and find out. I urged her to call for such participation if the idea had not yet been advanced. And I urged her to discuss with her committee the suggestion of mine that they call upon the Negro women far and wide to put on a magnificent exhibition either as a feature of the aforesaid Exposition or separately if that fails to materialize.

I argued that a concentration on their own archives for such a goal would do two things: educate their own women as nothing else could; promote the archives for the Center definitely.

I pointed out an analogy with the plan for a WCWA itself—dramatizing their materials in the interests of their women's recognition more fully.

The appeal seemed to "take." Today I have written a letter to Mrs. Thurman containing a summary of our conversation and its suggestions for united action. I had to agree to make a trip to the D.C. again in April to speak at a meeting to celebrate the launching of a Negro women's magazine sponsored by the National Council of Negro Women. It will not be easy for me to make the trip but I shall do so in the hope that this will help to iron out the trouble and possible misunderstanding of my position. Mrs. Bethune will of course be present (she was not in Washington this last week).

It must not happen that you and Mrs. Grove get a wrong idea of me and/or Washington. It is all a question as to whether we should run the risk of an awful row over a minority which might ruin WCWA. The most delicate diplomacy seems to be required unless our Board can make a decision which will lift it out of a dispute. If our Board refuses to do more or anything other than affirm its present By Laws, every white woman will resign in the D.C. and in their resignations we shall be accused of—well you know.

. . . In view of everything I hope that the Board will meet informally—not for the record—at a simple cheap luncheon somewhere at 12:30 or earlier—before the next regular Board meeting and discuss our situation thoroughly—prior to the decisions in the afternoon for the record. With

Miss Shouse absent we could even go into office affairs as we cannot do when she is present.

Unless we can have this extra time for informal discussion prior to our last Board meeting for months, I fear we shall wind up in a complete mess.

If we could get a little room at the Town Hall or somewhere—each of us paying for her own food—and paying for the private room to boot—perhaps we could hold our Board meeting right there too and save the time of traveling to your sweet domicile and save your expense of serving food again. We have been greedy and not confessed it.

There is one thing more at the moment. As you may know, the National Federation of Women's Clubs is collecting archives for a big anniversary—the 50th—a year or so ahead. We must try to get the archives pledged to WCWA for delivery after that event. There is no other institution to which they could be assigned with such profit to the Clubs. But they need to be aware of this now.

I asked the Washington women to do what they could at the Club headquarters there. But we must work all over the lot to gain this pledge. I can make the plea effectively in California, I think, for the woman who is now state president there may accept the state presidency of WCWA when her term ends for the Clubs. Mrs. Marsh can help in N.J. CAN you consult your NY friend-president about getting this put before the National Federation? Mrs. Hansl has been talking it up with Club leaders whom she knows. We should put in our claim immediately.

After these preliminaries we can have an official request go from our Board of course.

I "leave off" writing to you at this point for your own peace and happiness.

Affectionately, Mary R. B.

Miriam Holden and Mary Beard did not see eye to eye on the "Washington problem." In Holden's view, Beard had erred by deciding on her own how to handle the question of participation without consulting the black women themselves. Holden urged that the national board in New York be augmented by the addition of a distinguished Negro woman, such as Mrs. James Weldon Johnson. She thought that Beard was letting the white women in Washington off the hook too easily for their racism. Beard believed that the black women were satisfied with her decision and better off without knowing directly the exclusion they faced in the Washington unit.

At this point, Holden was less than satisfied with Beard's leadership on a number of issues. She did not favor Marjorie White as Beard did and was skeptical about other allies Beard made in local historical societies. She was positively angry at another researcher whom Beard encouraged: Jan Gay, a Latin-American specialist who had interfered in a way Holden disapproved in a Harlem exhibit in which they both were involved. Holden recognized that WCWA was in financial crisis. Moreover, she wanted to shift the emphasis of the center toward books and found Beard utterly and autocratically unsympathetic on that point.

Part of what Beard is responding to in the letter below is Holden's statement, in a prior letter, "To me the way we handle it (the Negro matter) is just about as important as whether we continue to have an archive center or not." Beard did not share those priorities. She was first and foremost for the survival of the archives. She was sufficiently frustrated and despondent about the future, however, to write to Marjorie White, on March 25, 1940, suggesting that White take over her own job as chairman of archives. She imagined that White together with a paid fundraiser and a field worker would make an ideal team. At the same time she knew that the funds to employ such a team were not in the center's purse.[11]

78. TO MIRIAM HOLDEN

New Milford
April 2, 1940

Dear Miriam Holden:

Your letter just received I am trying to answer at once but with the very best mind which I can utilize. This is to say I am attempting to think quietly and rationally about every item in it.

It is easy to cheer at your securing facilities for our meeting together as a Board in a long enough session this month to find out where each and all of us stand on all the essentials. I did not care about the Town Hall Club. I merely suggested that, not knowing we could get by ourselves in privacy at the City Club. Now I do hope and pray that we shall have a good turn out, for it is now or never respecting fundamentals.

I have always found you inclined to be impersonal. So you will let me be frank on points where frankness seems a little risky as friendship. This is to say that I do find you somewhat variable in your judgments of what I do. I refer to the matter of the Negroes. You haven't forgotten surely that you warmly commended our interview's outcome with Mrs. [James Weldon] Johnson. Well, I have merely been going forward on the principle, which you enthusiastically sanctioned, by inviting the committee appointed by Mrs. Bethune to work directly with my Committee on Archives. Mrs. Thurman appears to prefer having Mrs. Dorothy Porter chairman of that committee but she is a member. Mrs. Porter will be the representative of that committee on my committee presumably but this will be verified. If Mrs. Bethune approves this plan, the finest Negro women in the USA should soon be working to assemble their best archives. If Congressman Mitchell gets the appropriation for aid for a Great Negro Exposition at Chicago, and if the Negro women win the right to participate with a splendid Exhibit there, surely this will all be to the good of everybody.

As you saw in the copy of Mrs. Porter's letter which I sent you, she and her committee will draft a plan for their procedure subject to Mrs. Bethune's endorsement. This I had asked of Mrs. Thurman when she came to the office in the autumn and so we are back to first principles. Their plan we can make suggestions about if we have any. At any rate those Negro leaders will feel as they should feel at home at the center of our Center.

You would be willing to break up the whole w c w a for something else or something got in some other way? Well that is frank, my dear. . . .

You wonder what my plan of organization is? I have no plan which I am "putting over." I asked for a reconsideration of our arrangement for the branches because they just aren't acting under it. Washington quit pretty stone dead. . . . Finding the branches in distress over the financial set-up and as for the D.C. over other matters, I thought perhaps we could have a more elastic financial policy and relieve other distress through work directed by my Committee on Archives where the Negro women would meet with other grand members of that committee, such as Dr. Lynch, from time to time, and push hard for special archives. But if the attitude to be taken is that I am doing something myself or doing something wrong, then let me know openly at the coming informal discussion at lunch prior to the formal Board meeting.

. . . There was a finance committee, it is true. It had nothing positive to report. There may be nothing more to report in April. You have confessed to me, dear friend, that you don't like to ask people for money. Who does? Who will? I have tried to get it from everyone I thought could give. And I hear that Margaret Cuthbert is rooting for some for us. Mrs. Moffett's scheme still looks promising. But I begin to get more worried every hour as I confront more closely the issue of my financial obligation to this movement.

A committee could no doubt frame a nicer letter as a money appeal. But what committee? And could it ever decide to whom to mail the thing?

We are a flop as a Board because we won't organize for burdens. I try to keep the WCWA alive and keep it from ruin.

But if you still feel that your accusation of a year or so ago is still sound—that I am a Margaret Sanger unable to work with anybody else—then tell me so again and I shall get out of the way with pleasure. I have thought of doing that many times but refrained because it seemed so unfair to leave this important movement for you and the rest of the Board to carry alone. I felt I should be conscienceless if I did that both for your sakes and for the sake of all the women and men whom I have got interested in WCWA through my direct efforts. . . .

Unless at our coming luncheon, each woman will assume some task and stick to it, we are sunk. Otherwise everyone will merely knock me down and kick me. . . . I shall stop speaking for this thing as soon as I get through the April-May 3d meetings to which I am pledged. What's the use going on? The thing can't do with me or without me unless it can do without me. And how I wish it could!

Miss Gay knows that there is no hope of a position for her unless she and I can raise some money by ourselves for her to go on with her Latin-American project. Miss White has magnificently substituted for me in keeping the science project and Mrs. Mezerik at work and interested. I have written tons of letters, brought in money and members and friends. I have made hard train trips and tired myself speaking.

Then on a Negro issue, which does not have to be made an issue but can be taken care of so well that the Negro women will be the great gainers, you would let all this die? How do you know that in doing that and feeling that way you are doing anything for the Negroes? What reason have you for believing that you are a better friend to them than I am? If Mrs. Johnson comes on the Board, we shall have to add that as an issue when we have far more than we can manage now.

Oh God! Have mercy on my soul!
Affectionately as ever—Mary

In the following letter Beard laid her resolution of the Washington problem before an active (white) member of the Washington unit, Grace

Cooper. It was Cooper who had managed to secure an office for the group in the annex of the Library of Congress, because her uncle, Congressman Kent Keller of Illinois, chaired the House committee on the Library. By this point the continuance and vigor of the unit was an open question; it was functioning under an acting chair, Irene Wright, who was an assistant secretary in the State Department charged with improving Latin-American cultural relations.

79. TO MRS. GRACE KELLER COOPER

New Milford   Connecticut
April 29, 1940

Dear Mrs. Cooper:

I had a very fine conference with the Negro women in Washington on the 22d. Before the dinner at Howard University at which the magazine, Africamerican, was launched—the organ of the National Council of Negro Women—Mrs. Dorothy Porter, Mrs. Sue Bailey Thurman, Mrs. Sinclair, and a woman from Boston whose name I cannot repeat confidently (I have forgotten this name), talked with me for a long time about the problem of association with WCWA.

These are wonderful women indeed. Mrs. Porter is top-notch as a librarian with full knowledge of books on and by the people of her race. AND she has been given the task of providing the entire book exhibit for the Negro Exposition. I learned more about that Exposition: the fact that $75,000 are already available; the plan of the Exposition; the possibility that a good section can be reserved for the Negro Women and their Archives; the opportunities which a Congressional appropriation would enlarge.

We went over some possible items for the women's exhibit if it is to be a feature. Mrs. Porter will have the matter decided at once.

We also discussed the matter of drawing Negro women into state branches and it seemed to be the positive opinion of theirs that their women would be better off by working with our Center in NYC directly for the quest for their archives. The next step then, I think, is to ask the Washington leaders to call together a conference of the women who joined the Unit—calling it quietly and without excitement—and put before them this new and better plan. They know how to argue for it. They will be convincing with respect to its advantages. They have a lot of work to do in connection with the Exposition. The decision, I believe, will be in favor of their independent organization. This is the most democratic procedure and if it is approved by the conference, white and colored skies will both be clearer. I shall keep you informed of developments.

Meanwhile I hope that the majority members of the Washington Unit will proceed to collect the archives along the lines suggested in the original plan for the D.C. It is a unique plan for the country, as a plan for the nation's capital. The Negro women couldn't do much about collecting those materials but they should be asked to get everything they can about their lives and labor in the capital. I will stress this point with them while you all go after the materials of the majority folk.

It would be generous if some of you would subscribe to the new magazine—Africamerican. Mrs. Bailey is editor.

[M.R.B.]

Hitler's blitzkrieg—invading and overrunning Denmark, Norway, Holland, Belgium, Luxembourg, and France—began to strike on April 10, 1940. Mary Beard's sense of being beleaguered in her progress with the archives must have been exacerbated by the steady move of American intellectual and liberal opinion away from neutrality and noninterventionist sentiments. Charles Beard's vociferous opinions came under increasing and direct attack. Although the following letter to historian Merle Curti reflects none of this explicitly, it has a distinctly touchy tone—not untypical of Mary Beard's belief in her husband's wisdom and complexity (which no one could portray quite to her satisfaction) but surprisingly hostile, given the nature of Curti's question. Over the next decade and a half Mary Beard wrote to Curti, as a trusted friend, torrents of sharp criticisms of other male historians.

80. TO MERLE CURTI

[New Milford, Conn.]
May 14, 1940

Dear Professor Curti:

I find all the writings about CAB, with which I am familiar, either inadequate or rather vile.

[Max] Lerner's calling him just a village atheist was really vile.

Hubert Herring's sketch in Harper's made him a jitterbug rather than the hard-working scholar he has been all his adult life. That was surely inadequate.

Irwin Edman's tribute in his Journey of a Philosopher had the competence of a thoughtful student long associated with his teacher, although the adjective for his voice (one Edman applied to nearly all the rest) seemed inexact.

Certainly Johnny Chamberlain got CAB all wrong in his Farewell to Reform for CAB was never pro-Teddy Roosevelt.

A man who wanted to write a Profile for the New Yorker became very vexed with me because I wouldn't cooperate, as if I could join in a cartoon-making! He flung himself out of the house saying he wouldn't write it at all then. Well who wants just to appear in print for the sake of being there?

Herring wanted me to indulge in the personal and I refused. So this reply is the best I can give you respecting things that have been tried and written, which I have liked. I am sorry.

We surely must have another visit together.

Cordially, Mary R. Beard

Beard was facing the evaporation of the New York board's confidence in her, for what they saw as ill-advised forays into research when funds for the archives center did not exist. (She herself contributed a total of about three thousand dollars to the effort and was trying unique means to gain money to keep going: she initiated an arrangement with *McCall's* magazine in which five to seven outstanding women writers would contribute articles to the magazine and *McCall's* would pay the WCWA three thousand dollars for each—with fifteen hundred dollars up front. But the plan never materialized.) The attitude of one New York board member, Carol Willis Moffett, writing to Miriam Holden, was harsh but perhaps typical: she "appreciate[d] the contribution Mrs. Beard can make" but felt the board "must be absolved from responsibility for her erratic behavior." Moffett believed that "the idea of the archives is important, but not so important that I will drop all my other interests indefinitely in order to nurse it along in the face of recurrent personality problems." Holden clearly shared some similar misgivings.[12]

Meanwhile, in May 1940, just before the fall of France to the Nazis, Charles Beard's *A Foreign Policy for America* was published, restating his views on continentalism and neutrality, as against the internationalist intellectuals. Critics now lambasted him for moral indifference to the depravities of the Nazis and the ruthlessness of Japan. "The Irresponsibles," by Archibald MacLeish (*The Nation*, 150 [May 19, 1940]), which Mary

Beard notes below, was not an attack on her husband or any other specific individual but a wholesale condemnation of American intellectuals
for failing to confront the Nazis' repudiation of the forms of civilization
and moral understanding that intellectuals themselves lived by. MacLeish
attributed this egregious collective failing to the replacement of the "man
of letters," who had assumed a public responsibility, by the specialized
scholar and the aesthete.

81. TO MIRIAM HOLDEN

New Milford
May 25, 1940

Dear Miriam Holden:

That's a hard spanking you give me in your letter of the 22d. It comes
of course from your desire to keep me intelligent about the meaning of
wcwa and dignified in proposals for its advancement. Your spirit was
"well-intentioned" like that of the sensitive parent who flagellates a child
in its own interest. And though the average child does not take punish-
ment that way, I have had such disciplining that I do try my best to get the
other fellow's point of view.

. . . There is the issue of financing any archives project. The Board, I
suppose, has the right to examine and question and refuse any action of
mine looking to such financing. If such examining and criticising and refusing is to match the position taken respecting our Branches now in existence which I have mainly built up, then I may be completely stymied in
my archives work. I hear that the decision about branches may be brought
up for review on the ground that it was illegally taken. In this case they
may be voted out. And the Board may also reject any means I see of paying for archives projects which cannot be executed without pay. There is
the matter of Jan Gay's highly successful work for Latin-American documents which she carried handsomely forward last week in Washington on
my o.k. and partial financial aid. No one else can do for us what she is
doing and other people accept her without our anxiety about her domestic situation. I don't know what that is and I don't care except as I pity
(and respect) a young woman who is trying to keep her extraordinary
head above the storm. I also have a chance to get a rare California
woman of old Spanish ancestry, associated as curator with the Southwest
Museum, to document for us the women of the Spanish settlements in
that state, dead and living. She is widely recognized as the best person,
man or woman, in the State, to do this work. And I think I could relieve

her of her task at the Museum for a while to pursue this research with California money, *for our Center*.

But can I do any of these things as Chairman of Archives? Or is every single woman I bring into the picture to be destroyed for some reason assigned by other members of the Board? Have I any autonomy? LET THE BOARD SAY IN JUNE ONCE AND FOR ALL because I am helpless to do another thing in the present state of confusion about my function in WCWA.

In re Washington and the Negro women. The trouble there can be removed at once by the full and free consent of the Negro women, unless our Board refuses to let it be taken care of that way. Mrs. Thurman whom you met at our office, editor of the Africamerican Women's Journal, and the other women with whom I talked frankly in the D.C. in April, stated their feeling that their women would be lost or injured if they made an attempt to force their way into the local white groups. They said that in most states, certainly in the southern states, they would probably not have the quality for success in that business. BESIDES they are now so enthusiastic about studying themselves and working with the archives project that they acquired what is to me the utter DIGNITY of going forward with the widening and deepening of their own understanding as Mrs. Booker T. Washington the Third advised them to do. Thus they will outgrow their inferiority complex and command a sincere respect which the battle over archives on the social basis would never permit. BUT our Board from its own sense of "values" may, reviewing the decision of May, be so interventionist as to knock both the whites and the negroes in the head as of the archives? If it does, no one will be sorrier than those grand Negro women of the D.C. They are growing up.

There was a time not so long ago when all feminists felt compelled to force their way into every man's club and smoking car. That was the childhood of the sex in my opinion.

I would be in favor of inviting Mrs. Weldon Johnson to membership on our Board where she would learn to understand the total archives movement and help us to safeguard its purposes. I am also strongly in favor of solving the Washington dilemma in the way I have outlined, seeing no inconsistency but true statesmanship in that proposal.

Yes I read Macleish's Irresponsibles and thought it a maze of contradictions and grossly unfair to the Responsibles who have written all these years: i.e. Sinclair Lewis, "It Can't Happen Here." For this outburst I consider Macleish really disqualified to be the head of the Lib[rary of Congress]. He reveals no awareness of the literature of protest during re-

cent years. I hate to go back on him after adoring much that he has written himself. But I think this outburst rather disgraceful. No doubt it is
patterned somewhat on Benda's "La Trahison des Clercs" but Benda
wrote in the longer ago.

We're delighted that you like "A FOREIGN POLICY FOR AMERICA."
How CAB does get flayed in the press and elsewhere however! I do try to
refrain from writing you so much every time but there is always the need
of infinite explanation of my mind and manners. I AM NOT JUST STUB-
BORN and egoistic. If I am all wet however the Board can declare me so
in June and then I shall have its full understanding of what I am.

Yours as always   Mary R. Beard

Astonishingly, Mary Beard resigned from the effort she had nurtured for
five years. The failure of the board's confidence in her, as well as all the
foregoing problems, was undoubtedly the real cause. The precipitant was
Charles Beard's acceptance of a year-long teaching post at Johns Hopkins
University, which meant that Mary Beard would be in Baltimore for the
academic year. Beard had alerted Miriam Holden to her decision a few
weeks before the date of the letter below. Holden was utterly taken
aback. Peeved, unaware of Beard's agonizing over the project, she wrote
to another board member, "How can anyone walk out on their own
project so calmly and so freely I just can't imagine. Apparently no sense
of responsibility to us or the people who have sent their precious
archives." [13]

Though she was perhaps willfully deluding herself, Beard did not assume that the project would fold upon her withdrawal. She sustained
hope that either the New York or Washington group would continue the
work. It is puzzling, however, that in the letter below she seems willing to
leave the Archives in the hands of board member Eva von Baur Hansl,
whose career as an educator and vocational counselor Beard did not seem
to respect very much.

82. TO MEMBERS OF THE BOARD OF THE WORLD
CENTER FOR WOMEN'S ARCHIVES

New Milford   Connecticut
June 26, 1940
To my revered and beloved colleagues on the WCWA Board:
I abhor having to be away from Board meetings and having to give up

my direction of archives-collecting from this time forward but I positively must. I am deeply appreciative of your insistence that I remain at my post, but an absentee from the meetings and from the office cannot be either a Board director or a director of archives-collecting with any competence. I have been at work on this Center for five hard working years. I know a few women who can carry on my part of the work, as chairman of archives, if they can now be assigned to that job. I know a few women who could push organization and publicity if they can be given the conditions for doing so.

Unless strong new blood can be transfused into our movement's management, neither my continued service nor any other service, old or new, will carry us further toward our goal.

Mrs. Hansl and Marjorie White would make a fine team directing interest in and winning success with documents.

Mrs. Hansl and Miss Elsie Yellis of Allentown, Pennsylvania (whose correspondence with me is in the files), would make a fine organization and publicity team, I think. Miss Yellis would have to have a good salary however, even as Mrs. Hansl would. Miss Yellis is not well known in New York but she has qualifications which might elegantly offset that handicap. Her heart is so completely dedicated to wcwa and her business experience has been so exceptional that this combination is an asset. She was a very popular and efficient president of the International Quota Clubs and interested that entire organization in wcwa.

The suggested new members for the Board whose names were read at our June meeting do not impress me at all as good material for hard work for wcwa. I am afraid they will merely use words as we have all been so accustomed to do. Their advice will be excellent no doubt. But that is surely not enough. I do not believe that women identified with other historical societies, for that is [what] ours [is] really, will be tremendously active in pushing ours. Mrs. [James Weldon] Johnson will no doubt help us to get archives but can she help us get financial support?

I am resigning, in part, because I will not go on soliciting archives when there is no real push for money. The members of the Board never have brought in financial plans until I found Mrs. Moffett and she did. I forged ahead trying to get papers and support until I almost dropped dead with labor.

In my opinion we have marked time for months unnecessarily—by supposing that we could make a movement out of bookkeeping alone. The leadership of Miss Judson diverted a live thing into a deadish thing in my opinion and the moment that happened Miss Judson resigned even from membership in the movement, to say nothing of membership on the Board. I was never consulted about this decision to make good books the sole expenditure of our funds. While I honestly want no particular respect for my notions of the proprieties, it is honestly futile for me to try to lift our Center with my effort and get it considerably boosted and then have no other lifting done. The thing gets too lop-sided that way.

Other members of the Board have worked hard too. I do not overlook this truth or deny it for an instant. But sometimes they have done things on the assumption that those things had never been done or thought of before and sometimes they have thus unwittingly caused a check on work going ahead. WE HAVE NOT BEEN A WORKING-TOGETHER BOARD when we have been active. The fault has not all been mine.

If obstruction in what I saw to do and tried to do was rightfully exercised at times, yet it must be admitted by us all that rarely, if ever, was an efficient substitute provided wherewith publicity and organization could move along. I had to make nearly all the publicity myself, which we got, and I cannot go on doing that. It would wreck our movement if I did, for in that case everyone would get sick of the sight of my face and of my chatter.

If I were a rich woman I could set up this Center in a rapid way, I firmly believe. But I am not a rich woman. And for it to count large in the thought of women it should be set up by multitudes of women of course. Unfortunately for my enthusiasms, I am old and very tired physically. What is more to the point: I must leave the New York scene and its environs.

I'd like to commune personally with you, Mrs. Irwin, you, Mrs. Holden, and you, Mrs. Grove, to whom I am sending this message. But we are far apart now physically and that seems impossible. So please take my word for the deed of traveling to see you. I am yours forever and a day.

> With love and respect—
> Mary R. Beard

Just after Mary Beard's decision to resign from the World Center for Women's Archives, Rosika Schwimmer wrote to let her know that she had made a tentative arrangement to place her own archives and library in the New York Public Library and wanted to alert the board of the WCWA before the final settlement. Her closing lines were, "I have buried many dreams in these last decades. The World Center for Women's Archives goes now with the lot." [14] Mary Beard was still, willfully, somewhat more hopeful.

83. TO ROSIKA SCHWIMMER

> World Center for Women's
> Archives, Inc.
> New York City
> July 10, 1940

Dear Mme. Schwimmer:

I understand fully your feeling that your dreams are lost. I don't like to raise the question respecting the inevitability of shocks to dreaming but, as I now try to analyze the slow progress toward a great Women's Archive, I come to the conclusion that dreams must be subjected to sharp realities for their realization if anything approaching their designs is attained.

I have tried for five years to *force* the Archive into existence, my faith matching your dream. Now I realize that more groundwork must be laid—the reality. But I am also convinced that your-my dream of a great Women's Archive is not lost. In truth there is an active nucleus of the present Board membership which is determined to carry the idea and build up a visible collection of important archives of women. Though I have had to resign from the Board because of utter weariness, I am confident that the work will go on and I believe that it will go on better than if I were to continue my forced feeding.

On my part I shall try to strengthen the foundation in thought about women. I am going to have a new edition of my book called "On Understanding Women" this autumn reentitled WOMAN: CO-MAKER OF HISTORY. I hope to widen and deepen curiosity respecting what women have wanted of life and have tried to procure. For competence in such a report, I of course need your own archives and I regret beyond my power to say to you that World Center for Women's Archives, the idea of which you originated, is not functioning yet with your documents available to me.

As for purchasing them now, that is impossible it seems. I have spoken to all the persons I know who should have wanted to buy them for WCWA. The Board will not be able to get them within your ten day limit. It knows that you have invaluable papers. It does not have access to funds at this time. I can only rejoice that you are able to place them in a "New York institution". You will let us know what institution as soon as you can, I feel sure.

If some one else had been your spokesman for your dream, it is possible and probable that it might have borne fruit by this time. Obviously I have not been the perfect spokesman, if any good at all. Knowing my inadequacies I have been instrumental in turning over the task to other members of the Board who will now undertake to accomplish more than I could attain.

I wanted to call upon you on Monday night of this week which I spent in town. But my long day had been spent in placing the most important archives the Center has acquired in preserving wrappers, as the final step in my fiduciary trust. And I was so exhausted by night-fall that I just couldn't get to you.

I hope that you will be charitable toward me and my failure to find the benefactor who would endow the Center with your materials.

As for a peaceful world order, that dream I am completely powerless to discuss.

My affection for you and your sister is still sincere. I have gained in countless ways by being privileged to visit with you now and then. I would have seen more of you if I could have managed to extend this privilege. May the world approach the dream of order and decency as members of the WCWA Board are approaching the dream of a Women's Archive though admittedly it is a lesser dream.

Cordially as ever, Mary R. Beard

Imagining that the WCWA would continue without her, Mary Beard retained her confidence in Marjorie White and moved on to revising and supplementing her 1931 book, *On Understanding Women*, for a new edition. She had always felt it was "choked with typographical errors on which a critic could dwell with damaging effect," and when the publisher, Longmans, Green and Co., offered to bring out a corrected second edition, she took the opportunity to write a new first chapter.[15]

84. TO MARJORIE WHITE

World Center for Women's
Archives, Inc.
New York City
July 11, 1940

Dear Marjorie White:

The need for a "survey" of WCWA uptodate, pursued within the immediate weeks for basic decisions in the early autumn pertaining to the right kind of office, etc., is one which I recognize as an imperative. In the circumstances Mrs. Hansl is to study our history and our files and make the appraisal with the advice and aid of the executive committee.

I am resigning from all official responsibility and my release includes my release as archives chairman. On this account I am informing all the projects chairmen that the projects are to take a vacation until further notice comes in re Board decisions.

You and I together—mostly you—have created a fine legacy, as we know. I have every reason to believe that the Board will gradually understand what we have done. I have told Mrs. Hansl that, if questions arise as she goes into the survey of our movement, you, who are near at hand and who know everything else as well as I do and the filing system even better, can be consulted more profitably than anyone else. I have told her very positively that I have always found you utterly devoted to the interests of wcwa and that I could have done nothing without you.

I am leaving the directorate to others entirely now because I am just too weary to carry the load which I assumed any longer. But the load will be carried better, I am convinced, without my burden-bearing. I am not a good Board member of anything. I do not have the experience and sagacity for such team work; it requires infinite patience and conference and I have time and strength for neither. Luckily new members will be taken into the Board and a loyal and enthusiastic executive committee of the present Board seems to be hard at work to keep our ship on an even keel.

As advocate on the shore, I shall be the best rooter I can for wcwa hereafter.

Your relations and mine have given me deep pleasure based on our mutual concept of a great Center and our mutual effort to make it a realised fact. I hope that in the reorganization, your talents and fidelity and enthusiasm will be recognized and utilized.

Let us see each other when we can and commune on the overarching universe as we envisage it in our respective ways.

For a few weeks I must concentrate on the new edition of my book, On Understanding Women, which I am to have issued this autumn. I have promised to turn in the copy by the last of August, around the 20th if possible, and to carry out that pledge I must work with might and main, eschewing all temptations to leave this job.

If I have the sense, this revision will widen and deepen a foundation for thinking about women and history and thus about the universe. It is a high ambition. I am a low-brow. But if I can add a few stones to the understructure and strengthen its base, even a little, I shall still be doing my bit for WCWA. Give me your blessing and pray for my insight and vigor.

When I have sent in my copy, then come to the country for a visit with me where we can talk in peace and try to reason further together.

With genuine affection,
Mary R. Beard

●←—

The following postmortem of the New York situation from Mary Beard's point of view shows both how petty and how deep the organizational problems ran. It tends to confirm the view that Beard was deeply hurt by the board's unwillingness to place confidence in Marjorie White as well as herself.

85. TO MIRIAM HOLDEN

[New Milford, Connecticut]
August 15 [1940]

Dear Miriam:

I really can't bear to have us misunderstand each other after years now of close association. If I can just clear up one point at issue by this one more letter to you, my heart will be considerably lighter. This is still that miserable matter of Marjorie White. But it involves so much of our trouble that I bring it back just this once more. Please try to look at that affair through my eyes and then tell me once more where I err:

WCWA was supposed to work for Women's Archives.

It was not designed to be a library except insofar as some one might prefer to think of it in that way as having letters, manuscripts and other *source* materials (not printed stuff) as some libraries have. If we got books, we were glad but books were to be supplementary to the source materials and not the prime business of WCWA. Our first literature defined our aims and later literature explained the kind of materials we were seeking.

I was chairman of archives—

Unable to handle the whole quest for documents by myself, I pleaded for assistance and asked for M. White as the available secretary for *my* work.

I knew what she was doing when she was helping me. When the Board had too little money she volunteered because she was deeply interested and believed that my plan of research for important documents was on the right basis.

I was given no other help of any kind.

I was never asked whether M. Shouse could be of value to me. She was put in to her post, first by Miss Beatty, and then by Miss Judson, you and Mrs. Grove, as I understand, to keep books and run such office business as it was supposed she could run

I had to do what I could about archives by writing my own letters, with such help as I could get with interviews, letters, etc. from M. White alone.

When I saw that several of the Board were disliking her, I felt that my word of her value ought to be regarded as my competence on this matter. I felt that I was the one to be criticised if criticism was made. I tried to tell the Board on two or three occasions what she was doing for me but when I mentioned in one such report that she had got Mary Dreier's pledge of papers for instance, Miss Beatty declared that she had seen Miss Dreier and that was that. No doubt she did. I had written her and we are old old good friends but it took an interview by M. White to get the definite pledge. This is but an illustration of the difficulty I had both as to my position and as to my competence in knowing what I was doing.

I felt that to ask the Board to hear her tell of her work, when I barely got to talk myself about Archives, was not the right procedure and that if she was to be on the defensive, I was on the defensive first.

The winter I was in the South, I paid for M. White to carry on for me. We conferred constantly by mail and she made great headway at the office with ARCHIVES—

It was natural for her to like working at this particular thing for we both felt we were accomplishing real work, amid many difficulties, including M. Shouse's dislike of having the interviews, etc. take place at the office. As far as possible this was avoided and taken care of elsewhere.

I did not give M. White the office key. She may have asked M. Shouse for it. If she did, when she did it was because she could only get letters written and take care of interviews late in the day or on Saturdays with such persons as Dr. Clara Lynch who was not free to consult her about cooperation for my work at any other time. When I could be in town and stay for the last train, I was also present at interviews at those times. Without a key, they couldn't have been possible even for me. Miss White, having one, was some times able to receive such persons if I myself was a bit late. In this way Professor Reimer conferred with us—the only hour she could come.

Whatever the limitations of manner this woman possesses, as long as she was getting results for me, as chairman of archives, it still seems to me that if I had any value as chairman of Archives, I was the one to be disowned or reproved instead of my assistant. Or given another one more agreeable to others

But Miss White was used by you and others for other purposes now and then, whether I was paying her salary or not. Thus she acquired an anomalous position—made necessary in part by the lack of a staff sufficient to do all the necessary work of sorts other than the archives business

NOW isn't this picture of the past a correct one? Or is there something fundamentally wrong with it?

The fact is, I gradually learned, that your devotion lay in books. I was glad that the Gallant Am. Women [radio] program gave play to that interest of yours. I hope it will continue. I share it of course myself as my approach to this whole WCWA enterprise grew out of the years I had been reading books. But all that we need to know about women is by no means in books. And it is my knowledge of that truth PLUS my concern with the preserving of contemporary documents for books yet to be written that makes me so keen about WCWA.

Practically nothing has been written for many years on Women in Science. That is why I plugged away at the materials for it. But Mrs. Hansl got the idea that I was just trying, with M. White's help, to do a Who's Who on scientific women. That is not true.

No I am terribly sad to have WCWA fail and to be out of a movement which is so dear to me. But you cannot deny that I got precious little backing. You did all you could, dear Miriam. I am appreciative to the deeps of my being for your friendship and for our association for the idea which we were trying to realize—for the dream we were attempting to make come true.

Perhaps I should have come to the luncheon at Mrs. Hansl's. I am so moved to learn that those of you who did expressed your own strong affection for our movement. Perhaps too sensitively I felt that I had become a bete noire.

The future? Mrs. Moffett took us up a blind alley. Unintentionally of course. So we are stranded financially.

But I am hoping that Washington will still want to have the Center itself. That would be a dignified solution, don't you agree? Its interest may have petered out but I am trying to discover whether it is possible to revive its proclaimed desire to establish a great Women's Archive there.

This is more than a project for librarians. We are not ready for an archivist yet. No Historical Society, in my opinion, is the right patron at all.

When the Board reassembles in October, I shall come to the meeting